The Official EPAKS Guide to Long Form Two

© 2015 EPAKS Publications
Pompano Beach, FL USA

All Rights Reserved

No part of this work may be reproduced in any form or by any means - graphic, electronic, or mechanical, including (but not limited to) photocopying, recording, taping, or information storage and retrieval systems - without the express written permission of the publisher.

Products that are referred to in this document may be either trademarks, registered trademarks, and / or copyrights of the respective owners. The publisher and the author make no claim to these trademarks and / or copyrights.

While every precaution has been taken in the preparation of this document, the publisher, author, and / or contributors assume no responsibility for errors or omissions, or for damages or injuries resulting from the use of information contained in this document or from the use of videos from which this document may refer. In no event shall the publisher and the author be liable for any loss of profit or any other commercial and / or personal damage caused or alleged to have been caused directly or indirectly by this document.

The reader should consult a qualified doctor's approval before attempting any physical activities presented in this document.

ISBN: 978-0-9769823-4-0

Publisher
EPAKS Publishing

Author
Ken Herman

Illustrations
Ken Herman
Ed Parker Jr.
Marc Wolpert

Cover Design
Marc Wolpert
Ken Herman

Contributors / Proof Readers
Alexander Perez
Steven Saviano
Martin Seck
Richard Hartman
Noelle Perez

Special thanks to:

those who contributed their time and efforts toward the development of this publication. Your efforts are appreciated and were invaluable to its development. You should be proud.

Also, no EPAKS publication would be complete without a special thank you to the person who made this all possible - Senior Grand Master and founder of the American Kenpo system - Edmund Kealoha Parker Senior: You are greatly missed.

**In loving memory of our founder
SGM Edmund Kealoha Parker Senior
3/19/1931 - 12/15/1990**

Table of Contents

Part I	Introduction	14
Part II	History of Long Form Two	16
	2.1 During SGM Parker's Life	18
	2.2 After SGM Parker's Death	20
Part III	The Salutation and "Signifying"	22
	3.1 The Salutation	23
	Salutation Standard Execution	25
	Salutation Standard Execution - Illustration	29
	Salutation Variations	38
	3.2 "Signifying" a Form	39
	"Signifying" with Salutation - Standard Execution	41
	"Signifying" with Salutation - Illustration	45
	Variations	54
Part IV	Execution of Long Form Two	56
	4.1 Various "Standards"	58
	4.2 Form Standard Execution - No "V" Step	62

© 2015 EPAKS Publications

	4.3 Form Standard Execution - No "V" Step - Illustration	88
	4.4 Form Standard Execution - "V" Step	136
	4.5 Form Standard Execution - Video	137
	4.6 Form Pace	138
	4.7 Form Coordination	141
	Maneuver Coordination	144
	Base Set Coordination	146
	4.8 Form Standard Coordination	150
Part V	**Variations to Long Form Two**	**153**
	5.1 Form Execution - Variations	154
	5.2 Form Coordination - Variations	158
Part VI	**Understanding American Kenpo Forms**	**166**
	6.1 Understanding Long Form Two	169
Part VII	**Basics of Long Form Two**	**170**
	7.1 Quick Reference of Basics	172
	7.2 Basics Utilized in Long Form Two	177
Part VIII	**Focal Points of Long Form Two**	**187**

© 2015 EPAKS Publications

Contents

8.1 Common Focal Points	189
8.2 Less Common Focal Points	190
8.3 Obscure Focal Points	191

Part IX Analysis of Long Form Two — 192

9.1 Intra vs Inter Form Analysis	195
9.2 Beginning / Intermediate Analysis	196
Walk-Through Analysis	198
Form Overview Analysis	199
Inward Block Sequence	200
Transition - Inward / Outward	205
Outward Block Sequence	206
Transition - Outward / Upward	211
Upward Block Sequence	212
Transition - Upward / Downward	218
Downward Block Sequence	219
Half-knuckle Sequence	224
Inside-Downward, Palm up Block Sequence	229
Inside-Downward, Palm down Block Sequence	232
Push-Down Block Sequence	234

© 2015 EPAKS Publications

Inside, Vertical Forearm Strike Sequence	237
Inward, Overhead Elbow Strike Sequence	239
Elbow, Isolation Sequence	241
Form Close	245
Summary	**246**

9.3 Advanced Analysis — 252

Walk-Through Analysis	**254**
Form Overview Analysis	255
Inward Block Sequence	256
Transition - Inward / Outward	260
Outward Block Sequence	261
Upward Block Sequence	264
Transition - Upward / Downward	268
Downward Block Sequence	269
Half-knuckle Sequence	272
Inside-Downward, Palm up Block Sequence	275
Inside-Downward, Palm down Block Sequence	277
Push-Down Block Sequence	279
Inside, Vertical Forearm Strike Sequence	281
Inward, Overhead Elbow Strike Sequence	283

Contents

Elbow, Isolation Sequence	285
Form Close	288
Summary	289
9.4 Reverse / Opposite Analysis	296
Analysis	301
9.5 Principles / Rules / Theories / Concepts / Definitions Analysis	375

Part X Improving Your Execution of Long Form Two — 379

10.1 General Errors	382
Timing	383
Gaze	385
Breathing	386
10.2 Stance Errors	388
General Stance Errors	390
Meditating Horse	391
Neutral Bow	396
Forward Bow	402
45 Degree Cat	408
Offset Horse	414
Reverse Bow	420

© 2015 EPAKS Publications

Twist	427
10.3 Foot Maneuver Errors	**432**
General Foot Maneuver Errors	434
Step Out to Meditating Horse	435
Step Through	436
Twist Through	438
Crossover	439
Cover	440
10.4 Defensive Errors	**441**
General Defense Errors	443
Inward Block - Front Arm	445
Vertical Outward Block	448
Universal Block	451
Upward Block	454
Downward Block	457
Inside Downward - Palm up Block	460
Inside Downward - Palm down Block	463
Push-Down	465
10.5 Offensive Errors	**468**
General Offense Errors	470

Contents

Hand-sword	472
Horizontal Four-Finger Poke	477
Vertical Four-Finger Poke	482
Straight Punch	487
Vertical Punch (high)	497
Side Kick	502
Hammer-fist	507
Claw	512
Outward Back-knuckle	518
Inverted Vertical Back-knuckle	524
Straight Kick	529
Vertical Punch (middle)	534
Buckle	539
Half-knuckle	544
Instep Kick	549
Upward Horizontal Forearm	554
Vertical Two-Finger Poke	559
Vertical Back-knuckle	565
Outward Overhead Elbow	570
Inward Vertical Forearm	575

© 2015 EPAKS Publications

Inward Overhead Elbow	580
Inward Horizontal Elbow	585
Outward Horizontal Elbow	590
Upward Elbow	595
Back Elbow	600
10.6 Improvement Priorities	605

Part XI Frequently Asked Questions — 606

11.1 Why is this form call Long Form Two?	607
11.2 What is the timing of Long Form Two?	608
11.3 Why are the "two's" called the reverses of the "one's"?	609
11.4 What's the difference between isolating power principles and an isolation?	610
11.5 What is the purpose of the "cup and saucer" position in Long Form Two?	611
11.6 What is the difference between an opposite and a reverse?	612
11.7 Why should I do an instep kick instead of a crossover in this form?	613

Contents 11

11.8 Should I check with my alternate hand throughout the execution of the form? — 614

11.9 Why are there universal blocks in this form? — 615

11.10 Why are there no kicks in the forms until Long Form Two? — 616

11.11 Why are some vertical punches in Long Form Two to the middle height zone when it is a high height zone punch? — 617

11.12 We do Long Form Two differently - is that OK? — 618

11.13 Why are there a lot of downward type blocks in Long Form Two? — 619

11.14 Why are there three outward, overhead elbows but only two inward, overhead elbows in Long Form Two? — 620

11.15 Why do we step away on the first downward block of Long Form Two? — 621

11.16 How does leaning effect me? — 622

11.17 Did SGM Parker create Long Form Two? — 623

11.18 What is meant by a 'dictionary' form? — 624

© 2015 EPAKS Publications

11.19 Why shouldn't we visualize an opponent while executing this form? 625

11.20 If I'm not visualizing an imaginary opponent, where and what should I look at when doing the form? 626

Part XII Quizzes 627

12.1 Multiple Choice - Beginner / Intermediate 628

12.2 Fill in the Blank - Beginner / Intermediate 634

12.3 Multiple Choice - Advanced 637

12.4 Fill in the Blank - Advanced 643

Part XIII Appendix A - Quiz Answers 646

13.1 Multiple Choice Answers - Beginner / Intermediate 647

13.2 Fill in the Blank Answers - Beginner / Intermediate 648

13.3 Multiple Choice Answers - Advanced 649

13.4 Fill in the Blank Answers - Advanced 650

Part XIV Appendix B - The Kenpo Kards 651

14.1 The Front of the Kard 653

© 2015 EPAKS Publications

	Contents	13

14.2 The Back of the Kard 655

Part XV Appendix C - Body English 658

Part XVI Appendix D - Intent 663

Part XVII Addendums and Further Insights 666

© 2015 EPAKS Publications

Chapter 1 - Introduction

Long Form Two holds a very unique place in the American Kenpo system. First, like all the other forms after Short Form One, it encompasses and extends the foundation set by Short Form One. Second, it continues and in some cases completes some important physical and conceptual patterns that flowed through Short / Long Form One and Short Form Two. Third, it extends the definition of a long form introduced by Long Form One. Fourth, like Short Form Two, it emphasizes the reverses over the opposites established in Short / Long Form One. Fifth, it sets into motion some new physical and conceptual patterns that will be continued and expanded upon in future forms. And sixth, it is the last of the lower forms. Beyond this point in the forms, a lot changes.

Introduction

Since Long Form Two is a long form it follows the same rules and guidelines of a long form, which means one of its goals is to expand upon the base set of concepts and maneuvers introduced in Short Form Two. Because of this, Long Form Two has the same overall timing, is executed on the same physical pattern, and has generally the same look as Short Form Two.

Even though Long Form Two is considered a lower form, it is not very short, nor is it very easy to perform correctly. It has some relatively difficult physical maneuvers for a lower form, with a good number of the easily performed, dually timed maneuvers demonstrated in Short Form Two. This leaves the more difficult and awkward ones for this form. As such, this form has a reasonable number of areas where confusion and problems may arise. These facts make any inconsistencies, errors, and/or alterations very easy for an experienced eye to spot quickly.

One unfortunate observation about Long Form Two is that this form is where later generations of American Kenpo practitioners begin to implement some drastic variations from the traditional standard execution. Reasons and discussion about variations can be found in their respective chapters of this book.

As this book progresses it will explore and expose the many facets, nuances, and complexities of this form. The overall goal of this book is to not only help the reader perfect their knowledge and execution of and about Long Form Two, but to enhance their understanding of SGM Parker's purpose for the creation of this form and how it logically fits into the grand scheme of what we now call the American Kenpo system.

Chapter 2 - History of Long Form Two

Although the general history of Long Form Two is fairly well known, a precise history of one important date is not known - the exact creation date of the form. What is known, though, is that it was created by SGM Parker very early in the developmental stages of American Kenpo (in the mid to late 1950's). It is conjectured and probably true that SGM Parker got ample input and feedback from a number of sources during the form's development. Also, SGM Parker incorporated small changes and enhancements to the form over time, but all enhancements stopped by the mid 1960's.

History of Long Form Two

All formal documentation from SGM Parker shows Long Form Two as the fourth form of the American Kenpo system and was created to be a direct follow up to Short Form Two. Long Form Two is typically taught immediately after Short Form Two. Although, there are a few instructors that teach the lower forms (i.e. Short Form One - Long Form Two) in a slightly different order. Typically, they teach Short Form Two immediately after Short Form One, then teach Long Form One, followed by Long Form Two. But, regardless what order the lower forms are taught in, Long Form Two is always taught as the fourth form (i.e. the last of the lower forms). For more information as to why the lower form order is sometimes changed, please refer to the EPAKS Guide to Short Form Two / Long Form One - History section.

During SGM Parker's Life

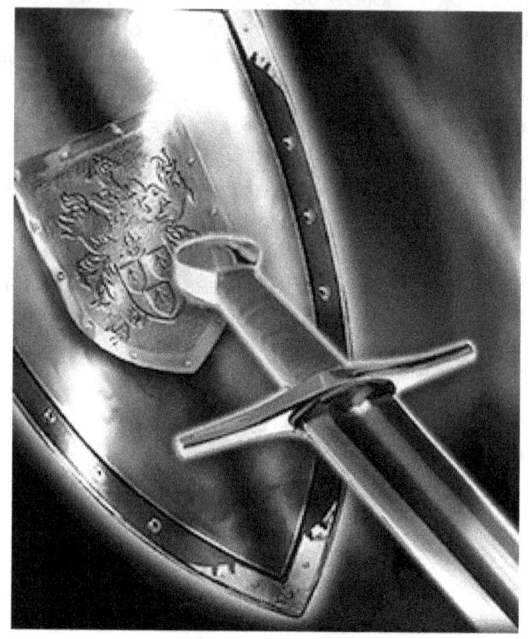

The IKKA Belt Sheets / Manuals (Pasadena School)
(Copyright 1970)
The Pasadena school belt manuals were never published, but were handed out to students to be used during their classes and for personal study. They were essentially a list of the basics, forms, sets, etc. that were to be learned as part of a specific rank curriculum, prior to moving onto a new rank. Many organizations, schools, and teachers still use similar sheets / manuals for their students. Long Form Two is listed in the Green belt curriculum manual.

The IKKA Accumulative Journal - Version 1.0

(Copyright 1972)
Technically speaking, this journal was never published for public consumption, but instead was supplied to IKKA affiliated studios with membership in the original IKKA organization. This is considered the first written explanation of Long Form Two execution. This reference also states that Long Form Two should be taught as part of the Blue belt curriculum.

The Infinite Insights into Kenpo - Book #5

(Copyright 1987)
This is the third written, but first publicly published reference to Long Form Two. Reference to Long Form Two is limited to the Web of Knowledge section (Chapter 5) and only states that the form should be taught as part of the Green belt curriculum.

After SGM Parker's Death

The Encyclopedia of Kenpo
Version 1.0
(Copyright 1992)
This is the fourth written and second publicly published reference to Long Form Two. The reference states that Long Form Two should be taught as part of the Blue belt curriculum.

The IKKA Accumulative Journal
Version 2.0
(Copyright 1992)

History of Long Form Two

This is the fifth, and last, official written reference to Long Form Two that can be somewhat attributed to SGM Parker's direct influence. It is an accumulation of revisions he was working on at the time of his death. It was compiled by his son Ed Parker Jr. This reference has Long Form Two listed as being taught as part of the Blue belt curriculum.

Chapter 3 - The Salutation and "Signifying"

In formal situations, the salutation and "signifying" are appended to the execution of a form. This practice adds clarity and formality to the form by allowing the viewer to not only determine the martial art style of the practitioner, but also the form which is intended to be performed; and whether the form will be modified from its standard execution.

The salutation is always appended to both the beginning and the end of the form. But, the signification gesture is only added to the beginning of the form.

The Salutation

The original Kenpo salutation dates back to the boxer rebellion in China. At that time, the salutation was used as a gesture to show that you where one of the individuals fighting to bring back the Ming dynasty. The left hand over right fist represented the sun and the moon, which in Chinese characters formed the symbol of the Ming dynasty.

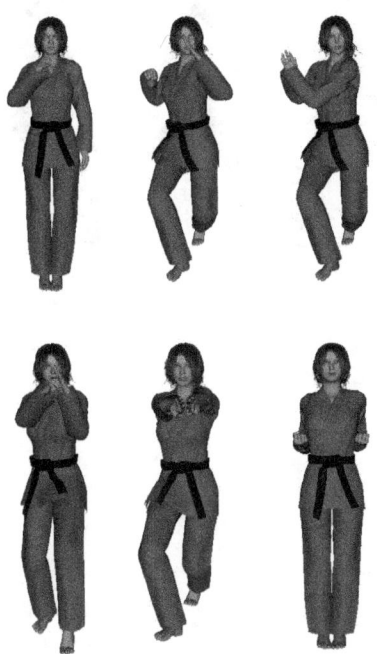

However, the salutation as executed today by American Kenpo practitioners is longer than the original and now only represents a linkage to its past heritage of Kenpo. The reason the modern day salutation is longer than the original is that SGM Parker added a "new" series of maneuvers to the end of the original salutation. This change was to represent a merging of the modern martial arts with those of the past.

Salutation Standard Execution

Note:
> H = Horizontal - Example: 6:00H
> V = Vertical - Example 12:00V

Note:
> Throughout the salutation, the foot and hand maneuver timing should be synchronized such that both start and come to a complete stop simultaneously.

---

1) From an attention stance (toward 12:00H), bow and raise your head.

Meaning:
> Show respect to the art of kenpo.

2) Step sideways, with your left foot (toward 9:00H), into a meditating horse stance (toward 12:00H) while simultaneously placing your left hand folded over (on a 1:30V - 7:30V line) your right fist (on a 10:30V - 4:30V line) parallel to your body in front of you, at chin level.

Meaning:
> Foot Maneuvers:
>> I cast off the weak.
>
> Hand Maneuvers:
>> I hide my treasure

3) Bow your head into meditation.

Meaning:
> The meditation may vary depending upon the purpose of the salutation:
>
> Opening a Form:
>> The practitioner is to clear the mind of any external thoughts.
>
> Closing a Form:
>> The practitioner is to meditate on the execution performance of the form.

4) Lift your head from meditation.
Meaning:
   You have finished meditation.

5) Raise both of your hands above your head (toward 12:00V), palms up (toward 12:00V), and without any loss of momentum draw your left foot (toward 3:00H) to your right foot while simultaneously lowering both of your hands in outward arches (left toward 9:00H - right toward 3:00H), ending into an attention stance (toward 12:00H).
Meaning:
   I draw the weak back to the strong.

Note:
   This is the point at which one would signify the form being performed.

6) Step forward with your right foot (toward 12:00H) into a right front twist stance (toward 12:00H) while simultaneously bringing both your right clenched fist and left open hand over your right shoulder with your right fist facing forward (toward 12:00H) and your left palm facing over your right shoulder (toward 6:00H) covering your right fist.
Meaning:
   The scholar and the warrior meet...

7) Step forward, with your left foot (toward 12:00H) into a left 45 degree cat stance (toward 12:00H) while simultaneously pushing both hands (maintaining contact with each other) forward (toward 12:00H) so your left open hand, palm facing downward (toward 4:30V) and to your right (toward 1:30H), covers your left side of fist, knuckles facing forward (toward 10:30H), in front of you, at chin level.
Meaning:
   and go forth into battle,...

The Salutation and "Signifying"

8) Rotate and open both of your hands (maintaining contact with each other), in opposite directions, so that both palms face away from each other (left toward 9:00H - right toward 3:00H).

Meaning:
   back to back they will work together...

9) Step back (left rear cross-over) with your left foot (toward 6:00H) into a right front twist stance (toward 12:00H) while simultaneously rotating both hands (still maintaining contact with each other) toward yourself, ending in a palm up position (toward 12:00V) in front of you at chin level. Draw your right foot back to your left foot (toward 6:00H) until both feet are side-by-side, while drawing and closing both hands simultaneously to chambered positions, palm up (toward 12:00V) at your sides, into a modified attention stance (toward 12:00H).

Meaning:
   to bring the country back to the people.

Note:
   Every move beyond this point was added by SGM Parker and is considered the "new" part of the salutation.

10) Step to your left with your left foot (toward 9:00H) into a horse stance while simultaneously raising both of your hands upward and in front of you (toward 12:00V) in slight outward arches, ending head high with palms away from you (toward 12:00H) and elbows slightly bent (far depth), while the thumbs and forefingers of both hands touch, forming a triangle [with the base of the triangle parallel to both the ground and your body (on a 9:00H - 3:00H line) and the tip of the triangle pointing straight upward (toward 12:00V)].

Meaning:
   I have no weapons.

11) Lower both hands (toward 6:00V) so your left folded over hand (on a 1:30V - 7:30V line) covers your right fist (on a 10:30V - 4:30V line) parallel to your body in front of you at chin level, with both elbows bent to the point that they are directly below the hands (medium depth).
Meaning:
　I hide my kenpo treasure

12) Continue the drop of your hands (toward 6:00V), to solar plexus level, while opening both of your hands simultaneously so the palms face each other (left toward 3:00H - right toward 9:00H) touching with the fingers pointing straight upward (toward 12:00V), as if praying; while simultaneously bending both elbows to the point that both hands are almost touching the lower chest area (close depth).
Meaning:
　I pray for forgiveness for having to use my karate.

13) Raise both of your hands above your head (toward 12:00V), palms up (toward 12:00V) and without any loss of momentum draw your left foot (toward 3:00H) to your right foot while simultaneously lowering both of your hands in outward arches (left toward 9:00H - right toward 3:00H), ending into an attention stance (toward 12:00H).
Meaning:
　Close of the salutation

14) Bow and raise your head.
Meaning:
　Show respect to the art of kenpo.

Salutation Standard Execution - Illustration

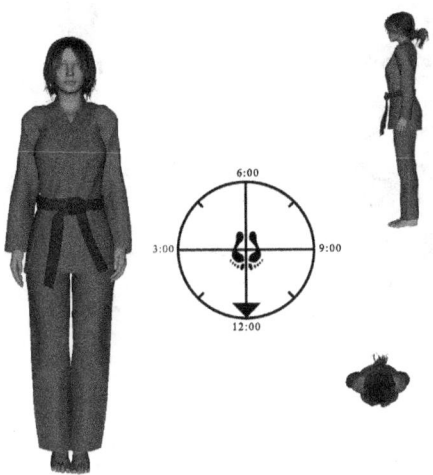

1) Opening Attention Stance

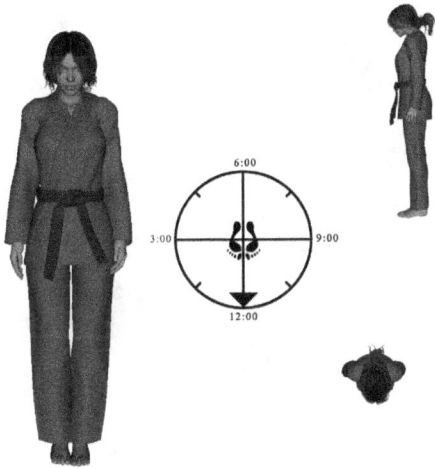

1b) Bow your head

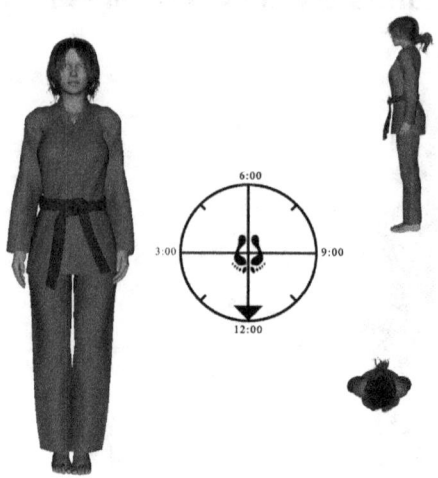

1c) Back to Attention Stance

2, 3 & 4) Meditating Horse

The Salutation and "Signifying" 31

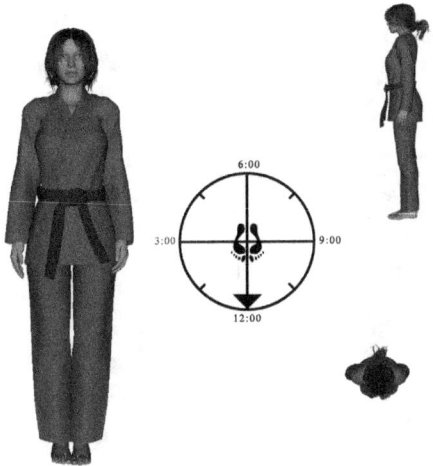

5) Back to Attention Stance

6a) the warrior

© 2015 EPAKS Publications

6b) and the scholar

6c) meet

The Salutation and "Signifying" 33

7) and go forth into battle

8) back to back they work

9) to bring the country back to the people

10) I have no weapons

The Salutation and "Signifying" 35

11) I hide my kenpo treasure

**12) I pray for forgiveness
(for having to use my martial art)**

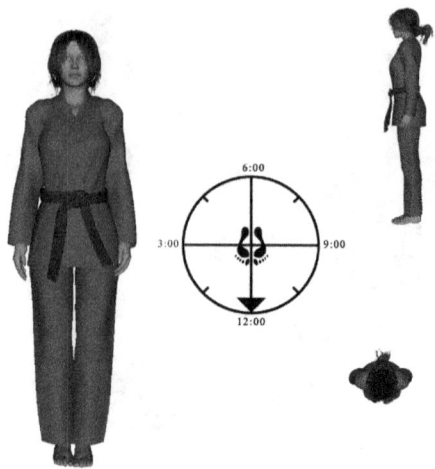

13) Back to Attention

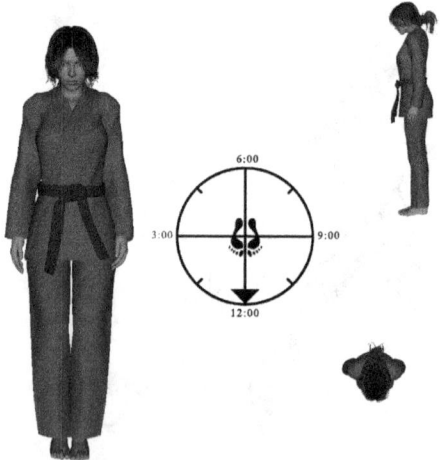

13a) Bow your head

The Salutation and "Signifying"

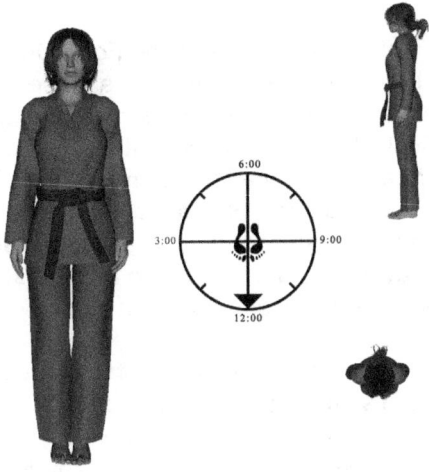

13b) Back to Attention

Salutation Variations

The first four forms (Short Form One, Long Form One, Short Form Two, Long Form Two) each start from a horse stance. Therefore, the salutation for each of these forms is generally executed up to the last meditating horse stance, without drawing back to the final attention stance. The form is then executed from that point in the salutation. But, if the practitioner draws back to the final attention stance, thus finishing the full salutation, they may simply step back into a horse stance and continue the execution of the form from that point.

One other common variation is the period of time meditation is performed during the salutation. This length of time can be skipped or can last for as long as a few seconds - but generally not longer, unless needed. This meditation is provided for the practitioner in order for them to become calm and focused in both body and mind. So meditation length will vary by individual.

The Salutation and "Signifying" | 39

"Signifying" a Form

Signifying (or signing) is a hand gesture that is displayed prior to executing a form. In the case of Long Form Two, the sign is two extended fingers (the index finger and middle finger) laid on top of the other opened hand (the backstop hand). This hand maneuver is typically done from an attention stance; displayed at waist level, facing front (i.e. perpendicular to the ground); and executed prior to the salutation. The backstop hand is positioned palm forward and fingers pointing to the ground. The signifying hand is placed perpendicular across the backstop hand, finger(s) pointing to the side, and palm facing the backstop hand.

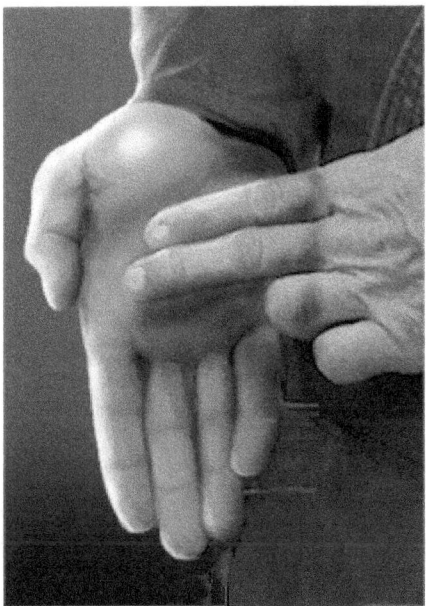

"Signifying" Long Form Two

© 2015 EPAKS Publications

The history of signifying a form comes from the early competition days (prior to the 1970's). At this time, the participant was not allowed to talk to the presiding judges. So, to inform the audience and judges as to which form was to be executed, the signification was added at the beginning. Also, the display was shown on both sides of the body, so as to cover a 180 degree radius.

"Signifying" with Salutation - Standard Execution

Note:
> H = Horizontal - Example: 6:00H
> V = Vertical - Example 12:00V

Note:
> Throughout the salutation, the foot and hand maneuver timing should be synchronized such that both start and come to a complete stop simultaneously.

---

1) From an attention stance (toward 12:00H), bow and raise your head.
Meaning:
> Show respect to the art of kenpo.

2) Step sideways, with your left foot (toward 9:00H), into a meditating horse stance (toward 12:00H) while simultaneously placing your left hand folded over (on a 1:30V - 7:30V line) your right fist (on a 10:30V - 4:30V line) parallel to your body in front of you, at chin level.
Meaning:
> Foot Maneuvers:
>> I cast off the weak.
>
> Hand Maneuvers:
>> I hide my treasure

3) Bow your head into meditation.
Meaning:
> The meditation may vary depending upon the purpose of the salutation:
>
> Opening a Form:
>> The practitioner is to clear the mind of any external thoughts.
>
> Closing a Form:
>> The practitioner is to meditate on the execution performance of the form.

4) Lift your head from meditation.
Meaning:
   You have finished meditation.

5) Raise both of your hands above your head (toward 12:00V), palms up (toward 12:00V), and without any loss of momentum draw your left foot (toward 3:00H) to your right foot while simultaneously lowering both of your hands in outward arches (left toward 9:00H - right toward 3:00H), ending into an attention stance (toward 12:00H).
Meaning:
   I draw the weak back to the strong.

Note:
   This is the point at which one would signify the form being performed.

6) Step forward, with your right foot (toward 12:00H) into a right front twist stance (toward 12:00H), while simultaneously bringing both your right clenched fist and left open hand over your right shoulder with your right fist facing forward (toward 12:00H) and your left palm facing over your right shoulder (toward 6:00H) covering your right fist.
Meaning:
   The scholar and the warrior meet...

7) Step forward, with your left foot (toward 12:00H) into a left 45 degree cat stance (toward 12:00H) while simultaneously pushing both hands (maintaining contact with each other) forward (toward 12:00H) so your left open hand, palm facing downward and to your right (toward 1:30H), covers your left side of fist, knuckles facing forward (toward 10:30H) in front of you, at chin level.
Meaning:
   and go forth into battle,...

The Salutation and "Signifying"

8) Rotate and open both of your hands (maintaining contact with each other), in opposite directions, so that both palms face away from each other (left toward 9:00H - right toward 3:00H).

Meaning:
   back to back they will work together...

9) Step back (left rear cross-over) with your left foot (toward 6:00H) into a right front twist stance (toward 12:00H) while simultaneously rotating both hands (still maintaining contact with each other) toward yourself, ending in a palm up position (toward 12:00V) in front of you at chin level. Draw your right foot back to your left foot (toward 6:00H) until both feet are side-by-side, while drawing and closing both hands simultaneously to chambered positions, palm up (toward 12:00V) at your sides, into a modified attention stance (toward 12:00H).

Meaning:
   to bring the country back to the people.

Note:
   Every move beyond this point was added by SGM Parker and is considered the "new" part of the salutation.

10) Step to your left with your left foot (toward 9:00H) into a horse stance while simultaneously raising both of your hands upward and in front of you (toward 12:00V) in slight outward arches, ending head high with palms away from you (toward 12:00H), while the thumbs and forefingers of both hands touch, forming a triangle [with the base of the triangle parallel to both the ground and your body (on a 9:00H - 3:00H line) and the tip of the triangle pointing straight upward (toward 12:00V)].

Meaning:
   I have no weapons.

11) Lower both hands (toward 6:00V) so your left hand folds over (on a 1:30V - 7:30V line) and covers your right fist (on a 10:30V - 4:30V line) parallel to your body in front of you at chin level.
Meaning:
   I hide my kenpo treasure

12) Continue the drop of your hands (toward 6:00V), to solar plexus level, while opening both of your hands simultaneously so the palms face each other (left toward 3:00H - right toward 9:00H) touching with the fingers pointing straight upward (toward 12:00V), as if praying.
Meaning:
   I pray for forgiveness for having to use my karate.

13) Raise both of your hands above your head (toward 12:00V), palms up (toward 12:00V) and without any loss of momentum draw your left foot (toward 3:00H) to your right foot while simultaneously lowering both of your hands in outward arches (left toward 9:00H - right toward 3:00H), ending into an attention stance (toward 12:00H).
Meaning:
   Close of the salutation

14)   Bow and raise your head.
Meaning:
   Show respect to the art of kenpo.

The Salutation and "Signifying" — 45

"Signifying" with Salutation - Illustration

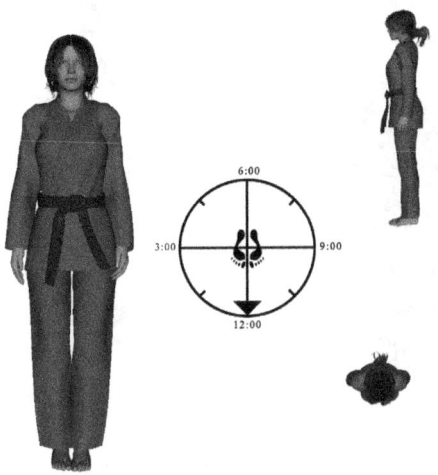

1) Opening Attention Stance

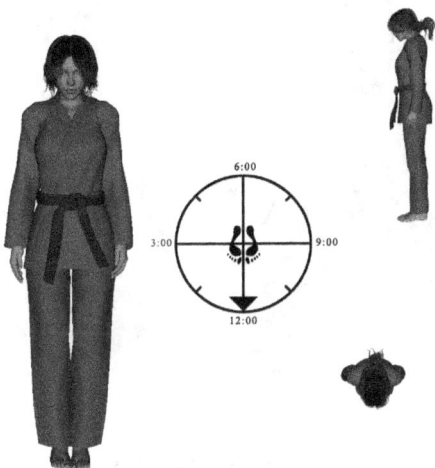

1b) Bow your head

1c) Back to Attention Stance

2, 3 & 4) Meditating Horse

The Salutation and "Signifying"   47

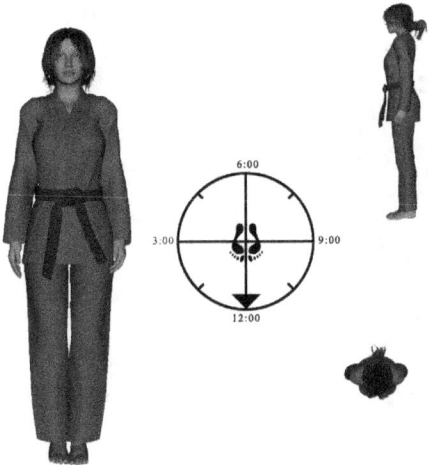

5) Back to Attention Stance

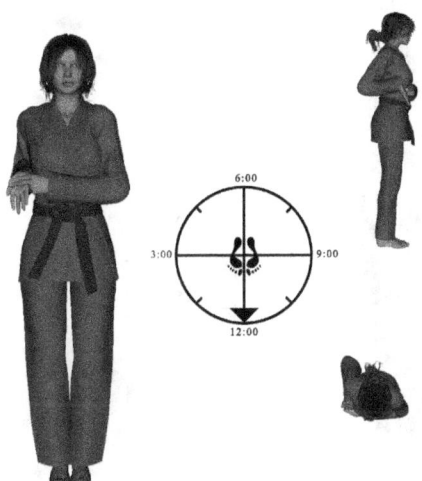

6) Signify on right side

© 2015 EPAKS Publications

7) Signify on left side

8a) the warrior

The Salutation and "Signifying"   49

8b) and the scholar

8c) meet

© 2015 EPAKS Publications

9) and go forth into battle

10) back to back they work

The Salutation and "Signifying" 51

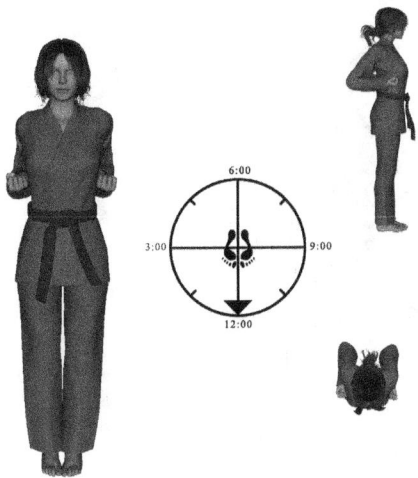

11) to bring the country back to the people

12) I have no weapons

13) I hide my kenpo treasure

14) I pray for forgiveness
(for having to use my martial art)

The Salutation and "Signifying" | 53

15) Back to Meditating Horse

Variations

The first variation is whether the form is signified at all. At first, only the upper forms (short three and above) were signified and utilized the salutation. But over time, signifying and the salutation were considered appropriate for all forms (but typically not sets). An added benefit to adding the signification and salutation to the lower forms was that it made the forms a great deal longer and gave the form a greater feeling of complexity. If compared to Short Form One, the signification and salutation, at least, double the execution time and complexity of the form. Also, the signification and salutation are typically only executed in formal situations, such as competitions and tests; otherwise, a form is executed alone – either from the horse stance (the lower forms) or the attention stance (the upper forms).

The next variation is whether the signifying hand touched or hovered over the backstop hand. If the signifying hand was touching the backstop hand, this indicated that the form being executed was modified from the standard execution. But, if the signifying hand hovered over the backstop hand, this indicated that the form was to be executed without modification. The exceptions to this rule are the forms five and six. The forms five and six would always have the signifying hand touch the backstop hand.

Another variation is to signify on both sides of the body or just a single side. Signifying on a single side of the body indicated that the form would be executed on only that side. For instance, if the signification was only given on the right side, then only the right side of the form would be executed. But, if given on both sides of the body, then both the left and right side of the form would be executed. This variation is specifically indicative of Short Form One - which is commonly executed on both the right and left side for competition.

The Salutation and "Signifying" — 55

On other common variation is the period of time meditation is performed during the salutation. This length of time can be skipped or can last for as long as a few seconds - but generally not longer, unless needed. This meditation is provided for the practitioner, in order for them to become calm and focused in both body and mind. So meditation length will vary by individual.

There are a number of other variations to the salutation and signifying that have appeared over time which have become part of the standard way of signifying a form. Some of the variations are widely used, some are not well known, but each of the variations is optionally applied as needed.

Chapter 4 - Execution of Long Form Two

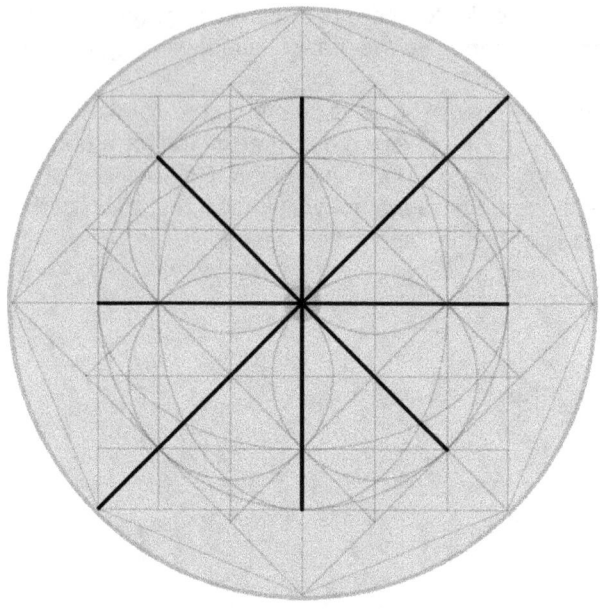

In this section, we will discuss the execution of Long Form Two. The execution presented, for the purposes of this discussion, will be considered the standard execution of the form. All information about the form will be derived from this standard of execution. This does not mean there are not legitimate variations to this standard.

Variations can be classified into two major groups: permanent and non-permanent. Non-permanent variations are variations that are made to a form for a specific purpose, such as for competition or for demonstration. Permanent variations are variations that are consciously or mistakenly made to a form, but ultimately end up being a permanent change to the standard execution of a form.

Non-permanent variations can be defined as any variation from the standard that is made to a form for any specific purpose - without the intent of changing the system of American Kenpo. In other words, this type of variation is made to a form without wanting to teach this variation as a "new" way of executing the standard form. Rather, it is executed and/or taught for a specific purpose: such as for tournament competition.

Permanent variations can be broken down into two types: destructive and non-destructive.

Destructive variations can be defined as a variation that detracts from or eliminates some information that is intended to be demonstrated during the execution of the form. This can include: missing maneuvers, new maneuvers, altered maneuvers, and/or improperly executed maneuvers. Because, by definition, these types of variations effect, alter, change, or otherwise detract from the intended information of a form, destructive variations should be avoided and eliminated.

Non-destructive variations can be defined as a variation that changes the form in some way, but does not interfere with the information that is intended to be demonstrated during the execution of the form. These variations are completely acceptable, but should be noted as a variation from the standard.

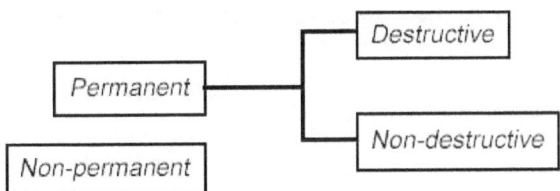

Form variation types

Various "Standards"

As a general rule, all American Kenpo forms will have various "correct" ways of execution. This is due to a number of factors. But, each factor can be whittled down to one common and important characteristic, they each affect the "standard" execution of the form. Now, carry any of these change factors out a couple of instructor-to-student generations, and you get a resulting form with variations from the beginning of the cycle. But, each generation will swear that they do the form correctly. And, in their mind they are correct. Who is to say otherwise?

Why is the word "standard" in quotes in this section? Because standardization, as it relates to American Kenpo, can be a relative thing. Even Mr. Parker would change the execution of various forms for various reasons. Most of the time for one demonstration, but sometimes permanently.

For example, American Kenpo, as a style that we recognize today, was developed and evolved over a number of decades. During this time, SGM Parker got a large amount of feedback from a great number of direct and indirect students. Whenever he found feedback that was sound and reasonable, he would roll that feedback into his system. But, doing so would leave a number of students that were already taught the form with a slight variation from the now current "standard." Granted, this was infrequent, but it did happen.

Another reason for alternate "standards" of a form is that Mr. Parker would sometimes vary a form slightly while teaching it to a specific individual. This is called giving the form a signature. This practice was done so that when a new individual would come to Mr. Parker making claims as to their lineage, Mr. Parker could "test" the individual by having them perform a single or series of forms. From what he saw, SGM Parker could determine whether or not they were being truthful. With this knowledge, he could quickly determine the relative reliability of the individual. But, this practice has a serious side effect - the signature became a "standard." Why? Because that is how the practitioner learned the form from SGM Parker; and, the individual can correctly say that SGM Parker taught them to do the form that specific way. And, they are correct.

A third reason for a "standard" is the, "doesn't affect the information in the form" reason. This comes about because American Kenpo forms can be considered "books" of information about the system. But, certain moves and/or maneuvers can be altered slightly without information being lost or altered in the form. These changes are considered acceptable to the instructor, and as a new generation is taught the form, they will learn it slightly differently from the previous generation, generally without any information about the original version and reason for the change.

Probably the most common reason for a "standard" comes about from human error. The scenario goes like this: Mr. Parker teaches a student a form. The person goes home and practices the form, but forgets or accidentally varies the form in some way. But, they never get any further correction and/or feedback from SGM Parker about the "new" way of doing the form. They now teach it to a student with the change, each believing it is the correct and original way of executing the form. And, the cycle continues.

Two Distinct Standards

To demonstrate how a form can have distinct "standards" we will illustrate the two most common ways in which Long Form Two can be executed. Each with its own advantages and disadvantages.

The major difference between the two execution methods of Long Form Two breaks down to whether you transition through a transitory cat stance on the upward and downward block sections of the form. Transitions through the transitory cat stance at these points in Long Form Two is commonly referred to as "V" stepping. It gets this name because of the shape that is made during the execution of the step. There are two trains of thought on whether to execute a "V" step at these points in the form - the for and against. What follows is a summary of the arguments for each.

For

- The "V" step adds a transitory reverse cat stance that would not be demonstrated otherwise.
- The "V" step keeps the theme of demonstrating the cat stance (Intersection Position) between each transition.

Against

- The "V" step breaks the general rule: always step directly to the new location, when moving forward: therefore, the "V" step breaks the principle of Economy of Motion - i.e. stepping directly is quicker.
- The "V" step causes the practitioner to eliminate rotation (specifically on the downward blocks), causing the isolation of Torque to be compromised with the introduction of Back-up mass.

Execution of Long Form Two

So, more importantly than if you "V" step or not in the execution of Long Form Two, is whether you understand the arguments presented above - and draw your own conclusion. To be truly versatile, be able to execute the form both ways, depending upon how you WANT to execute it at that point in time.

Form Standard Execution - No "V" Step

Note:
    H = Horizontal - Example: 6:00H
    V = Vertical - Example 12:00V

From a meditating horse stance...

Execution of Long Form Two

1)
a) Step forward, with your right foot (toward 12:00H) into a right neutral bow (facing 12:00H) with a right, hammering, inward block (toward 10:30H) (major), while simultaneously retracting your left hand (toward 6:00H) into a left chambered position, palm up (toward 12:00V).

b) Execute a right, hammering, outward, downward diagonal hand-sword (toward 12:00H / 4:30V) (minor), while simultaneously settling (toward 6:00V) into your right neutral bow (facing 12:00H).

c) Without any loss of motion, rotate forward (clockwise H) into a right forward bow (facing 12:00H) with a left, thrusting, horizontal, four finger poke (major) (toward 12:00H), palm down (toward 6:00V), at eye level, while simultaneously continuing to retract your right hand (toward 6:00H) into a right chambered position, palm up (toward 12:00V).

d) Rotate backward (counter-clockwise H) returning to a right neutral bow (facing 12:00H) with a right, thrusting, vertical, four finger poke (major) (toward 12:00H), palm facing to the left (toward 9:00V), at rib level, while simultaneously retracting your left open hand (toward 6:00H) into a left chambered position, palm up (toward 12:00V).

2)
a) Step forward, with your left foot (toward 12:00H), into a left neutral bow (facing 12:00H) with a left, thrusting, inward block (toward 1:30H) (major), while simultaneously retracting your right hand (toward 6:00H) into a right chambered positioned, palm up (toward 12:00V).

b) Execute a left, hammering outward, downward, diagonal hand-sword (toward 12:00H / 7:30V) (minor), while simultaneously settling (toward 6:00V) into your left neutral bow (facing 12:00H).

© 2015 EPAKS Publications

c) Without any loss of motion, rotate forward (counter-clockwise H) into a left forward bow (facing 12:00H) with a right, thrusting, horizontal, four finger poke (major) (toward 12:00H), palm down (toward 6:00V), at eye level, while simultaneously continuing to retract your left hand (toward 6:00H) into a left chambered position, palm up (toward 12:00V).

d) Rotate backward (clockwise H) returning into a left neutral bow (facing 12:00H) with a left, thrusting, vertical, four finger poke (major) (toward 12:00H), palm facing to the right (toward 3:00V), at rib level, while simultaneously retracting your right open hand (toward 6:00H) into a right chambered positioned, palm up (toward 12:00V).

Execution of Long Form Two

3)
a) Draw your left foot backward (toward 6:00H) toward your right foot into a left 45 degree cat (facing 12:00H), while simultaneously retracting both of your fists with palms facing each-other (toward 6:00H), to your right side, at hip level.

Note: The right fist closes to a right chambered position, palm up (toward 12:00V), while your left fist completes its retraction ending horizontally cocked across your lower abdomen, palm down (toward 6:00V), left fist positioned directly on top of the right fist (a.k.a."cup and saucer position").

b) Step your left foot to your left (toward 9:00H) into a left, offset, fighting horse (facing 9:00H), while simultaneously executing a left, vertical, outward block (toward 6:00H) (major) with a right, thrusting, straight punch (toward 9:00H) (major).

Note: The offset, fighting horse is positioned such that the feet are offset aligned (toe-heel alignment - like a neutral bow), both feet and body point directly perpendicular to the Point of Reference (like a horse, but with the Point of Reference directly to the side), and with the head turned to look at the Point of Reference (where an imaginary opponent would be - like a neutral bow).

c) Execute a left straight thrust punch (toward 9:00H) (major), at chin level, while simultaneously retracting your right fist (toward 3:00H) to your right upper chest region, palm facing upward (toward 12:00V) and knuckles facing to your left (toward 9:00H).

d) Execute a right straight thrust punch (toward 9:00H) (major) at chin level, while simultaneously retracting your left fist (toward 3:00H) to your left shoulder region, palm facing toward your right (toward 12:00H).

Note: Your left knuckles should try to keep relative line of sight towards 9:00H.

e) Execute a left, snapping, vertical punch (toward 9:00H) (at chin level), simultaneously with a left, snapping, side kick (toward 9:00H) (at shin level), while also retracting your right fist (toward 3:00H) to a right chambered position, palm up (toward 12:00V).

4)
a) Draw your right foot toward your left foot (toward 9:00H) into a right 45 degree cat (facing 12:00H), while simultaneously retracting both of your fists with palms facing each-other (toward 6:00H), to your left side, at hip level.

Note: The left fist completes its retraction into a left chambered position, palm up (toward 12:00V), while your right fist completes its retraction ending horizontally cocked across your lower abdomen, palm down (toward 6:00V), right fist positioned directly on top of the left fist (a.k.a."cup and saucer position").

Note: The during the retraction of the right foot the left foot should be simultaneously rotated (counter-clockwise H) until on a 45 degree angle (on a 10:30H / 4:30H line) to create proper cat stance foot positioning.

b) Step your right foot to your right (toward 3:00H) into a right, offset, fighting horse (facing 3:00H), while simultaneously executing a right, vertical, outward block (toward 6:00H) (major) with a left, thrusting, straight punch (toward 3:00H) (major).

Note: The offset, fighting horse is positioned such that the feet are offset aligned (toe-heel alignment - like a neutral bow), both feet and body point directly perpendicular to the Point of Reference (like a horse, but with the Point of Reference directly to the side), and with the head is turned to look at the Point of Reference (where an imaginary opponent would be - like a neutral bow).

c) Execute a right straight thrust punch (toward 3:00H) (major), at chin level, while simultaneously retracting your left fist (toward 9:00H) to your left upper chest region, palm facing upward (toward 12:00V) and knuckles facing to your right (toward 3:00H).

d) Execute a left straight thrust punch (toward 3:00H) (major) at chin level, while simultaneously retracting your right arm (toward 9:00H) to your right shoulder region, palm facing toward your left (toward 12:00H).

Note: Your right knuckles should try to keep relative line of sight towards 3:00H.

e) Execute a right, snapping, vertical punch (toward 3:00H) (at chin level), simultaneously with a right, snapping, side kick (toward 3:00H) (at shin level), while also retracting your left fist (toward 9:00H) to a left chambered position, palm up (toward 12:00V).

Execution of Long Form Two | 69

5)
a) Draw your left foot toward your right foot (toward 3:00H), into a left 45 degree cat stance (facing 12:00H), while simultaneously retracting both of your fists with palms facing each-other (toward 6:00H), to your right side.

Note: The right fist completes its retraction into a right chambered position, palm up (toward 12:00V), while your left fist completes its retraction ending horizontally cocked across your lower abdomen, palm down (toward 6:00V), left fist positioned directly on top of the right fist (a.k.a."cup and saucer position").

Note: The during the retraction of the left foot the right foot should be simultaneously rotated (clockwise H) until on a 45 degree angle (on a 1:30H / 7:30H line) to create proper cat stance foot positioning.

b) Step your left foot backwards (toward 5:30H) into a left modified rear twist stance (facing 6:00H). Immediately after stabilizing your base, rotate to your left (counter-clockwise H) into a left neutral bow (facing 6:00H), while simultaneously executing a left, hammering, downward block (major) (toward 3:00H) with a right, thrusting, inward block (major) (toward 4:30H) (a.k.a universal block).

c) Shift forward (counter-clockwise H) into a left forward bow (facing 6:00H) with a left, thrusting, upward block (major) (toward 12:00V / 6:00H), simultaneously with a right, hammering, forward, diagonally upward, hammer-fist (major) (toward 6:00H / 1:30V).

Note: The hammer-fist realistically travels on a vertical rotation downward and away from your body on a perpendicular axis (counter-clockwise V).

© 2015 EPAKS Publications

d) Shift backward (clockwise H) into a left neutral bow (facing 6:00H) with left, overhead claw (major) (toward 6:00H / 6:00V), palm forward (toward 6:00H), simultaneously with a right, outward back-knuckle (major) (toward 7:30H), at head level.

Note: The shift should be timed such that it completes at the same time as back-knuckle. Also, the outward back-knuckle should be timed such that it replaces the overhead claw's spacial position (at temple level) as the overhead claw descends to just below chin level (i.e. finger tips just below chin level).

e) Execute a left outward back-knuckle (major) (toward 4:30H), at head level, while simultaneously retracting your right fist (toward 6:00H) to your left side, at lower chest level, palm facing you (toward 12:00H).

f) Execute a right outward back-knuckle (major) (toward 7:30H), at head level, while simultaneously retracting your left fist (toward 6:00H) to your right side, at lower chest level, palm facing you (toward 12:00H).

6)
a) Step your right foot backwards (toward 1:30H) into a right modified rear twist stance (facing 12:00H). Immediately after stabilizing your base, rotate to your right (clockwise H) into a right neutral bow (facing 12:00H), while simultaneously executing a right, hammering, downward block (major) (toward 3:00H) with a left, thrusting, inward block (major) (toward 1:30H) (a.k.a. universal block).

b) Shift forward (clockwise H) into a right forward bow (facing 12:00H) with a right, thrusting, upward block (major) (toward 12:00V / 12:00H), simultaneously with a left, hammering, forward, diagonally upward, hammer-fist (major) (toward 12:00H / 1:30V).

Note: The hammer-fist realistically travels on a vertical rotation downward and away from your body on a perpendicular axis (clockwise V).

c) Shift backward (counter-clockwise H) into a right neutral bow (facing 12:00H) with right, overhead claw (major) (toward 12:00H / 6:00V), palm forward (toward 12:00H), simultaneously with a left, outward back-knuckle (major) (toward 10:30H), at head level.

Note: The shift should be timed such that it completes at the same time as back-knuckle. Also, the outward back-knuckle should be timed such that it replaces the overhead claw's spacial position (at temple level) as the overhead claw descends to just below chin level (i.e. finger tips just below chin level).

d) Execute a right outward back-knuckle (major) (toward 1:30H), at head level, while simultaneously retracting your left fist (toward 6:00H) to your right side, at lower chest level, palm facing you (toward 6:00H).

e) Execute a left outward back-knuckle (major) (toward 10:30H), at head level, while simultaneously retracting your right fist (toward 6:00H) to your left side, at lower chest level, palm facing you (toward 6:00H).

Execution of Long Form Two 73

7)
a) From your previous position, step your right foot (toward 10:30H) into a right modified reverse bow (facing 4:30H), while maintaining the position of you arms (body fusion). Immediately after stabilizing your base, rotate (counter-clockwise H) into a left neutral bow (facing 4:30H) with a right, double factor, inside downward, block (minor) (toward 1:30H), palm up (toward 12:00V) - while simultaneously cocking your left fist (toward 7:30H) to your right hip region, palm up (toward 12:00V). Without any loss of motion, settle (toward 6:00V) into a left neutral bow (facing 4:30H) with a left, hammering, downward block (major) (toward 1:30H), while simultaneously retracting your right fist (toward 10:30H) to a right chambered position, palm up (toward 12:00V).

Note: The above moves should be executed to maximize torque for the downward block with emphasis on the left downward block (the major) not the inside, downward block (the minor).

b) Without any loss of motion from the previous move, execute a left, thrusting, inverted, vertical, back-knuckle (major) (toward 7:30H).

c) Shift forward (counter-clockwise H) into a left forward bow (facing 4:30H) with a right, thrusting, straight punch (major) (toward 4:30H), at solar plexus level, while simultaneously retracting your left fist (toward 10:30H) to a left chambered position, palm up (toward 12:00V).

d) Execute a right, snapping, step through, ball kick (major) (toward 4:30H), at groin level, with a left, thrusting straight punch (major) (toward 4:30H), at solar plexus level, simultaneously with the retraction of your right fist (toward 10:30H) to a right chambered position, palm up (toward 12:00V). Without any loss of motion from the previous moves, plant (toward 6:00V) your right foot forward (toward 4:30H) into a modified right forward bow (facing 4:30H).

© 2015 EPAKS Publications

e) Immediately after stabilizing your base, shift (counter-clockwise H) into a right fighting horse (facing 4:30H) with a right, thrusting, vertical punch (major) (toward 4:30H), at rib height, while simultaneously retracting your left fist (toward 10:30H) to a left chambered position, palm up (toward 12:00V).

Note: The vertical punch should be executed such that the forearm remains relatively parallel to the ground with the elbow being backed up by your ribs.

Note: The rotation into the fighting horse should also rotate the front leg, creating a buckling effect. This buckle would be directed against an opponent's forward knee/shin - thus creating a two-in-one timing with the punch.

Execution of Long Form Two | 75

8)
a) From your previous position, step your right foot (toward 7:30H) into a right neutral bow (facing 7:30H) with a left, double factor, inside downward block (minor) (toward 10:30H), palm up (toward 12:00V), while simultaneously cocking your right fist (toward 4:30H) to your left hip region, palm up (toward 12:00V). Without any loss of motion, settle (toward 6:00V) into a right neutral bow (facing 7:30H) with a right, hammering, downward block (major) (toward 10:30H), while simultaneously retracting your left fist (toward 1:30H) to a left chambered position, palm up (toward 12:00V).

Note: The above moves should be executed to maximize torque for the downward block.

b) Without any loss of motion from the previous move, execute a right, thrusting, inverted, vertical, back-knuckle (major) (toward 4:30H).

c) Shift forward (clockwise H) into a right forward bow (facing 7:30H) with a left, thrusting, straight punch (major) (toward 7:30H), at solar plexus level, while simultaneously retracting your right fist (toward 1:30H) to a right chambered position, palm up (toward 12:00V).

d) Execute a left, snapping, step through, ball kick (major) (toward 7:30H), at groin level, with a right, thrusting straight punch (major) (toward 7:30H), at solar plexus level, simultaneously with the retraction of your left fist (toward 1:30H) to a left chambered position, palm up (toward 12:00V). Without any loss of motion from the previous moves, plant (toward 6:00V) your left foot forward (toward 7:30H) into a modified right forward bow (facing 7:30H).

e) Immediately after stabilizing your base, shift (clockwise H) into a left fighting horse (facing 7:30H) with a left, thrusting, vertical punch (major) (toward 7:30H), at rib height, while simultaneously retracting your right fist (toward 1:30H) to a right chambered position, palm up (toward 12:00V).

© 2015 EPAKS Publications

Note: The vertical punch should be executed such that the forearm remains relatively parallel to the ground with the elbow being backed up by your ribs.

Note: The rotation into the fighting horse should also rotate the front leg, creating a buckling effect. This buckle would be directed against an opponent's forward knee/shin - thus creating a two-in-one timing with the punch.

Execution of Long Form Two | 77

9)
a) Execute a left, thrusting, instep (arch) kick (major) (toward 1:30H), at shin level, with a left, hammering, close-fist half-knuckle strike (major) (toward 1:30H / 4:30V), at nose level, while maintaining the position of your right fist (chambered). Without any loss of motion from the previous maneuver, plant (toward 6:00V) your left foot forward (toward 1:30H) into a left front twist (facing 1:30H).

b) Immediately after stabilizing your base, step through forward with your right foot (toward 1:30H) into a right neutral bow (facing 1:30H) with a right uppercut punch (minor) (toward 12:00V / 1:30H), at chin level, while simultaneously retracting your left fist (toward 7:30H) to a left chambered position, palm up (toward 12:00V). Without any loss of motion (sophisticated basic), execute a right, thrusting, upward horizontal forearm strike (major) (toward 12:00V / 1:30H), palm forward (toward 3:00V / 1:30H), at chin level.

c) Execute of a left, thrusting, vertical two-finger poke (major) (towards 1:30H), at eye level, while maintaining the position of your right arm.

d-1) While maintaining the shape (vertical, two-finger poke), position (extended), and directionality (fingers pointing towards 1:30H) of your left hand, retract your right hand (toward 7:30H) to your right upper chest region by bending your right elbow directly downward (toward 6:00V) at the elbow (i.e. anchored) with the simultaneous closing of your right hand to a vertical, two-finger poke formation (toward 1:30H / 3:00V), in preparation for the next move (Line of Sight).

d-2) Immediately, execute a right, thrusting, vertical two-fingered poke (major) (toward 1:30H) with the retraction of your left hand (toward 7:30H) to your left upper chest region - while also maintaining the left hand's shape (vertical, two-finger poke) and directionality (fingers pointing towards 1:30H), in preparation for the next move (Line of Sight).

© 2015 EPAKS Publications

e) Execute a left, thrusting, vertical two-fingered poke (major) (toward 1:30H) with the retraction of your right hand (toward 7:30H) to the right upper chest region (back to its original position) - while also maintaining the shape (vertical, two-finger poke) and directionality (fingers pointing towards 1:30H) of the right hand.

Execution of Long Form Two

10)
a) Execute a right, thrusting, instep (arch) kick (major) (toward 10:30H), at shin level with a right, hammering, close-fist half-knuckle strike (major) (toward 10:30H / 7:30V), at nose level, while simultaneously retracting your left fist (toward 7:30H) to a left chambered position, palm up (toward 12:00V). Without any loss of motion from the previous maneuver, plant (toward 6:00V) your right foot forward (toward 10:30H) into a right front twist (facing 10:30H).

b) Immediately after stabilizing your base, step through forward with your left foot (toward 10:30H) into a left neutral bow (facing 10:30H) with a left uppercut punch (minor) (toward 12:00V / 10:30H), at chin level, while simultaneously retracting your right fist (toward 4:30H) to a right chambered position, palm up (toward 12:00V). Without any loss of motion (sophisticated basic), execute a left, thrusting, upward horizontal forearm strike (major) (toward 12:00V / 10:30H), palm forward (toward 9:00V / 10:30H), at chin level.

c) Execute of a right, thrusting, vertical two-finger poke (major) (towards 10:30H), at eye level, while maintaining the position of your left arm.

d-1) While maintaining the shape (vertical, two-finger poke), position (extended), and directionality (fingers pointing towards 10:30H) of your right hand, retract your left hand (toward 4:30H) to your left upper chest region by bending your left elbow directly downward (toward 6:00V) at the elbow (i.e. anchored) with the simultaneous closing of your left hand to a vertical, two-finger poke formation (toward 10:30H / 9:00V), in preparation for the next move (Line of Sight).

d-2) Immediately, execute a left, thrusting, vertical two-fingered poke (major) (toward 10:30H) with the retraction of your right hand (toward 4:30H) to your right upper chest region - while also maintaining the right hand's shape (vertical, two-finger poke) and directionality (fingers pointing towards 10:30H), in preparation for the next move (Line of Sight).

© 2015 EPAKS Publications

e) Execute a right, thrusting, vertical two-fingered poke (major) (toward 10:30H) with the retraction of your left hand (toward 4:30H) to the left upper chest region (back to its original position) - while also maintaining the shape (vertical, two-finger poke) and directionality (fingers pointing towards 10:30H) of the left hand.

11)
a) Step your left foot (passing behind the right leg) backward (toward 4:30H) into a right front twist (facing 10:30H), with a left, hammering, inside downward palm up (toward 1:30V) block (major) (toward 4:30H), while simultaneously retracting your right fist (toward 4:30H) to a right chambered position, palm up (toward 12:00V).

b) Unwind (counter-clockwise H) into a right neutral bow (facing 10:30H) with a right, snapping vertical punch (major) (toward 10:30H), at lower rib level, while simultaneously retracting your left fist (toward 4:30H) to a left chambered position, palm up (toward 12:00V).

12)
a) Step your right foot (passing behind the left leg) backward (toward 4:30H) into a left front twist (facing 10:30H), with a right, hammering inside downward palm up (toward 1:30V) block (major) (toward 4:30H), while simultaneously retracting your left fist (toward 4:30H) to a left chambered position, palm up (toward 12:00V).

b) Unwind (clockwise H) into a left neutral bow (facing 10:30H) with a left, snapping vertical punch (major) (toward 10:30H), at lower rib level, while simultaneously retracting your right fist (toward 4:30H) to a right chambered position, palm up (toward 12:00V).

Execution of Long Form Two

13)
a) Step your right foot to your left (toward 7:30H) (clockwise H) into a left neutral bow (facing 1:30H) with a left, hammering, inside downward palm down (toward 7:30V) block (major) (toward 4:30H), while maintaining the position of your right arm (chambered).

b) Without any loss of motion from the previous move, continue the circular path (counter-clockwise V) of your left fist until completely vertical, fist upward (toward 12:00V) and palm facing you (toward 7:30H),

Note: The above move should be executed using the elbow as the primary pivot point. Therefore, the elbow should maintain the same relative position throughout the entire move. This move should resemble the execution of a vertical outward block.

c) Without any loss of motion from the previous move, execute a left, snapping, vertical back-knuckle thrust (minor) (toward 1:30H / 1:30V), at face level.

Note: The position of your right arm should remain unchanged (chambered) throughout the execution of all of the above maneuvers in this section.

14)
a) Left step through reverse (toward 7:30H) into a right neutral bow (facing 1:30H) with a right, hammering, inside downward palm down (toward 7:30V) block (major) (toward 10:30H), while simultaneously retracting your left fist (toward 7:30H) to a left chambered position, palm up (toward 12:00V).

b) Without any loss of motion from the previous move, continue the circular path (clockwise V) of your right fist until completely vertical, fist upward (toward 12:00V) and palm facing you (toward 7:30H),

Note: The above move should be executed using the elbow as the primary pivot point. Therefore, the elbow should maintain the same relative position throughout the entire move. This move should resemble the execution of a vertical outward block.

c) Without any loss of motion from the previous move, execute a right, snapping, vertical back-knuckle thrust (minor) (toward 1:30H / 1:30V), at face level.

Note: The position of your left arm should remain unchanged (chambered) throughout the execution of all of the above maneuvers in this section.

Execution of Long Form Two

15)
a) Rotate forward (clockwise H) into a right forward bow (facing 1:30H) with a left push-down block (major) (toward 1:30H / 6:00V), at groin level, while simultaneously retracting your right fist (toward 7:30H) to a right chambered position, palm up (toward 12:00V).

b) Immediately, rotate (clockwise H) forward into a right front twist (facing 1:30H), while simultaneously allowing your left arm to cock across your body (toward 7:30H).

Note: The above move should be executed using body fusion. Therefore, the arm is cocked by the rotation of the body.

c) Left step through forward (toward 1:30H) into a left neutral bow (facing 1:30H) with a left, hammering, outward, overhead elbow (major) (toward 1:30H / 6:00V), at face level.

d) Without any loss of motion, settle (toward 6:00V) into the left neutral bow (facing 1:30H) with a left, hammering, overhead claw (major), palm forward (toward 1:30H), at face level.

Note: The above move is executed by extending the elbow, lowering the strike with the shoulder, and settling into the stance - simultaneously. With each motion listed in the order of its contribution to the power generation of the strike respectively.

Note: Once the right arm is chambered at the beginning of this section it maintains the same relative position throughout the execution of the entire section.

16)
a) Rotate forward (counter-clockwise H) into a left forward bow (facing 1:30H) with a right push-down block (major) (toward 1:30H / 6:00V), at groin level, while simultaneously retracting your left fist (toward 7:30H) to a left chambered position, palm up (toward 12:00V).

b) Immediately, rotate (counter-clockwise H) forward into a left front twist (facing 1:30H), while simultaneously allowing your right arm to cock across your body (toward 7:30H).

Note: The above move should be executed using body fusion. Therefore, the arm is cocked by the rotation of the body.

c) Right step through forward (toward 1:30H) into a right neutral bow (facing 1:30H) with a right, hammering, outward, overhead elbow (major) (toward 1:30H / 6:00V), at face level.

d) Without any loss of motion, settle (toward 6:00V) into the right neutral bow (facing 1:30H) with a right, hammering, overhead claw (major), palm forward (toward 1:30H), at face level.

Note: The above move is executed by extending the elbow, lowering the strike with the shoulder, and settling into the stance - simultaneously. With each motion listed in the order of its contribution to the power generation of the strike respectively.

Note: Once the left arm is chambered at the beginning of this section it maintains the same relative position throughout the execution of the entire section.

Execution of Long Form Two

17)
a) Rotate forward (clockwise H) into a right forward bow (facing 1:30H) with a left push-down block (major) (toward 1:30H / 6:00V), at groin level, while simultaneously retracting your right fist (toward 7:30H) to a right chambered position, palm up (toward 12:00V).

b) Immediately, rotate (clockwise H) forward into a right front twist (facing 1:30H), while simultaneously allowing your left arm to cock across your body (toward 7:30H).

Note: The above move should be executed using body fusion. Therefore, the arm is cocked by the rotation of the body.

c) Left step through forward (toward 1:30H) into a left neutral bow (facing 1:30H) with a left, hammering, outward, overhead elbow (major) (toward 1:30H / 6:00V), at face level.

d) Without any loss of motion, settle (toward 6:00V) into the left neutral bow (facing 1:30H) with a left, hammering, overhead claw (major), palm forward (toward 1:30H), at face level.

Note: The above move is executed by extending the elbow, lowering the strike with the shoulder, and settling into the stance - simultaneously. With each motion listed in the order of its contribution to the power generation of the strike respectively.

Note: Once the right arm is chambered at the beginning of this section it maintains the same relative position throughout the execution of the entire section.

18)
a) Shift forward (counter-clockwise H) into a left forward bow (facing 1:30H) with the execution of a right, thrusting straight punch (major) (toward 1:30H), at solar plexus level, while simultaneously cocking your left arm (toward 7:30H) to the left shoulder region, fist closed and palm facing forward (toward 1:30H).

Note: The left arm should maintain its vertical alignment and move simultaneously with the body's rotation (i.e. body fusion).

b) Rotate backward (clockwise H) into a left neutral bow (facing 1:30H) with a left, hammering, vertical, inside forearm strike (major) (toward 3:00H), while simultaneously retracting your right fist (toward 7:30H) to a right chambered position, palm up (toward 12:00V).

19)
Left step through reverse (toward 7:30H) into a right neutral bow (facing 1:30H) with a right, hammering, inward overhead elbow (major) (toward 1:30H / 6:00V), while simultaneously retracting your left fist (toward 7:30H) to a left chambered position, palm up (toward 12:00V).

20)
Right step through reverse (toward 7:30H) into a left neutral bow (facing 1:30H) with a left, hammering, inward overhead elbow (major) (toward 1:30H / 6:00V), while simultaneously retracting your right fist (toward 7:30H) to a right chambered position, palm up (toward 12:00V).

21)
Step your left foot backward (toward 9:00H) into a modified right twist (facing 1:30H) but with the Point of Reference toward 12:00H). Immediately after planting the left foot, rotate (counter-clockwise H) into a horse stance (facing 12:00H) with a right, inward, horizontal, elbow sandwich (major) (toward 12:00H), at jaw level.

Execution of Long Form Two

22)
Note: The remaining moves are executed as an isolation.

a) Cock both open hands (left over right) (left toward 3:00H) (right toward 9:00H) across your body (parallel to both your body and the ground) at the upper chest level, palms down (toward 6:00V). Immediately, reverse the path of the previous moves, executing double, thrusting outward elbows (major) (left toward 9:00H) (right toward 3:00H), palms down (toward 6:00V), while simultaneously transitioning your open hands to closed fists.

Note: The closing of the hands should be coordinated with the execution of the outward elbows such that each move is completed simultaneously with one another (synced).

b) Execute a left upward elbow (major) (toward 12:00H / 12:00V), palm facing to the right (toward 3:00V), with a right backward elbow (major) (toward 6:00H / 3:00V), palm up (toward 12:00V).

c) Bring both arms to a meditating horse (facing 12:00H) by placing your left open hand (on a 1:30V - 7:30V line) over your right fist (on a 10:30V - 4:30V line) parallel to your body in front of you, at chin level.

Closing salutation...

Form Standard Execution - No "V" Step - Illustration

Opening Meditating Horse

1a) Right Hammering Inward Block

Execution of Long Form Two   89

1b) Right Outward Hand-sword

1c) Left Thrusting Horizontal Four-Finger Poke

1d) Right Thrusting Vertical Four-Finger Poke

2a) Left Thrusting Inward Block

Execution of Long Form Two — 91

2b) Left Outward Hand-sword

2c) Right Thrusting Horizontal Four-Finger Poke

© 2015 EPAKS Publications

2d) Left Thrusting Vertical Four-Finger Poke

3a) Left 45 degree Cat - "Cup and Saucer" Position

Execution of Long Form Two 93

3b) Left Vertical Outward Block with Right Straight Punch

3c) Left Straight Punch

© 2015 EPAKS Publications

3d) Right Straight Punch

**3e) Left Vertical Punch with Left Side Kick
(before planting of foot)**

Execution of Long Form Two 95

4a) Right 45 degree Cat - "Cup and Saucer" Position

4b) Right Vertical Outward Block with Left Punch

4c) Right Straight Punch

4d) Left Straight Punch

Execution of Long Form Two   97

4e) Right Vertical Punch with Right Side Kick
(before planting of foot)

5a) Left 45 degree Cat - "Cup and Saucer"
Position

5b - 1) Left Rear Twist - "Cup and Saucer"
(Transitory)

5b - 2) Left Neutral Bow with Right Inward / Left
Downward Universal Block

Execution of Long Form Two 99

5c) Left Forward Bow with Left Upward Block and Right Forward Hammer-fist

5d - 1) Left Forward Bow with Left Overhead Claw

5d - 2) Left Neutral Bow with Right Outward Back-knuckle

5e) Left Neutral Bow with Left Outward Back-knuckle

Execution of Long Form Two — 101

5f) Left Neutral Bow with Right Outward Back-knuckle

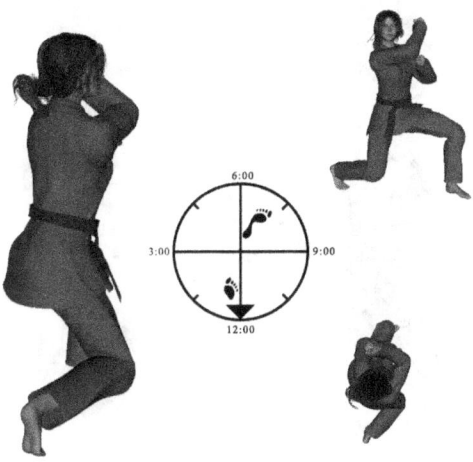

6a - 1) Right Rear twist (Transitory)

© 2015 EPAKS Publications

6a - 2) Right Neutral Bow with Left Inward / Right Downward Universal Block

6b) Right Forward Bow with Right Upward Block and Left Forward Hammer-fist

Execution of Long Form Two 103

6c - 1) Right Formward Bow with Right Overhead Claw

6c - 2) Right Neutral Bow with Left Outward Back-knuckle

6d) Right Neutral Bow with Right Outward Back-knuckle

6e) Right Neutral Bow with Left Outward Back-knuckle

Execution of Long Form Two

7a - 1) Left Reverse Bow with Right, Inside-Downard, Palm-up, Block
(Transitional - Shown in motion)

7a - 2) Left Netral Bow with Left Downward Block

7b) Left Inverted, Vertical Back-knuckle

7c) Left Forward Bow with Right Straight Punch

Execution of Long Form Two | 107

7d) Right Straight Kick with Left Straight Punch

7e - 1) Right Forward Bow with Left Extended Arm

© 2015 EPAKS Publications

7e - 2) Right Side Horse with Right Vertical Punch / Buckle

8a - 1) Right Neutral Bow with Left, Inside-Downard, Palm-up, Block
(Transitional - Shown in motion)

Execution of Long Form Two 109

8a - 2) Right Netral Bow with Right Downward Block

8b) Right Inverted, Vertical Back-knuckle

8c) Right Forward Bow with Left Straight Punch

8d) Left Straight Kick with Right Straight Punch

Execution of Long Form Two   111

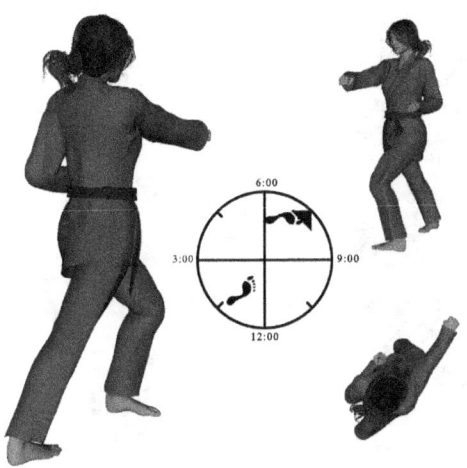

8e - 1) Left Forward Bow with Right Extended Arm

8e - 2) Left Side Horse with Left Vertical Punch / Buckle

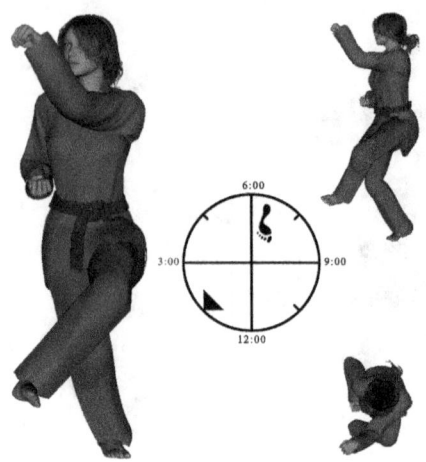

9a) Left Instep (arch) Kick with Left, Downward, Diagonal Half-knuckle

9b - 1) Right Neutral with Right Uppercut Punch

Execution of Long Form Two 113

9b - 2) Right Neutral with Right Upward, Horizontal Forearm

9c) Right Neutral with Left, Vertical, Two-Finger Poke

9d-1) Right Neutral with Left and Right hands in Vertical, Two-Finger Poke positioning

9d-2) Right Neutral with Right, Vertical, Two-Finger Poke

Execution of Long Form Two 115

9e) Right Neutral with Left, Vertical, Two-Finger Poke

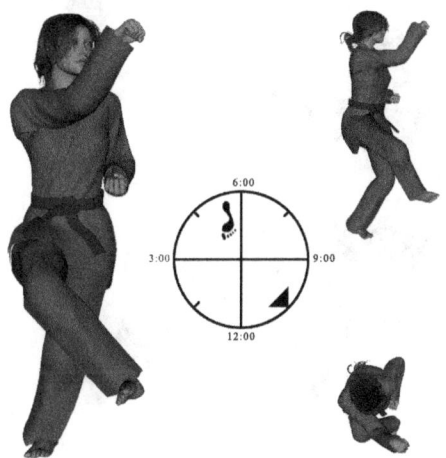

10a) Right Instep (arch) Kick with Right, Downward, Diagonal, Half-knuckle

10b - 1) Left Neutral with Left Uppercut Punch

10b - 2) Left Neutral with Left Upward, Horizontal Forearm

Execution of Long Form Two   117

10c) Left Neutral with Right, Vertical, Two-Finger Poke

10d-1) Left Neutral with Left and Right hands in Vertical, Two-Finger Poke positioning

© 2015 EPAKS Publications

10d-2) Left Neutral with Left, Vertical, Two-Finger Poke

10e) Left Neutral with Right, Vertical, Two-Finger Poke

11a) Right Twist wih Left, Inside, Downward, Palm-up Block

11b) Right Neutral with Right, Snapping Vertical Punch

11a) Left Twist wih Right, Inside, Downward, Palm-up Block

12b) Left Neutral with Left, Snapping Vertical Punch

Execution of Long Form Two — 121

13a) Left Neutral wih Left, Inside, Downward, Palm-down Block

13b) Left Neutral with Positioning for Left, Vertical, Back-Knuckle Punch

13c-1) Left Neutral with Left, Snapping, Vertical, Back-Knuckle Punch

13c-2) Left Neutral with Positioning after Left, Snapping, Vertical, Back-Knuckle Punch

14a) Right Neutral wih Right, Inside, Downward, Palm-down Block

14b) Right Neutral with Positioning for Right, Vertical, Back-Knuckle Punch

14c-1) Right Neutral with Right, Snapping, Vertical, Back-Knuckle Punch

14c-2) Right Neutral with Positioning after Right, Snapping, Vertical, Back-Knuckle Punch

Execution of Long Form Two — 125

15a) Right Forward with Left Push-down Block

15b) Right Twist with Left Push-down Block
(rotated for next move)

15c) Left Neutral with Left, Outward, Overhead Elbow

15d) Left Neutral with Left Overhead Claw

Execution of Long Form Two — 127

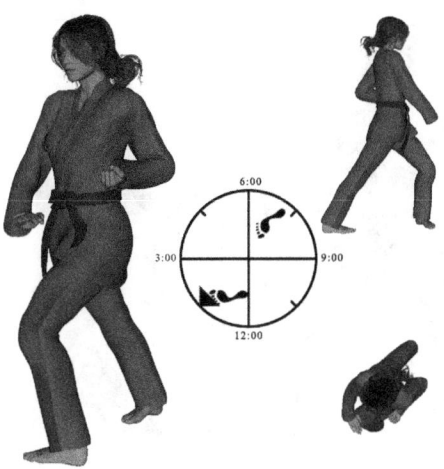

16a) Left Forward with Right Push-down Block

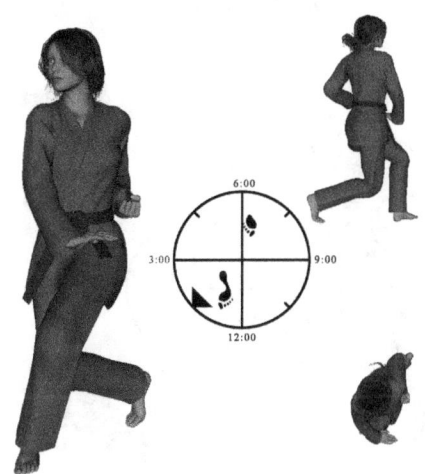

**16b) Left Twist with Right Push-down Block
(rotated for next move)**

© 2015 EPAKS Publications

16c) Right Neutral with Right, Outward, Overhead Elbow

16d) Right Neutral with Right Overhead Claw

Execution of Long Form Two

17a) Right Forward with Left Push-down Block

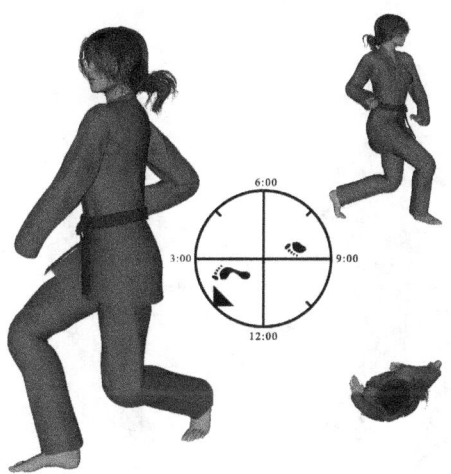

**17b) Right Twist with Left Push-down Block
(rotated for next move)**

17c) Left Neutral with Left, Outward, Overhead Elbow

17d) Left Neutral with Left Overhead Claw

18a) Left Forward with Right Straight Punch

18b) Left Neutral with Left, Inside, Vertical, Forearm

19) Right Neutral with Right, Inward, Overhead Elbow

20) Left Neutral with Left, Inward, Overhead Elbow

Execution of Long Form Two   133

21a) Right Modified Twist with Positioned Left,
Inward, Overhead Elbow
(Transitory)

21b) Horse with Right, Inward Elbow Sandwich

22a-1) Horse with Left and Right Positioning for Double Outward Elbows (Transition)

22a-2) Horse with Double Outward Elbows (Isolation)

Execution of Long Form Two — 135

22b) Horse with Right Backward and Left Upward Elbows (Isolation)

Closing Meditating Horse

Form Standard Execution - "V" Step

Due to the fact that both the "V" step and non-"V" step "standards" are illustrated and analyzed in their entirety in the Short Form Two guide book, a conscience choice was made to only illustrate one of the "standards" in this book. The non-"V" step version of Long Form Two was chosen, since it is the most commonly executed "standard' of the form. Using the illustrations from the Short Form Two guide book the reader can easily transpose the same changes to the same locations in Long Form Two to compose the "V" step "standard." But, the main reason for the decision to illustrate only one version of Long Form Two was space. In order to keep this guide book to a readable and manageable size it was felt that illustrating both "standards" was redundant and didn't add any information that was not already thoroughly presented and graphically demonstrated in the Short Form Two guide book.

Execution of Long Form Two | 137

Form Standard Execution - Video

EPAKS has produced a number of videos that have been uploaded to YouTube. The purpose of these videos is to demonstrate the execution of American Kenpo forms and self-defense techniques. They are not intended to be perfect. Instead, they are intended to be reasonably good examples of execution which the viewer can use as a benchmark. Among the videos is one demonstrating Long Form Two. It may be viewed here:

https://youtu.be/j6nKMeesasg

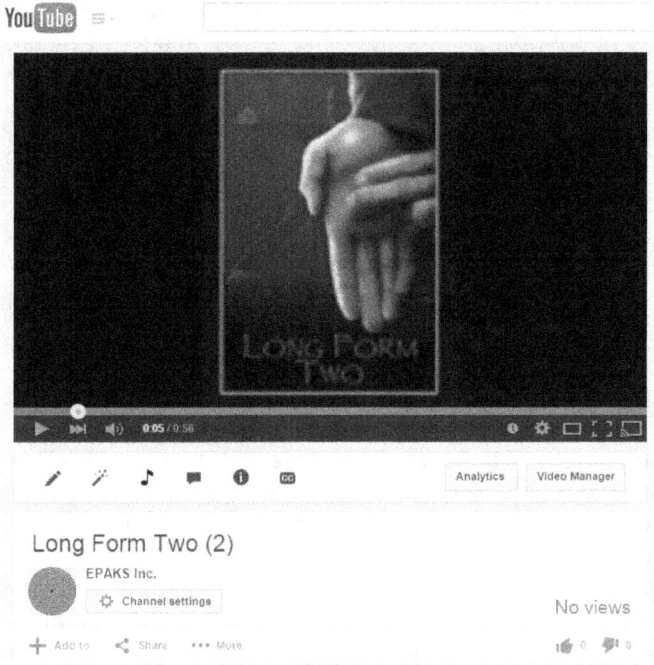

© 2015 EPAKS Publications

Form Pace

Competent and successful execution of a form does not end at proper execution of each of the physical maneuvers of the form. There are a number of other factors that determine whether a form is executed well. One such factor is pace.

The strict definition of pace is: a measure, quantity or frequency compared to another measure, quantity or frequency.

This definition, although precise, can be very vague and confusing and requires further explanation in order to understand how it relates to forms. For our purposes pace can either be looked at from the perspective of the time it takes to execute the entire form compared against other times it takes to complete the form; or from the perspective of the time it takes to complete any subset of the form compared against the time completing the entire form, other subsets of the form, and/or other executions of the same subset. But, from either perspective; if a predefined set of maneuvers are executed, that execution requires a specific amount of time to complete. That specific time can then be used to compare against other specific times. That comparison gives pace.

In non-technical and real world terms, we humans can repeatedly observe maneuvers being executed, innately determine an average speed of the executions observed, and then use that estimated speed to compare it against future executions of the same or similar maneuvers. We, as individuals, can almost definitively say that the execution currently being observed is faster than, slower than, or relatively the same as the one we internally use as our reference. We can do this for a small subset of the form or for the form as a whole. We can do this because humans, by our very nature, are wired to recognize patterns. There are many studies on how and why humans see patterns instinctively. But, that is beyond the scope of this guide. Suffice it to say that pattern recognition is one thing that humans do very well. And, pace is a pattern.

Execution of Long Form Two

In fact, we recognize patterns so well that we base entire martial arts styles upon these patterns. Specific styles have specific paces at which they execute their forms. For instance, Tai-Chi is know for its slow pace, where Wushu (and many other kung-fu styles) is know for its quicker pace. In comparison, American Kenpo forms tend to have a very practical pace. The pace of the execution of a form should be within a range where each of the maneuvers are effective and distinctive. Also, where other styles may have dramatically varying paces throughout the execution of a form, American Kenpo forms have a relatively consistent pace of execution. As a general rule, once a pace is set, that relative pace is maintained throughout the entire execution of the form.

The correct pace of an American Kenpo form is a relative and subjective thing. It depends upon a number of factors, such as: experience, taste, and/or style. In a general sense, less experience with a form means a slower pace. More experience means a faster pace, up to the point that the pace is determined to be optimal. It is at this point - i.e. the optimal pace, that things become subjective. What some might consider to be the optimal pace, others might consider the pace to be too slow, too fast, or just right. Unfortunately, there really is no universal optimal pace. It is left up to the general consensus of a group, or the lead instructor of the group, to determine optimal. But, fortunately, there are general rules which limit the maximum and minimum pace with which one should execute any form.

From the maximum pace perspective, the general rule is:

One should only execute a form as fast as it can be executed correctly.

In other words, if the pace of the form is so fast that the execution of each of the individual maneuvers in the form are not correct and distinctive, then the pace is too fast. This race condition is often referred to as mumble motion.

From the minimum pace perspective, the general rule is:

One should always execute a form fast enough such that each maneuver is effective.

In other words, if the pace of the form is slow enough to detract from the effectiveness of any maneuver, then the pace is too slow.

To get more on the subject of pace and correctness of form execution, see "Improving Your Execution of Long Form Two / General Errors - Pace".

One final note: pace should not to be confused with timing. Timing deals with the coordination of different maneuvers to achieve a specific goal - such as effectiveness, emphasis, intent, etc. Although, pace can affect timing, it is not timing.

Form Coordination

An important aspect of form execution, which is often overlooked or under-appreciated is coordination. Coordination is just as important an element as proper physical dimensions, formation, alignments, etc. to the proper execution of a form. Changes in coordination can dramatically change your, your opponent's, and/or an observer's understanding of, opinion of, reaction to, interaction with, and/or characterization of the maneuver(s) in question.

Even though coordination is extremely important to the execution of (a) maneuver(s), coordination is typically considered non-destructive. This means that even though coordination changes can change the emphasis point on maneuver(s) or alter whether an individual maneuver's execution is maximized or not, the general information contained within the movement(s) is typically not altered.

Coordination should not be confused with method. Where coordination concerns synchronization of (a) maneuver(s), method refers to the manner in which (i.e. how) (a) maneuver(s) is/are executed. For example, changing a maneuver's Method of Execution from Thrusting to Snapping, would, by definition, change the effect, intent, and information pertaining to the maneuver; but a change of method does not necessarily necessitate a change to the coordination of the maneuver. Also, as stated earlier, where as a change in coordination is typically non-destructive to the information presented in a form, a change to method is typically destructive.

In the context of forms, coordination can be viewed from two different perspectives:

1. coordination within the execution of an individual maneuver
2. coordination between the execution of a predefined set of maneuvers

© 2015 EPAKS Publications

For the purpose of this analysis, individual maneuver coordination will be referred to as Maneuver Coordination, while coordination between multiple maneuvers will be referred to as Base Set Coordination. The term "base set" is chosen because SGM Parker frequently referred a base set of moves as - a predetermined set of moves which formed a single unit for the purpose of analysis.

Note: To read more about coordination refer to Infinite Insight into Kenpo - Book 4 / Chapter 7.

So why is coordination important to the overall execution of the form? Well, lets assume the entire form was executed with exact same coordination throughout. The entire form would have no emphasis or coordination variations whatsoever. That would make for a very boring form to watch. Plus, it would give an observer no indication as to what elements of the form where intended to be important. It would be like listening to a speech where the speaker used a monotone voice and cadence throughout the entire speech. That would make for a very bad and very boring speech - no matter what was being said. But, if the same speaker were to add emphasis and voice inflections to parts of the speech, it would make for a very different speech. Even though the exact same words would have been used, the difference in what and whether people paid attention to what was being said would have been dramatic.

Another example of coordination would be to music. It is often said that the one element that is just as important to music as the notes is the space in between the notes. Image any piece of music that you remember. Now envision that music being executed with the exact same spacing between notes throughout the piece. Again, the change would dramatically alter the intention of the composer. But, technically the music wouldn't be changed, because all the notes would remain the same. This is why some famous performers are better than other non-famous performers even though they can sometimes play the same music. One may be very technical and boring, while the other 'puts their soul into the music'. It is the same for form execution. It can make the difference between a form that is boring or average to one that is exciting and stands out.

Maneuver Coordination

Maneuver coordination concerns synchronization related to a specific maneuver and its execution. To be more specific, this is coordination that is limited to - just before, during, and just after the execution of a specific maneuver; not multiple maneuvers. It refers to the precise syncing of and focusing of movement, mind, and breath to maximize results.

Maneuver coordination is what most practitioners would usually be referring to when talking about coordination in a general sense. It is the coordination of a single maneuver with all of its components, such as body maneuvers, foot maneuvers, defensive maneuvers, offensive maneuvers, mind, breath, etc. In relation to forms, proper coordination is defined as upper body maneuvers, lower body maneuvers, breath, and attention to be focused at precisely the same time.

Maneuver Coordination Manipulation

As a general rule when executing forms, maneuver coordination can be said to be correct if:
- the upper body and lower body are in sync
- the extremities and head are in sync with the rest of the body
- the body and breath are in sync
- the body and mind are in sync

For example, hand and foot coordination should be synchronized such that upper body maneuvers complete execution at approximately the same time as the lower body maneuvers. This allows for the upper body maneuvers to have a solid base upon execution. If one were to block too soon, the block would complete without having a solid base. In contrast, if one were to step, pause, and then block, the block would be considered delayed. In either case, the block would be considered not maximized for the maneuver, and the coordination would need to be corrected.

Also, another thing to consider is extremity and head coordination within a maneuver. Any (re)positioning of the arms / hands - legs / feet - head should be executed in-sync with the rest of the maneuver. Bad coordination of these elements of the maneuver can throw off the coordination of the entire maneuver.

It should become apparent that maneuver coordination is an objective goal that is definable, observable, and reproducible. And, with experience and practice, one should be able to discern a precisely and correctly executed maneuver from one that is incorrectly coordinated. If this skill is not acquired and honed, one will not be able to distinguish properly executed maneuvers from improperly executed maneuvers, and therefore, never be able to properly achieve proper coordination of the form.

Base Set Coordination

Base set coordination concerns the synchronization between multiple maneuvers (i.e. a group of maneuvers). This perspective relates to a base set of maneuvers and how coordination changes effect them. A base set of maneuvers can number as few as two or as many as all of the maneuvers in the form. This perspective allows for small groups of maneuvers to be analyzed independently of one-another; or as a sub-set of the whole. In other words, analysis can be done on a specific number of maneuvers in the form (i.e. a specific section) and look at how changes in coordination effect just that section, without concern for the rest of the form.

For the purposes of this analysis, each "base set" (i.e. section) of the form will correspond to the numbers designated in the written and visual illustration of the form. In other words, each number in the "Execution of Long Form Two - Form Standard Execution" or "Execution of Long Form Two - Form Standard Execution - Illustration" will be considered a Base set and analyzed as such.

As stated earlier, even though coordination is an extremely important aspect of the form, changes in Base Set Coordination generally fall into the non-destructive category of modifications. The reason for this is because coordination changes typically don't add or take away information in the form. Rather form coordination changes typically add emphasis to specific information in a form.

Just as a kiai adds audible and physical emphasis to a specific maneuver, coordination changes can be just as effective by adding visual, physical, and intent emphasis (see Appendix D - Intent). And, sometimes changes in coordination are also executed with a kiai, to add further emphasis. See "Improving Your Execution of Long Form Two / General Errors - Breathing" for more information on this subject.

Execution of Long Form Two

Base Set Coordination Manipulation

To illustrate how coordination can change emphasis, lets look at the first base set of the form (i.e. section #1 of the illustration) and analyze how coordination can change which maneuvers get emphasis with each change. Rather than re-write out the entire illustration or shorthand the description to cryptic abbreviations, a description short enough to discern what each maneuver of the base set is doing will be used.

So, each maneuver of base set #1 of the form will be written as follows:

Step-Block-Chamber
Chop
Shift-Poke-Chamber
Shift-Poke-Chamber

This should be enough information to build a mental visualization of the maneuvers in the form as it progresses. The only thing left is to represent the coordination between each of the maneuvers of the base set. The following legend will explain each symbol that will be used:

Symbol	Meaning
:	simple rest (i.e. single beat rest)
..	long rest (i.e. more than single beat rest)
...	undetermined rest (i.e. rest is a long as needed)
/	executed together (i.e. two or more moves executed simultaneously)
-	executed within a single beat (i.e. two or more moves executed within the approximate time span of a single move)
+	executed without delay between moves (i.e. executed continuously)
"	literal word (i.e. not a symbol - word contains symbol)

With this, there is enough information to succinctly write a coordination chart for the section of the form under discussion. For example, if the following were written:

Step-Block-Chamber : Chop : Shift-Poke-Chamber : Shift-Poke-Chamber

each maneuver in this base set would not contain any emphasis. Each maneuver of the form would contain the same amount of emphasis as each of the other maneuvers of the base set.

But, if the same section was written as follows:

Step-Block-Chamber : Chop+Shift-Poke-Chamber .. Shift-Poke-Chamber

this would denote the following:

1. the last maneuver was delayed (to emphasize that maneuver)
2. the middle two maneuvers where de-emphasized by making their individual timings shorter
3. the chop could have been changed from a major move to a minor move (if it started as a major)

Head Maneuvers

One thing that still needs to be discussed with base set coordination, looking (i.e. head turning) between base sets. When a change of direction is required, the standard and more dramatic head maneuver is to turn both the head and the eyes prior to re-positioning into the next base set. This is done even if the new direction can be viewed with just turning the eyes. This gives the observer(s) an indication as to the direction of the next base set to be executed and adds an element of flare to the form.

But, there is also a negative to the practice or emphasizing head turning in a real world scenario. This can be summed up with one word - telegraphing. There is a general rule in American Kenpo not to telegraph any maneuvers and some practitioners also obey this rule during form execution.

Either scenario has its merits. It is left up to the individual practitioner to decide how to handle head maneuvering. More important than the actual execution or not is the understanding of the pro's and con's of the maneuver. Some practitioners come to a compromise where-in the lower forms (i.e. the One's and Two's) are executed with the head maneuver, since they are the more basic and elementary forms, and left out of the upper forms (i.e. the remaining forms), since they contain more realistic and advanced maneuvering.

Form Standard Coordination

Although Long Form Two can be executed with a number of different coordination patterns, one should be chosen as the standard. This does not mean that the form cannot be executed correctly using a different coordination pattern; just that this is the most common pattern and makes the most sense as it relates to the information that this form is intended to convey.

Symbol Legend:

Symbol	Meaning
:	simple rest (i.e. single beat rest)
..	long rest (i.e. more than single beat rest)
...	undetermined rest (i.e. rest is a long as needed)
/	executed together (i.e. two or more moves executed simultaneously)
-	executed within a single beat (i.e. two or more moves executed within the approximate time span of a single move)
+	executed without delay between moves (i.e. executed continuously)
"	literal word (i.e. not a symbol - word contains symbol)

From a meditating horse stance...

1) - (toward 12:00H)
Step-Block-Chamber : Chop+Shift-Poke-Chamber .. Shift-Poke-Chamber :

2) - (toward 12:00H)
Step-Block-Chamber : Chop+Shift-Poke-Chamber .. Shift-Poke-Chamber :

© 2015 EPAKS Publications

Execution of Long Form Two   151

3) - (primarily toward 9:00H)
Cat/Chamber :
Step-Block/Punch : Punch : Punch .. Punch/Kick-Chamber
   +Plant :

4) - (primarily toward 3:00H)
Cat/Chamber :
Step-Block/Punch : Punch : Punch .. Punch/Kick-Chamber
   +Plant :

5) - (primarily toward 6:00H)
Cat/Chamber :
Step-Rotate-Block/Block : Shift-Block/"Hammer-fist" ..
Claw-"Back-knuckle" : "Back-knuckle" : "Back-knuckle" :

6) - (primarily toward 12:00H)
Step-Rotate-Block/Block : Shift-Block/"Hammer-fist" ..
Claw-"Back-knuckle" : "Back-knuckle" : "Back-knuckle" :

7) - (primarily toward 4:30H)
Step+Block-Punch-Chamber :
Shift-Punch-Chamber : Kick/Punch-Chamber : Plant+Shift-
   Punch-Buckle-Chamber :

8) - (toward 7:30H)
Step+Block-Punch-Chamber :
Shift-Punch-Chamber : Kick/Punch-Chamber : Plant+Shift-
   Punch-Buckle-Chamber :

9) - (toward 1:30H)
Kick/Punch+Plant : Step+Punch-Chamber+Forearm ..
Poke : Position : Poke : Poke :

10) - (toward 10:30H)
Kick/Punch-Chamber+Plant : Step+Punch-Chamber+Forearm ..
Poke : Position : Poke : Poke :

11) - (toward 10:30H)
Step-Block-Chamber : Untwist-Punch-Chamber :

© 2015 EPAKS Publications

12) - (toward 10:30H)
Step-Block : Untwist-Punch-Chamber :

13) - (toward 1:30H)
Step-Block+Position : "Back-knuckle" :

14) - (toward 1:30H)
Step-Block-Chamber+Position : "Back-knuckle" :

15) - (toward 1:30H)
Shift-"Push-down"-Chamber : Twist/Position : Step-Elbow+Claw :

16) - (toward 1:30H)
Shift-"Push-down"-Chamber : Twist/Position : Step-Elbow+Claw :

17) - (toward 1:30H)
Shift-"Push-down"-Chamber : Twist/Position : Step-Elbow+Claw :

18) - (toward 1:30H)
Shift-Punch/Cock : Shift-Forearm-Chamber :

19) - (toward 1:30H)
Step-Settle/Elbow-Chamber :

20) - (toward 1:30H)
Step-Settle/Elbow-Chamber :

21) - (primarily toward 12:00H)
Step-Shift/Elbow Sandwich +

22) - (toward 12:00H)
Position+Elbows : Elbows :

Meditating Horse ...

Chapter 5 - Variations to Long Form Two

As implied earlier in this guide, there are a vast number of variations that can occur during the execution of Long Form Two. These variations can range from destructive to non-destructive, from physical to mental, to anything in between. There is no possible way to highlight each and every variation, explain it, justify it, discredit it, and/or rationalize it. Rather, only some of the most common and important variations will be further discussed and analyzed. So, one should not be alarmed or distressed if a variation that is familiar to them is not discussed and/or highlighted in this chapter.

© 2015 EPAKS Publications

Form Execution - Variations

As mentioned earlier in the 'Execution of Long Form Two' section, variations to a form fall into one of two categories: destructive or non-destructive. This section will give examples of some common variations and explain how these variations fit into these categories. Consult the 'Execution of Long Form Two' for more insights into variations.

Non-destructive variations

Non-destructive variations are alterations to the standard execution of the form that do not detract from the information intended to be exposed in the form. These variations tend to be more palatable to a scrutinizing audience than destructive variations. There also tend to be far less non-destructive variations than destructive variations. This is due to the fact that it is much harder to alter the standard execution of the form without detracting from the standard information. Because of this fact, non-destructive variations tend to be more 'known' by well traveled, senior instructors.

1) Position of unused hand throughout the execution of the form.
In general, Long Form Two is considered a non-advanced form, i.e. a basic form: even though it is the most advanced of the 'dictionary' forms. So, most of the time the unused hand is retracted into chamber. Although realistic positioning was introduced in Short Form Two, it is still not executed as a standard maneuver in Long Form Two, even though it is demonstrated as standard positioning in various parts of the form.

Variations to Long Form Two

The most common areas where cocking the unused hand becomes an issue is:
Section #1 / #2 - at the end of sequence
Section #3 / #4 - as part of the sequence
Section #7 / #8 - at the end of sequence
Section #18 - as part of the sequence
Section #19 / #20 - as part of sequence

Each of these sections has at least one position where the unused arm can be chambered or not, some with multiple positions. For preferred hand / arm positioning, see the section 'Execution of Long Form' / 'Form Standard Execution' in this guide.

2) Open or closed Chambered Hand
Also, with the above stated sequences there is a decision as to whether the cocked hand is open or closed. For preferred hand posture, see the section 'Execution of Long Form' / 'Form Standard Execution' in this guide.

3) The Kiai
In general, American Kenpo forms, by default, don't have kiai's. That does not mean that one cannot nor should not add a kiai to a form. Kiai's have very practical value in defensive situations. But, they can also be used to add intensity and/or emphasis to a form and should be added, if desired.

Note: To read more about the kiai and breathing as it relates to American Kenpo refer to Infinite Insight into Kenpo - Book 4 / Chapter 3.

Destructive Variations

Destructive variations are alterations to the standard execution of the form that detract from the information intended to be exposed in the form. Because of this, destructive variations are discouraged from also becoming permanent variations. Permanent variations are variations to the standard execution of the form that are taught from instructor to student as the standard execution of the form.

One of the main reasons for the creation of a destructive variation is for competition. Variations can be used to 'spice up' a form in an attempt to get higher scores. Where this is perfectly acceptable and accounted for in the system (see the Salutation and "Signifying" - "Signifying Variations" section), it can also be abused to the point where the standard form is no longer recognizable - at which point it is arguable that one is still performing the same form.

Also, destructive variations are almost innumerable. Although some variations are popular and easily recognizable by the well traveled instructor, others are far more obscure and limited to a specific group of practitioners. What follows are some of the more common destructive variations.

Note: for further research in what information is demonstrated in the standard execution as it relates to the variation, see the "Analysis of Long Form Two" section.

1) Changing the foot maneuver angles in the form
This destructive variation alters the standard pattern of the form. Since Long Form Two is an extension of Short Form Two, and builds upon Short / Long Form One, it needs to maintain the same pattern. Also, the foot pattern fits with higher forms. Altering the foot pattern would disrupt this flow.

Variations to Long Form Two

2) Section #7 / #8 - not executing an inverted vertical back-knuckle
This destructive variation alters the intention of creating a blocking circle / striking sequence category. Altering this sequence would disrupt the completion of the category, leaving this category incomplete.

3) Section #7 / #8 - not executing a buckle
One of the main reasons the buckle with punch at the end of the sequence is necessary is that it fulfills a two-in-one and intent (see Appendix D) category that is demonstrated throughout the form. This destructive variation is common, because the buckle is easily overlooked as just a rotation into a horse. Lack of information about this maneuver can lead to another common variation - landing directly into a neutral bow; which would completely eliminate the two-in-one timing of this maneuver.

4) Section #9 / #10 - not executing an instep kick
This maneuver is typically replaced with a simple front crossover (then step out). The instep kick is needed because it is an integral part of a number of major categories demonstrated in the form.

5) Section #9 / #10 - execution the upward forearm as an upward block
One major reason this maneuver needs to follow the standard execution is because it is an integral part of an intent category that is demonstrated throughout the form.

Form Coordination - Variations

A characteristic question that might pop into one's mind about further analyzing coordination pattern variations might be - why? With the implied logic being - coordination pattern changes are typically non-destructive and don't effect the information in the form. So what is to be gained by analyzing these variations?

Some of the primary reasons for analysis of coordination pattern variations are:
    1) further clarifying the rationale of the standard coordination patterns
    2) illustrate some legitimate variations to coordination patterns
    3) explain the logic behind variations in coordination patterns
    4) validate why practitioners may want to execute the form with different coordination patterns
    5) convey important information about the form in relation to its coordination patterns
    6) uncover some of the diverse set of thoughts that exist about the form
    7) expose some of the nuances that exist within American Kenpo and its forms

The symbol legend used for timing is:

Variations to Long Form Two

Symbol	Meaning
:	simple rest (i.e. single beat rest)
..	long rest (i.e. more than single beat rest)
...	undetermined rest (i.e. rest is a long as needed)
/	executed together (i.e. two or more moves executed simultaneously)
-	executed within a single beat (i.e. two or more moves executed within the approximate time span of a single move)
+	executed without delay between moves (i.e. executed continuously)
"	literal word (i.e. not a symbol - word contains symbol)

Note: For simplicity of analysis, each base set of maneuvers in this section corresponds numerically with the base set from the section "Execution of Long Form Two - Form Standard Coordination".

1/2) The standard coordination pattern is:
    Step-Block-Chamber : Chop+Shift-Poke-Chamber .. Shift-Poke-Chamber :

The primary rationale behind this pattern is to put emphasis on the major themes of this form - i.e. to
    1) draw a link back to the previous forms - by maintaining the same relative coordination pattern
    2) highlight the physical reverse to Long Form One - via the last maneuver
    2) pause allows for kiai (i.e. more emphasis) on last maneuver

one common pattern variation is:
    Step-Block-Chamber .. Chop+Shift-Poke-Chamber : Shift-Poke-Chamber :

© 2015 EPAKS Publications

The primary rationale behind this pattern change is to:
1) emphasize the link back to previous forms - by the pause after the first maneuver
2) remove emphasis to the physical reverse of Long Form One - by not pausing before the last maneuver
3) "hide in plain sight" the reverse information of the last maneuver - by not emphasizing it

3/4) The standard coordination pattern is:
Cat/Chamber : Step-Block/Punch : Punch : Punch .. Kick/Punch-Chamber :

The primary rationale behind this pattern is:
1) to draw attention to the kick/punch - by pausing before last maneuver
2) pause allows for kiai (i.e. more emphasis) on last maneuver

one common pattern variation is:
Cat/Chamber .. Step-Block-Punch : Punch : Punch : Kick/Punch-Chamber :

The primary rationale behind this pattern is:
1) to emphasize the link back to Short Form Two - by the pause after the first maneuver
2) even out the emphasis to the four punches of the sequence - by eliminating pauses

5/6) The standard coordination pattern is:
Cat/Chamber (5 only) :
Step-Block/Block : Block/Strike ..
Claw-Strike + Strike + Strike :

The primary rationale behind this pattern is:
1) to draw attention to the triple back-knuckle strikes - by pausing before sequence

© 2015 EPAKS Publications

Variations to Long Form Two

one common pattern variation is:
    Cat/Chamber (5 only) ..
    Step-Block/Block : Block/Strike :
    Claw-Strike + Strike + Strike :

The primary rationale behind this pattern is:
    1) to emphasize the link back to Short Form Two - by pausing after first maneuver
    2) even out the emphasis to the back-knuckle sequence - by eliminating pauses

7/8) The standard coordination pattern is:
    Step-Block-Punch-Chamber :
    Punch-Chamber : Kick/Punch-Chamber :
    Plant+Shift-Punch-Buckle-Chamber :

The primary rationale behind this pattern is:
    1) to not put emphasis to any specific maneuver - by eliminating pauses
    2) no pauses means each maneuver has equal importance

one common pattern variation is:
    Step-Block-Punch-Chamber ..
    Punch-Chamber .. Kick/Punch-Chamber ..
    Plant : Shift-Punch-Buckle-Chamber :

The primary rationale behind this pattern is:
    1) to emphasize each maneuver of the section - by adding pauses
    2) has same effect as standard, but opposite way of obtaining results
    3) adds slightly more emphasis to two-in-one maneuvers
    4) pauses allows for kiai (i.e. more emphasis) on highlighted maneuvers

9/10) The standard coordination pattern is:
    Kick/Punch (-Chamber [10 only]) : Step+Punch-Chamber +Strike ..
    Poke : Position : Poke : Poke :

© 2015 EPAKS Publications

The primary rationale behind this pattern is:
   1) to put emphasis on the pokes - by pausing before maneuvers
   2) slight pause for positioning allows for less mumbled motion (with stance shifts and strikes)

one common pattern variation is:
   Kick/Punch (-Chamber [10 only]) : Step+Punch-Chamber +Strike :
   Poke : Position .. Poke : Poke :

The primary rationale behind this pattern is:
   1) to keep emphasis on the pokes, but allow more time for proper positioning - by adding pauses

11/12) The standard coordination pattern is:
   Step-Block-Chamber : Untwist-Punch-Chamber :

The primary rationale behind this pattern is:
   1) to not put emphasis on any specific maneuver - by eliminating pauses

one common pattern variation is:
   Step-Block-Chamber .. Untwist-Punch-Chamber :

The primary rationale behind this pattern is:
   1) to put emphasis on the two maneuvers - by adding a pause between
   2) pause allows for kiai (i.e. more emphasis) on strike

13/14) The standard coordination pattern is:
   Step-Block (-Chamber [14 only])+Position : Strike :

The primary rationale behind this pattern is:
   1) to not put emphasis on any specific maneuver - by eliminating pauses

one common pattern variation is:
   Step-Block (-Chamber [14 only])+Position .. Strike :

Variations to Long Form Two — 163

The primary rationale behind this pattern is:
1) to put emphasis on the two maneuvers - by adding a pause between
2) pause allows for kiai (i.e. more emphasis) on strike

15/16/17) The standard coordination pattern is:
Shift-Block-Chamber : Twist/Position : Step-Elbow+Claw :

The primary rationale behind this pattern is:
1) to not put emphasis on any specific maneuver - by eliminating pauses

one common pattern variation is:
Shift-Block-Chamber .. Twist/Position .. Step-Elbow+Claw :

The primary rationale behind this pattern is:
1) to put emphasis on each of the maneuvers - by adding a pause between
2) pause allows for kiai (i.e. more emphasis) on last maneuver

18) The standard coordination pattern is:
Shift-Punch/Cock : Shift-Strike-Chamber :

The primary rationale behind this pattern is:
1) to not put emphasis on any specific maneuver - by eliminating pauses

one common pattern variation is:
Shift-Punch/Cock .. Shift-Strike-Chamber :

The primary rationale behind this pattern is:
1) to put emphasis on the two maneuvers - by adding a pause between
2) pause allows for kiai (i.e. more emphasis) on strike

19/20) The standard coordination pattern is:
Step-Settle/Strike-Chamber :

The primary rationale behind this pattern is:
    1) to not put emphasis on any specific maneuver - by eliminating pauses

one common pattern variation is:
    Step .. Settle/Strike-Chamber :

The primary rationale behind this pattern is:
    1) to put emphasis on each of the maneuvers - by adding a pause between
    4) pause allows for kiai (i.e. more emphasis) on strike

21) The standard coordination pattern is:
    Step-Shift/Strike +

The primary rationale behind this pattern is:
    1) to not put emphasis on any specific maneuver - by eliminating pauses
    2) continue motion into isolation maneuvers

one common pattern variation is:
    Step .. Shift/Strike +

The primary rationale behind this pattern is:
    1) to put emphasis on each of the maneuvers - by adding a pause between
    2) pause allows for kiai (i.e. more emphasis) on strike
    3) separates first elbow from isolation sequence

22) The standard coordination pattern is:
    Position+Strike : Strike :

The primary rationale behind this pattern is:
    1) to put emphasis on elbow strikes
    2) separate ending meditation horse from form

one common pattern variation is:
    Position : Strike : Strike +

Variations to Long Form Two

The primary rationale behind this pattern is:
1) to put emphasis on each of the maneuvers - by adding a pause between
2) pauses allow for kiai (i.e. more emphasis) on strikes
3) blends closing meditation horse into form

The standard coordination pattern is:
Meditating Horse .. (salutation)

The primary rationale behind this pattern is:
1) to put emphasis on the meditation
2) separate ending meditation horse from salutation

one common pattern variation is:
Mediating Horse + (salutation)

The primary rationale behind this pattern is:
1) to create a more dynamic closure to the form
2) blends closing meditating horse with salutation

Chapter 6 - Understanding American Kenpo Forms

The most important thing to understand about an American Kenpo form is that it should not be thought of as an imaginary fight between the performer and (an) imaginary opponent(s). Many people make the assumption that is the way one must think about American Kenpo forms. This assumption comes from a couple of venues. For one, most self-defense systems structure their forms this way. For another, almost everyone visualizes an opponent in some way while executing their form. Visualization of an opponent is often used to focus strikes and maneuvers while also helping to provide psychological motivation. Also, visualization of an opponent is often used while learning and/or teaching a form.

Understanding American Kenpo Forms

In contrast to other styles of self-defense, American Kenpo forms are defined as:

A predefined series of maneuvers that:
1) show the rules and principles of motion,
2) that everything has a reverse and an opposite,
3) by giving an example

Another way to look at it is: an American Kenpo form can be thought of as a packet of information, exposed as movement, used to convey some of the information that shapes the framework of the American Kenpo system. This information is to be learned along with the movements, thus continuing an unbroken line of succession from instructor to student.

One common way to begin understanding the information presented in American Kenpo forms is to first break the forms down into their respective categories. Through some simple analysis one of the first things that should to begin become apparent is that their appears to be three different types of forms. This appearance is correct. The name of the concept associated with this observation is called the Dictionary / Encyclopedia / Appendix analogy. Whereas dictionaries define individual words encyclopedias explain things and concepts in greater detail. But, appendices expand and expound upon a small or focused area of information. Using this explanation, one can create a one-to-one correlation to the observed three categories of forms.

The first four forms (the one's and the two's) appear to have a slightly different style than the higher forms. These forms fall into the 'dictionary' category. They are commonly referred to as defining motion. By this it is meant that these forms concentrate more on the basics and demonstrating their opposites and reverses, and less upon the concepts and theories.

© 2015 EPAKS Publications

The higher forms (the three's and up) appear to be far more complex than the lower forms. These forms fall into the 'encyclopedia' category. These forms, in contrast to the dictionary forms, lean more toward concentrating on the concepts and theories of American Kenpo and less towards the physical opposites and reverses.

The remaining type of form (the set) is very different from all the other forms. Sets are so different, in fact, that they even have a different name - i.e. sets. These forms fall into the 'appendix' category. By this it is meant that these forms have a very narrow scope. In other words, these forms concentrate and explore the information present within specific genre of information/motion.

Understanding Long Form Two

So, how does Long Form Two fit into the Dictionary / Encyclopedia / Appendix analogy?

First, Long Form Two begins from a Meditating Horse stance. As a matter of fact, all forms up through Long Form Two begin from a Meditating Horse stance. Next, Long Form Two starts with a Right, Hammering, Inward Block and copies the In / Out / Up / Down sequence set in Short Form One. Again, all forms up through Long Form Two share these properties. Therefore one can safely say: all Dictionary forms start from a Meditating Horse stance; begin with a Right, Hammering, Inward Block; and work on an In / Out / Up / Down sequence.

Next, Long Form Two builds on the foundation which was set in place by Short Form One. Specifically, it extends the demonstration of the concept of opposites (left / right, up / down, in / out, etc) and reverses (forward / backward, inward / outward, clockwise / counter-clockwise, etc). An important thing to notice about Long Form Two extending the foundation is that even though the extension is primarily focused on physical motion - in this case, reverse physical motion, it also includes conceptual opposites.

As an example: an opposite to a closed hand is an open hand - physical motions. Whereas an opposite to understanding is not understanding - a concept.

© 2015 EPAKS Publications

Chapter 7 - Basics of Long Form Two

In order to properly analyze Long Form Two, one must first become aware of all the basics that are employed in its execution. Since the first four forms (the one's and the two's) are considered the "dictionary" forms (i.e. they define motion), the emphasis on highlighting the basics is of greater significance than in the higher forms. In contrast, the higher forms (Short Form Three and above) tend to have more emphasis on theories and concepts over basics.

Basics of Long Form Two 171

Also, by clarifying the utilized basics in Long Form Two, one can begin to see how it expands upon the basics of Short Form One and Short Form Two. Glancing at the "Quick Reference of Basics" section, one can also see a fairly high degree of uniformity and consistency throughout this form. This symmetry is not quite to the same degree as Short Form One nor Short Form Two. But, nearly every maneuver, or maneuver series, in this form has a matching counterpart, with only a few exceptions. This is similar to Long Form One, which also has a few maneuvers that have no complement (within the form).

The "Basics Utilized in Long Form Two" section gives a more detailed analysis to each employed basic. This detail is provided to help in understanding the implementation and emphasis of each basic (by providing intent and method) and for remembering each step of the form (by providing direction, position, focus, and side). With this analysis, it is fairly straightforward to re-assemble the correct execution of Long Form Two.

Quick Reference of Basics

Stances:
  Major
      Meditating Horse
      Neutral Bow
          Right / Left
      45 degree Cat
          Front
              Left / Right
      Fighting Horse (Offset)
          Left / Right
      Twist
          Left / Right
  Minor (Transitory)
      45 degree Cat
          Front
              Left / Right
      Forward Bow
          Right / Left

Basics of Long Form Two

Blocks:
  Major
    Inward
      Front Hand
        Right (Hammering) / Left (Thrusting)
    Vertical Outward
      Front Hand
        Left / Right
    Universal (Inward/Outside Downward)
      Right / Left
    Upward
      Front Hand
        Left / Right
    Outside Downward
      Front Hand
        Palm Down
          Left / Right
    Inside Downward
      Front Hand
        Palm Up
          Left / Right
        Palm Down
          Left / Right
    Push Down
      Rear Hand
        Left / Right
  Minor
    Positional Cover
      Rear Hand
        Left / Right
    Inside Downward (Double Factor)
      Palm Up
        Rear Hand
          Right / Left

© 2015 EPAKS Publications

Strikes:
   Hammering
      Outward Hand-Sword
         Right / Left
      Vertical Claw
         Left / Right
      Downward, Diagonal Half-Knuckle
         Right / Left
      Inward, Vertical Forearm
         Left
      Outward, Overhead Elbow
         Left / Right
      Inward, Overhead Elbow
         Left / Right
      Back Elbow
         Right
   Thrusting
      Horizontal, Four-Finger Poke
         Left / Right
      Vertical, Four-Finger Poke
         Right / Left
      Straight Punch (90 degree)
         Right / Left
      Vertical, Punch
         Right / Left
      Side Kick
         Left / Right
      Back-Knuckle
         Right / Left
      Inverted, Vertical Back-knuckle
         Left / Right
      Straight Punch
         Right / Left
      Front Kick
         Right / Left
      Instep Kick
         Left / Right
      Uppercut Punch
         Right / Left
      Upward, Horizontal Forearm

Basics of Long Form Two

    Right / Left
  Vertical, Two-Finger Poke
    Left / Right
  Inward, Horizontal Elbow
    Right
  Outward, Horizontal Elbow
    Left / Right
  Upward Elbow
    Left

Snapping
  Vertical, Punch
    Left / Right
  Vertical Back-Knuckle
    Left / Right

Foot Maneuvers:
   Individual
      Step Through
         Forward
            Right / Left
         Reverse
            Left / Right
      90 degree Cover
         Left / Right
      180 degree Cover
         Left / Right
      225 degree Cover
         Left
   Combinations
      Draw to Cat - Cover Step
         Draw Backward / Step Forward
            90 degree
               Left / Right
            180 degree
               Left
      Cross-over / Step out
         Forward
            Right / Left
      Cross-over / Twist out (Twist-thru)
         Reverse
            Left / Right
      Twist / Step out (Twist-thru)
         Forward
            Right / Left

Basics Utilized in Long Form Two

Presented in execution order

Stances	Side	Intent	Direction	Method/Area	Focus
Meditating Horse		Major			12:00H
Neutral Bow	Right	Major	Forward (12:00H)	Step Through (Forward)	12:00H
Forward Bow	Right	Major	Forward (12:00H)	Shift (Clockwise)	12:00H
Neutral Bow	Right	Major	Backward (6:00H)	Shift (Counter-Clockwise)	12:00H
Neutral Bow	Left	Major	Forward (12:00H)	Step Through (Forward)	12:00H
Forward Bow	Left	Major	Forward (12:00H)	Shift (Counter-Clockwise)	12:00H
Neutral Bow	Left	Major	Backward (6:00H)	Shift (Clockwise)	12:00H
Cat Stance 45 degree	Left	Major	Backward (6:00H)	Shift (Reverse)	12:00H
Fighting Horse (Offset)	Left	Major	Forward (9:00H)	90 degree Cover	9:00H
Cat Stance 45 degree	Right	Major	Backward (9:00H)	Shift (Reverse)	12:00H
Fighting Horse (Offset)	Right	Major	Forward (3:00H)	90 degree Cover	3:00H
Cat Stance 45 degree	Left	Major	Backward (3:00H)	Shift (Reverse)	12:00H
Rear Twist	Left	Minor	Backward (6:00H)	Step (Reverse)	6:00H
Neutral Bow	Left	Major	Forward (6:00H)	180 degree Cover (Counter-Clockwise)	6:00H
Forward Bow	Left	Major	Forward (6:00H)	Shift (Counter-Clockwise)	6:00H
Neutral Bow	Left	Major	Backward (12:00H)	Shift (Clockwise)	6:00H
Rear Twist (Modified)	Right	Minor	Backward (12:00H)	Step (Reverse)	12:00H
Neutral Bow	Right	Major	Forward (12:00H)	180 degree Cover (Clockwise)	12:00H

© 2015 EPAKS Publications

The Official EPAKS Guide to Long Form Two

Stances	Side	Intent	Direction	Method/Area	Focus
Forward Bow	Right	Major	Forward (12:00H)	Shift (Clockwise)	12:00H
Neutral Bow	Right	Major	Backward (6:00H)	Shift (Counter-Clockwise)	12:00H
Reverse Bow	Left	Minor	Backward (10:30H)	Step (Reverse)	4:30H
Neutral Bow	Left	Major	Forward (4:30H)	Shift (Counter-Clockwise)	4:30H
Forward Bow	Left	Major	Forward (4:30H)	Shift (Counter-Clockwise)	4:30H
Forward Bow (Modified)	Right	Minor	Forward (4:30H)	Step Through (Forward)	4:30H
Fighting Horse	Right	Major	Forward (4:30H)	Shift (Counter-Clockwise)	4:30H
Cat Stance 45 degree	Right	Minor	Backward (1:30H)	Shift (Clockwise)	7:30H
Neutral Bow	Right	Major	Forward (7:30H)	90 degree Cover (Clockwise)	7:30H
Forward Bow	Right	Major	Forward (7:30H)	Shift (Clockwise)	7:30H
Forward Bow (Modified)	Left	Minor	Forward (7:30H)	Step Through (Forward)	7:30H
Fighting Horse	Left	Major	Forward (7:30H)	Shift (Clockwise)	7:30H
Front Twist	Left	Major	Forward (1:30H)	Front Crossover (Forward)	1:30H
Neutral Bow	Right	Major	Forward (1:30H)	Step out (Forward)	1:30H
Forward Bow	Right	Major	Forward (1:30H)	Shift (Clockwise)	1:30H
Neutral Bow	Right	Major	Backward (7:30H)	Shift (Counter-Clockwise)	1:30H
Front Twist	Right	Major	Forward (10:30H)	Front Crossover (Forward)	10:30H
Neutral Bow	Left	Major	Forward (10:30H)	Step out (Forward)	10:30H
Forward Bow	Left	Major	Forward (10:30H)	Shift (Counter-Clockwise)	10:30H
Neutral Bow	Left	Major	Backward (4:30H)	Shift (Clockwise)	10:30H

© 2015 EPAKS Publications

Basics of Long Form Two 179

Stances	Side	Intent	Direction	Method/Area	Focus
Front Twist	Right	Major	Backward (4:30H)	Front Crossover (Reverse)	10:30H
Neutral Bow	Right	Major	Backward (4:30H)	Unwind (Counter-Clockwise)	10:30H
Front Twist	Left	Major	Backward (4:30H)	Front Crossover (Reverse)	10:30H
Neutral Bow	Left	Major	Backward (4:30H)	Unwind (Clockwise)	10:30H
Neutral Bow	Left	Major	Backward (7:30H)	90 degree Cover	1:30H
Neutral Bow	Right	Major	Backward (7:30H)	Step Through (Reverse)	1:30H
Forward Bow	Right	Major	Forward (1:30H)	Shift (Clockwise)	1:30H
Front Twist	Right	Major	Forward (1:30H)	Shift (Clockwise)	1:30H
Neutral Bow	Left	Major	Forward (1:30H)	Step out (Forward)	1:30H
Forward Bow	Left	Major	Forward (1:30H)	Shift (Counter-Clockwise)	1:30H
Front Twist	Left	Major	Forward (1:30H)	Shift (Counter-Clockwise)	1:30H
Neutral Bow	Right	Major	Forward (1:30H)	Step out (Forward)	1:30H
Forward Bow	Right	Major	Forward (1:30H)	Shift (Clockwise)	1:30H
Front Twist	Right	Major	Forward (1:30H)	Shift (Clockwise)	1:30H
Neutral Bow	Left	Major	Forward (1:30H)	Step out (Forward)	1:30H
Forward Bow	Left	Major	Forward (1:30H)	Shift (Counter-Clockwise)	1:30H
Neutral Bow	Left	Major	Reverse (7:30H)	Shift (Clockwise)	1:30H
Neutral Bow	Right	Major	Reverse (7:30H)	Step Through (Reverse)	1:30H
Neutral Bow	Left	Major	Reverse (7:30H)	Step Through (Reverse)	1:30H
Front Twist (Modified)	Right	Major	Reverse (7:30H)	Crossover (Reverse)	1:30H

© 2015 EPAKS Publications

Stances	Side	Intent	Direction	Method/Area	Focus
Meditating Horse		Major	Reverse (7:30H)	Shift (Counter-Clockwise)	12:00H

Blocks	Side	Intent	Direction	Position	Method/Area	Focus
Inward	Right	Major	Inward (10:30H)	Front	Hammering	12:00H
Inward	Left	Major	Inward (1:30H)	Front	Thrusting	12:00H
Vertical Outward	Left	Major	Outward (6:00H)	Front	Thrusting	9:00H
Vertical Outward	Right	Major	Outward (6:00H)	Front	Thrusting	3:00H
Universal (Inward / Downward)	Right / Left	Major	Inward (10:30H) / Downward (9:00H)	Front / Rear	Hammering	6:00H
Upward	Left	Major	Upward (12:00V / 6:00H)	Front	Thrusting	6:00H
Universal (Inward / Downward)	Left / Right	Major	Inward (1:30H) / Downward (3:00H)	Front / Rear	Thrusting / Hammering	12:00H
Upward	Right	Major	Upward (12:00V / 12:00H)	Front	Thrusting	12:00H
Inside Downward (Palm Up)	Right	Minor	Inward (1:30H) / Downward (6:00V)	Rear	Hammering	4:30H
Outside Downward (Palm Down)	Left	Major	Downward (6:00V) / Outward (1:30H)	Front	Hammering	4:30H
Inside Downward (Palm Up)	Left	Minor	Inward (10:30H) / Downward (6:00V)	Rear	Hammering	7:30H
Outside Downward (Palm Down)	Right	Major	Downward (6:00V) / Outward (7:30H)	Front	Hammering	7:30H
Inside Downward (Palm Up)	Left	Major	Inward (4:30H) / Downward (6:00V)	Front	Hammering	10:30H
Inside Downward (Palm Up)	Right	Major	Inward (4:30H) / Downward (6:00V)	Front	Hammering	10:30H
Inside Downward	Left	Minor	Inward (4:30H) / Downward (6:00V)	Front	Hammering	1:30H

Basics of Long Form Two

Blocks	Side	Intent	Direction	Position	Method/Area	Focus
(Palm Down) Inside Downward (Palm Down)	Right	Major	Inward (10:30H) / Downward (6:00V)	Front	Hammering	10:30H
Push-Down	Left	Major	Downward (6:00V)	Rear	Hammering (Pressing)	1:30H
Push-Down	Right	Major	Downward (6:00V)	Rear	Hammering (Pressing)	1:30H
Push-Down	Left	Major	Downward (6:00V)	Rear	Hammering (Pressing)	1:30H

Strikes	Side	Intent	Direction	Position	Method/Area	Focus
Outward Hand-Sword	Right	Major	Outward (3:00H) Downward Diagonal (4:30V)	Front	Hammering	12:00H
Horizontal, Four Finger Poke	Left	Major	Forward (12:00H)	Rear	Thrusting	12:00H
Vertical, Four Finger Poke	Right	Major	Forward (12:00H)	Front	Thrusting	12:00H
Outward Hand-Sword	Left	Major	Outward (9:00H) Downward Diagonal (7:30V)	Front	Hammering	12:00H
Horizontal, Four Finger Poke	Right	Major	Forward (12:00H)	Rear	Thrusting	12:00H
Vertical, Four Finger Poke	Left	Major	Forward (12:00H)	Front	Thrusting	12:00H
Straight Punch	Right	Major	Forward (9:00H)	Rear	Thrusting	9:00H
Straight Punch	Left	Major	Forward (9:00H)	Front	Thrusting	9:00H
Straight Punch	Right	Major	Forward (9:00H)	Rear	Thrusting	9:00H
Vertical Punch	Left	Minor	Forward (9:00H)	Front	Snapping	9:00H
Side Kick	Left	Minor	Forward (9:00H)	Front	Snapping	9:00H
Straight Punch	Left	Major	Forward (3:00H)	Rear	Thrusting	3:00H
Straight Punch	Right	Major	Forward (3:00H)	Front	Thrusting	3:00H
Straight Punch	Left	Major	Forward (3:00H)	Rear	Thrusting	3:00H
Vertical Punch	Right	Minor	Forward (3:00H)	Front	Snapping	3:00H
Side Kick	Right	Minor	Forward (3:00H)	Front	Snapping	3:00H
Hammer-fist	Right	Major	Forward (6:00H)	Rear	Hammering	6:00H

© 2015 EPAKS Publications

Strikes	Side	Intent	Direction	Position	Method/Area	Focus
			Upward Diagonal (1:30V)			
Claw	Left	Minor	Downward (6:00V)	Front	Clawing	6:00H
Back-Knuckle	Right	Major	Outward (1:30H)	Rear	Thrusting	6:00H
Back-Knuckle	Left	Major	Outward (10:30H)	Front	Thrusting	6:00H
Back-Knuckle	Right	Major	Outward (1:30H)	Rear	Thrusting	6:00H
Hammer-fist	Left	Major	Forward (12:00H)	Rear	Hammering	12:00H
			Upward Diagonal (1:30V)			
Claw	Right	Minor	Downward (6:00V)	Front	Clawing	12:00H
Back-Knuckle	Left	Major	Outward (10:30H)	Rear	Thrusting	12:00H
Back-Knuckle	Right	Major	Outward (1:30H)	Front	Thrusting	12:00H
Back-Knuckle	Left	Major	Outward (10:30H)	Rear	Thrusting	12:00H
Inverted, Vertical Back-knuckle	Left	Major	Forward (7:30H)	Front	Round-housing	4:30H
Straight Punch	Right	Major	Forward (4:30H)	Rear	Thrusting	4:30H
Straight Punch	Left	Major	Forward (4:30H)	Front (to Rear)	Thrusting	4:30H
Ball Kick	Right	Minor	Forward (4:30H)	Rear (to Front)	Snapping	4:30H
Vertical Punch	Right	Major	Forward (4:30H)	Front	Thrusting	4:30H
Shin Buckle	Right	Minor	Forward (3:00H)	Front	Pressing	4:30H
Inverted, Vertical Back-knuckle	Right	Major	Forward (4:30H)	Front	Round-housing	7:30H
Straight Punch	Left	Major	Forward (7:30H)	Rear	Thrusting	7:30H
Straight Punch	Right	Major	Forward (7:30H)	Front (to Rear)	Thrusting	7:30H
Ball Kick	Left	Minor	Forward (7:30H)	Rear (to Front)	Snapping	7:30H
Vertical Punch	Left	Major	Forward (7:30H)	Front	Thrusting	7:30H
Shin Buckle	Left	Minor	Forward (9:00H)	Front	Pressing	7:30H
Half-Knuckle	Left	Major	Forward (1:30H) Downward Diagonal (4:30V)	Rear	Hammering	1:30H

Basics of Long Form Two — 183

Strikes	Side	Intent	Direction	Position	Method/Area	Focus
Instep (arch) Kick	Left	Major	Forward (1:30H)	Rear	Thrusting	1:30H
Uppercut Punch	Right	Minor	Upward (1:30H) / (1:00V)	Front	Thrusting	1:30H
Upward, Horizontal Forearm	Right	Major	Upward (1:30H) / 1:00V)	Front	Thrusting	1:30H
Vertical, Two-Finger Poke	Left	Major	Forward (1:30H)	Rear	Thrusting	1:30H
Vertical, Two-Finger Pole	Right	Major	Forward (1:30H)	Front	Thrusting	1:30H
Vertical, Two-Finger Pole	Left	Major	Forward (1:30H)	Rear	Thrusting	1:30H
Half-Knuckle	Right	Major	Forward (10:30H) Downward Diagonal (4:30V)	Rear	Hammering	10:30H
Instep (arch) Kick	Right	Major	Forward (10:30H)	Rear	Thrusting	10:30H
Uppercut Punch	Left	Minor	Upward (10:30H) / 1:00V)	Front	Thrusting	10:30H
Upward, Horizontal Forearm	Left	Major	Upward (10:30H) / (1:00V)	Front	Thrusting	10:30H
Vertical, Two-Finger Poke	Right	Major	Forward (10:30H)	Rear	Thrusting	10:30H
Vertical, Two-Finger Poke	Left	Major	Forward (10:30H)	Front	Thrusting	10:30H
Vertical, Two-Finger Poke	Right	Major	Forward (10:30H)	Rear	Thrusting	10:30H
Vertical Punch	Right	Major	Forward (10:30H)	Front	Thrusting	10:30H
Vertical Punch	Left	Major	Forward (10:30H)	Front	Thrusting	10:30H
Vertical, Back-Knuckle	Left	Minor	Upward (1:30H) / (1:30V)	Front	Snapping	1:30H
Vertical Back-Knuckle	Right	Minor	Upward (1:30H) / (1:30V)	Front	Snapping	1:30H
Outward, Overhead Elbow	Left	Major	Downward (1:30H) / (5:00V)	Front	Hammering	1:30H

© 2015 EPAKS Publications

Strikes	Side	Intent	Direction	Position	Method/Area	Focus
(Heel-Palm) Claw	Left	Major	Downward (1:30H) / (5:00V)	Front	Hammering	1:30H
Outward, Overhead Elbow	Right	Major	Downward (1:30H) / (5:00V)	Front	Hammering	1:30H
(Heel-Palm) Claw	Right	Major	Downward (1:30H) / (5:00V)	Front	Hammering	1:30H
Outward, Overhead Elbow	Left	Major	Downward (1:30H) / (5:00V)	Front	Hammering	1:30H
(Heel-Palm) Claw	Left	Major	Downward (1:30H) / (5:00V)	Front	Hammering	1:30H
Straight Punch	Right	Major	Forward (1:30H)	Rear	Thrusting	1:30H
Inside, Vertical Forearm	Left	Major	Forward (3:00H)	Front	Hammering	1:30H
Inward, Overhead Elbow	Right	Major	Downward (1:30H) / (6:00V)	Front	Hammering	1:30H
Inward, Overhead Elbow	Left	Major	Downward (1:30H) / (6:00V)	Front	Hammering	1:30H
Inward Elbow (Sandwich)	Right	Major	Inward (10:30H)		Thrusting	12:00H
Outward Elbow	Left	Major	Outward (9:00H)		Thrusting	12:00H
Outward Elbow	Right	Major	Outward (3:00H)		Thrusting	12:00H
Upward Elbow	Left	Major	Upward (12:00H) / (12:00V)		Thrusting	12:00H
Back Elbow	Right	Major	Backward (6:00H)		Hammering	12:00H

Foot & Body Maneuvers	Side	Intent	Direction	Focus
Step Through	Right	Major	Forward (12:00H)	12:00H
Shift (Reach)	Right	Major	Forward (Clockwise) (12:00H)	12:00H
Shift (Power)	Right	Major	Backward (Counter-Clockwise) (6:00H)	12:00H
Step Through	Left	Major	Forward (12:00H)	12:00H
Shift (Reach)	Left	Major	Forward (Counter-Clockwise) (12:00H)	12:00H

© 2015 EPAKS Publications

Basics of Long Form Two — 185

Foot & Body Maneuvers	Side	Intent	Direction	Focus
Shift (Power)	Left	Major	Backward (Clockwise) (6:00H)	12:00H
Shift (Distance)	Left	Major	Backward (6:00H)	12:00H
90 degree Cover	Left	Major	Forward (9:00H)	9:00H
Step (Re-plant)	Left	Major		9:00H
Shift (Distance)	Right	Major	Backward (9:00H)	12:00H
180 degree Cover	Right	Major	Forward (3:00H)	3:00H
Step (Re-plant)	Right	Major		3:00H
Shift (Distance)	Left	Major	Backward (3:00H)	12:00H
Step	Left	Minor	Forward (6:00H)	6:00H
180 degree Cover	Left	Major	Forward (12:00H)	12:00H
Shift (Reach)	Left	Major	Forward (Counter-Clockwise) (6:00H)	6:00H
Shift	Left	Major	Backward (Clockwise) (12:00H)	6:00H
Step	Right	Minor	Forward (12:00H)	12:00H
180 degree Cover	Right	Major	Forward (12:00H)	12:00H
Shift (Reach)	Right	Major	Forward (12:00H)	12:00H
Shift	Right	Major	Backward (Counter-Clockwise) (6:00H)	12:00H
Step	Right	Minor	Backward (10:30H)	4:30H
225 degree Cover	Left	Major	Forward (4:30H)	4:30H
Shift (Reach)	Left	Major	Forward (Counter-Clockwise) (4:30H)	4:30H
Step Through	Right	Major	Forward (4:30H)	4:30H
Shift (Power)	Right	Major	Forward (4:30H)	4:30H
Shift (Distance)	Right	Minor	Backward (1:30H)	7:30H
90 degree Cover	Right	Major	Forward (7:30H)	7:30H
Shift (Reach)	Left	Major	Forward (7:30H)	7:30H
Step Through	Right	Major	Forward (7:30H)	7:30H
Shift (Power)	Right	Major	Forward (7:30H)	7:30H
Crossover	Left	Major	Forward (1:30H)	1:30H
Step out	Right	Major	Forward (1:30H)	1:30H
Shift (Reach)	Right	Major	Forward (Clockwise) (1:30H)	1:30H
Shift	Right	Major	Backward (Counter-Clockwise) (7:30H)	1:30H
Crossover	Right	Major	Forward (10:30H)	10:30H
Step out	Left	Major	Forward (10:30H)	10:30H
Shift	Left	Major	Forward (Counter-Clockwise) (10:30H)	10:30H
Shift	Left	Major	Backward (Clockwise) (4:30H)	10:30H
Step	Left	Major	Backward (4:30H)	10:30H

© 2015 EPAKS Publications

Foot & Body Maneuvers	Side	Intent	Direction	Focus
Shift (Power)	Right	Major	(Counter-Clockwise)	10:30H
Step	Right	Major	Backward (4:30H)	10:30H
Shift (Power)	Left	Major	(Clockwise)	10:30H
90 degree Cover	Left	Major	Backward (Clockwise) (7:30H)	1:30H
Step Through	Left	Major	Backward (7:30H)	1:30H
Shift (Reach)	Right	Major	Forward (Clockwise) (1:30H)	1:30H
Shift (Positional)	Right	Minor	(Clockwise)	1:30H
Step out	Left	Major	Forward (1:30H)	1:30H
Shift (Reach)	Left	Major	Forward (Counter-Clockwise) (1:30H)	1:30H
Shift (Positional)	Left	Minor	(Counter-Clockwise)	1:30H
Step out	Right	Major	Forward (1:30H)	1:30H
Shift (Reach)	Right	Major	Forward (Clockwise) (1:30H)	1:30H
Shift (Positional)	Right	Minor	(Clockwise)	1:30H
Step out	Left	Major	Forward (1:30H)	1:30H
Step Through	Left	Major	Backward (7:30H)	1:30H
Step Through	Right	Major	Backward (7:30H)	1:30H
Step	Left	Minor	Backward (7:30H)	1:30H
Shift		Major	(Counter-Clockwise) (12:00H)	12:00H

Chapter 8 - Focal Points of Long Form Two

Each American Kenpo form adds something to the overall system as a whole. This is done in such a way as to add to the knowledge base set down by previous forms. Therefore it is logical to conclude that each form has specific areas / maneuvers that can be considered highlights, themes, spotlights, focal points, etc. which help to fulfill this goal. Long Form Two is no exception.

These focal points in a form can be broken down into any number of groups, depending upon how one wishes to categorize them. For the purposes of this guide, the categories will be as follows:

1) Common - i.e. items that are generally known and taught
2) Less Common - i.e. items that are know and sometimes taught, but generally to advanced or experienced practitioners
3) Obscure - i.e. items that are often overlooked, forgotten, not taught, and/or obscure in nature

One thing to keep in mind with this type of breakdown of Long Form Two: it is not intended to be an all encompassing analysis of the form. But, rather to call out the focal points of the form. Instead, the "Analysis of Long Form Two" section of this guide is intended for the purpose of comprehensive analysis. In other words, this section can be construed more as a trivia like section, rather than an actual analysis section.

Common Focal Points

1) **The beginning sequence of the form is a constant continuation of the same sequence started in Short Form One.**
This begins with the inward block and continues building all the way up to the sequence in Long Form Two. Even though the basics are not exactly the same, each sequence is logically and physically building upon the previous sequence.

2) **The In / Out / Up / Down sequence binds the forms Short Form One - Long Form Two together.**
The first four forms keep this pattern as their fundamental sequence, even though each form continues to expand, in some unique way, upon the sequence.

3) **The first four forms are usually group together.**
Short Form One - Long Form Two can be categorized together to form the 'dictionary' forms. This distinction means that the emphasis of this group of forms is upon basics - not theories. This group ends with Long Form Two, leaving different groupings for the remaining forms / sets.

4) **Long Form Two form introduces kicking.**
These maneuvers add the opposite end of the body introduced at the first move of Short Form One. It is added in the last of the 'beginning' forms, because kicking is considered more of an advanced basic - due to destabilizing of the base during the execution of the maneuver.

5) **Long Form Two introduces Universal Blocks.**
This maneuver adds two-in-one timing with blocks. It also can be categorized with the two-in-one kick/strike maneuvers.

© 2015 EPAKS Publications

Less Common Focal Points

1) **Long Form Two adds the twist through foot maneuver.**
The step through foot maneuver, if broken down, consists of both distance and rotation. But, the twist through foot maneuver is designed to highlight each of these elements, by executing them independently of each other. Either by doing distance first, then rotation - or by doing rotation first, then distance.

2) **The blocking sequence in the second half of Long Form Two contains the blocking sequence of the isolation in Long Form One.**
But, the sequence is out of order. Long Form One's is: Inside-downward palm-down, Inside-downward palm-up, push down. Long Form Two's sequence is: Inside-downward palm-up, Inside-downward palm-down, push down.

3) **The triple back-knuckles compliment the triple blocks of Long Form One.**
But, they demonstrate the opposite concept - i.e. they are offensive.

Obscure Focal Points

1) Long Form Two completes a step / block sequence started in Short Form One.
The first downward block of each of the dictionary form creates the following category:
- Short Form One - step away with left foot / block with right arm
- Long Form One - step in with right foot / block with right arm
- Short Form Two - step in with left foot / block with left arm
- Long Form Two - step away with right foot / block with left arm

2) The elbows of Long Form Two are isolated to the second half of the form.
This is to help flow this form into the next form seamlessly.

3) Long Form Two adds striking to all three height zones.
Created by:
- Back-knuckles - high zone
- punches - middle zone
- kicks - low zone

4) Long Form Two adds two-in-one timing for striking and body side
Created by:
- kick with punch - front with front
- kick with punch - front with back (and left with right)
- kick with half-knuckle - back with back
- elbow with elbow - neither (but, left with right)
- elbow with elbow - neither (but, front with back)

© 2015 EPAKS Publications

Chapter 9 - Analysis of Long Form Two

In order to analyze Long Form Two, one must first answer two simple questions:

1) What is it that is being analyzed?
2) What is the purpose of the analysis?

What is being analyzed?

The obvious answer is Long Form Two is being analyzed. But what is Long Form Two? In the most fundamental terms, Long Form Two is a series of basics executed together to create a form. But, what is the purpose of creating a form? As mentioned earlier in this guide, American Kenpo forms are not to be thought of as a choreographed fight between the practitioner and (an) imaginary opponent(s) for demonstration purposes. American Kenpo forms are defined as:

A predefined series of maneuvers that:
1) show the rules and principles of motion,
2) that everything has a reverse and an opposite,
3) by giving an example

Provided with the above information, one can move on to the second question posed.

What is the purpose of the analysis?

Again, the obvious answer is to expose the information presented in Long Form Two. But, what information is being exposed? From the definition derived above, one can refine their analysis to concentrate on the three elements that compose the definition. And, highlight and/or clarify any pertinent information or contextual data about the information that can help to achieve a complete analysis.

Presenting the analysis

This now leaves one major follow-up question - "how will this information be presented?"

The information exposed from Long Form Two will be broken down into four sections:

Beginner / Intermediate Information
This analysis section summarizes and details information for which a beginner to intermediate practitioner should be exposed to about the form. This section is useful to the practitioner because it allows them to check what they know against what should be known about the form at the beginner to intermediate level. The section is also useful to the instructor by providing a filtered, detailed analysis of what information should be conveyed to both the beginning and intermediate student when teaching and reviewing the form.

Advanced Information
This section summarizes and details the information for which an advanced practitioner / instructor should be exposed to about the form. This section is intended for the both advanced practitioner and the instructor. It covers some of the lesser known or often overlooked information present in the form.

Reverse / Opposite Analysis
This section collates and exposes the reverse / opposite information present in the form. This section is important because, by definition, American Kenpo forms give an example of reverses and opposites. This section is intended to help simplify this type of analysis by exposing the reverses and opposites present throughout the form.

Principles / Rules / Theories / Concepts / Definitions
This section summarizes the American Kenpo terms related to the form. Each term will need to be further researched by the reader. This section is provided mainly as a starting point into further analysis of American Kenpo terminology, concepts, theories, rules, and principles.

Intra vs Inter Form Analysis

When analyzing any form, one must first consider the scope of their analysis. Does the analysis only include the form itself, or does the analysis include other forms in the system? Any analysis should first start with the form itself, and then expand to include the rest of the forms in the system.

In other words, each form can be thought of as both a self-contained entity, and a component of a larger structure. By thinking of the forms in this way, one can build boundaries in which to perform their analysis. Analysis contained within the boundaries of the form is referred to as intra-form analysis. Analysis outside of the boundaries of the form is referred to as inter-form analysis.

One suggested way in which to progress through the analysis of a form is to begin by examining each element of the form, comparing and contrasting it to other elements of the form, to ultimately build up an analysis of the entire form. The next step would be to expand the analysis to the earlier forms, looking to find ways in which the current form completes missing information, while also adding to the knowledge base of the lower forms. Next, as new forms are learned, this method of analysis should repeat itself with this newly learned form. And for the final step, the practitioner should go back to each of the previously known forms, filling in any newly discovered pieces of information that were previously overlooked or not known until exposed by the learning of the new form.

In the case of Long Form Two, inter-form analysis is easier than in higher forms. This is mainly due to the fact that Long Form Two, in essence, contains a great deal of the information presented in Short Form One, Long Form One, and Short Form Two.

© 2015 EPAKS Publications

Beginning / Intermediate Analysis

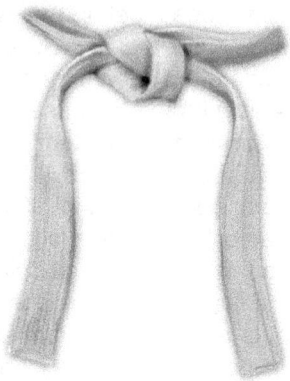

This section will cover the analysis of Long Form Two from the perspective of what should be known, learned and / or taught to the novice to intermediate practitioner. One would be justified in asking why not just analyze Long Form Two in one overarching section? Why segment out the analysis into two major sections - Beginner / Intermediate and Advanced? There are a number of reasons for this format.

First, by splitting the analysis in this way, a beginning to intermediate reader can be exposed to just the information for which they should be aware; without being mired down in information that is way beyond their current knowledge level of the American Kenpo system. Secondly, from an instructor's perspective by splitting the analysis in this manner this guide book can be used to summarize the information that an instructor should be imparting to their students about the form at the appropriate level.

Also, since the American Kenpo system is composed of many principles, rules, theories, concepts, ideas, definitions, and maneuvers, it is very easy for the beginning to intermediate practitioner to be overwhelmed with information about a seemingly easy form. By segmenting the information, it makes exposure to the comprehensive knowledge base of the American Kenpo system less intimidating and overwhelming. This methodology is also applicable to the instructor as they teach the information about Long Form Two to their student(s). Too much information in a short period of time can sometimes be just as bad as too little.

Finally, the information in this section tends to be information that is commonly presented. In other words, information in this section is more openly taught by instructors about the form. The information in the Advanced Analysis section tends more towards self-exposed information - that is, information that the practitioner them-self should be able to deduce on their own, with little to no help from an instructor. That being said, this section is a building block for the Advanced Analysis section. By using the method of analysis presented in this section, much of the information presented in the Advanced Analysis section should be deducible through self-analysis of the form on one's own.

As a final note: It is advisable that the beginner to intermediate practitioner review the information presented in this section numerous times. By doing this, the reader will be able to reflect on and get comfortable with any new information learned from this section. Then, at a future date, come back to this same section, review the reflected upon information, and hopefully glean more new information through each repeated exposure to this section - until all of the information presented in this section is easily recalled and understood.

Walk-Through Analysis

The design of the lower four (4) American Kenpo forms (aka the 'dictionary' forms) is to start with the information presented in Short Form One and build upon it with each progressive form. One of the best ways to illustrate how this is accomplished is to step through the form and explain the information exposed from each maneuver - exposing how it compounds the information from the previous forms. Through this approach the reader will be presented with both the obvious information and the not so obvious and/or often overlooked information. This not so obvious information is 'hidden' in plain sight, and it consists of information that is demonstrated during the execution of the form, but not necessarily explained. Or if explained, not explained thoroughly or often explained in a purposely vague manner.

© 2015 EPAKS Publications

Analysis of Long Form Two

Form Overview Analysis

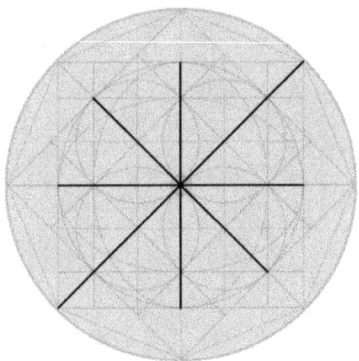

An overview of this form exposes the following themes:
- two-in-one timing
- one-in-one timing
- simultaneous strikes
- simultaneous blocks
- simultaneous defense / offense
- minor angles (in addition to major angles)
- advancing (as reverse of retreating)

An analysis overview of this form exposes that the form introduces:
- new strikes: fingers, knuckles, forearm, elbows, kicks
- new blocks: universal
- new stances: transitory reverse bow
- new foot maneuvers: twist through

Inward Block Sequence

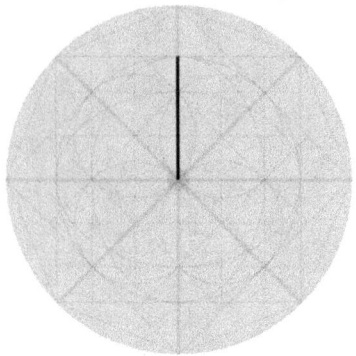

The inward block sequence is as follows:
1) step forward into a right neutral bow while delivering a hammering, right, inward block to the front while drawing the left hand to a left chambered position, in a fist, at the your left side
2) slightly settle into stance with the execution of a right, hammering outward hand-sword to the front at neck level
3) continue the previous motion of your right hand until it draws to your right side, palm-up and in a fist, while simultaneously rotating to your right into a right forward bow with a left, thrusting, horizontal, four finger poke at eye level
4) rotate to your left, returning to a right neutral bow with a right, forward, thrusting, vertical, four finger spear hand at rib level, while simultaneously retracting your left hand into a left chambered position, hand open and palm up
5) step through forward into a left neutral bow, repeating the above steps on the opposite side (toward 12:00H)

Analysis of Long Form Two

The obvious information derived from this sequence is:
- it only advances
- it utilizes the neutral bow stance and the forward bow stance
- it utilizes both the front and rear hand
- it shows both closed and open hands
- it does not have positional covers - like Short Form Two
- all blocks are executed with closed hands
- all strikes are executed with open hands
- strikes are executed to different height zones
- non-used hands are sometimes left open
- there is no cover or transition between the first and second sequence execution
- it demonstrates both sides of the sequence (opposites)

Analyzing this sequence further exposes the following information:
- it uses the power principle of torque and back-up mass
- it introduces both the horizontal and vertical, four finger poke
- the rotation of stances shows both the same and reverse direction of rotation in Long Form One
- the foot maneuver sets one of the major themes of the form - reverse direction of both Short / Long Form One

Inward Block Specific Information

The obvious information derived from the Inward Blocks is:
- it is defensive
- it is executed using linear path of travel (horizontally)
- the blocking maneuver (upper body) is executed exactly the same as in Short / Long Form One, not Short Form Two (covering hand)
- the foot maneuver (lower body) is executed exactly the same as Short Form Two, not Short / Long Form One

Right / Left Inward Block Specific Information

The obvious information derived from the two Inward Blocks is:
- the first block (right) uses the hammering Method of Execution
- the second block (left) used the thrusting Method of Execution

Hand-sword Specific Information

The obvious information derived from the Hand-swords is:
- it is offensive
- it is executed using the same arm as the block
- it is executed to mid-range extension
- it uses a hammering Method of Execution
- it is execute using circular path of travel (diagonally)
- it does not stop at potential point of contact

Analyzing this maneuver further exposes the following information:
- it demonstrates an offense with the front hand (opposite of Long Form One)
- offense is the opposite of defense
- the hand-sword (open hand) is an opposite of the punch (closed hand)

Horizontal, Four-Finger Poke Specific Information

The obvious information derived from the Horizontal, Four-Finger Poke is:
- it is offensive
- it is executed using the opposite hand of the previous strike (hand-sword)
- it (hand rotation) is executed on a horizontal plane
- it is executed open handed
- it is executed to long range
- it uses a thrusting Method of Execution
- it is executed using linear line of travel (diagonally)
- it is executed with a Forward Bow rotation
- it is similar to the punch of Long Form One, but with an open hand and to a different height zone

Analyzing this maneuver further exposes the following information:
- it (stance rotation) is in the reverse direction of the block (stance rotation)
- the poke (open hand) is an opposite of the punch (closed hand)
- the poke introduces a new point of contact for a strike (tips of fingers)

Vertical, Four-Finger Poke Specific Information

The obvious information derived from the Vertical, Four-Finger Poke is:
- it is offensive
- it is executed using the opposite hand of the previous strike (poke)
- it (hand rotation) is executed on a vertical plane
- it is open handed
- it is executed to short range
- it uses a thrusting Method of Execution
- it is executed using linear line of travel (horizontally)
- it is executed with a Neutral Bow rotation

Analyzing this maneuver further exposes the following information:
- the poke (open hand) is an opposite of the punch (closed hand)
- this poke is to a different plane and height zone of the previous strike (poke)
- this rotation is in the reverse direction of the previous rotation (and Long Form One)

Transition - Inward / Outward

The transition between the inward and outward block sequence is as follows:
1) draw the left foot toward the right into a right forty five degree cat stance while simultaneously retracting both arms to the right side in a 'cup and saucer' position.

The obvious information derived from this maneuver is:
- it highlights one of the major themes of the form - the intersection position
- it shows the opposite side (cat) of Long Form One (with different arm positioning)

Analyzing this information further exposes the following information:
- the cat stance exposes the intersection position of the stances
- the maneuver, along with the following foot maneuver, demonstrates one of the major purposes of the intersection position - mainly changing direction

Outward Block Sequence

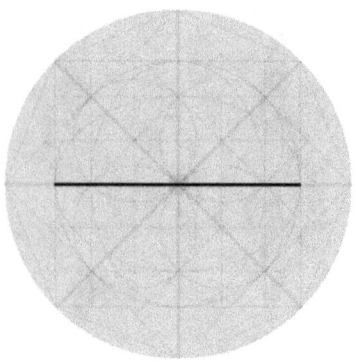

The outward block sequence is as follows:
1) step to the left with the left foot with the execution of both a left vertical outward block and a right ninety degree straight punch
2) execute a left straight thrust punch, at head level, while simultaneously retracting your right arm to your right upper chest area
3) execute a right straight thrust punch, at head level, while simultaneously retracting your left arm to your left shoulder area
4) execute a left, snapping, vertical punch, at head level, simultaneously with a left, snapping, side kick, at shin level
5) draw the right foot toward the left into a right forty five degree cat stance while simultaneously retracting both arms to the left side in a 'cup and saucer' position
6) step to the right with the right foot, repeating the above sequence on the opposite side (toward 3:00H)

Analysis of Long Form Two

The obvious information derived from this sequence is:
- it advances from the transitory (cat) position
- it only utilizes the offset horse stance (excluding the transition)
- it introduces the execution of front with front weapon
- it introduces punching with the front hand
- it introduces offense with offense
- it introduces execution of upper with lower weapon
- it introduces kicking
- it demonstrates defense with offense
- it demonstrates the execution of front with rear weapon
- it demonstrates both sides of the sequence (opposites)
- the two sides of the sequence are execution in reverse directions

Analyzing this sequence further exposes the following information:
- it uses the power principles of back-up mass (punch) with torque (block)
- it isolates the power principle of back-up mass
- it introduces punching to the high zone
- it is executed to the horizontal plane
- it demonstrates circular with linear execution
- it demonstrates linear with linear execution
- it introduces triple striking (offense) to match triple blocking (defense) of Long Form One
- it demonstrates triple linear strikes

Outward Block / Punch Specific Information

The obvious information derived from the maneuver is:
- the block is defensive
- the block is executed using the thrusting Method of Execution
- the block is executed using circular path of travel (horizontally)
- the punch is offensive
- the punch is executed to short range (because of no stance rotation)
- the punch is executed using the thrusting Method of Execution
- the punch is executed using linear line of travel (horizontally)

Analyzing this maneuver further exposes the following information:
- it demonstrates execution of front with rear weapon
- it demonstrates defense with offense
- it demonstrates circular with linear motion
- it demonstrates execution of middle with middle zone

© 2015 EPAKS Publications

Punch #2 Specific Information

The obvious information derived from the punch is:
- it is offensive
- it is executed to long range
- it is executed to the high zone
- it is executed using the thrusting Method of Execution
- it is executed using linear line of travel (horizontally)

Analyzing this maneuver further exposes the following information:
- the strike introduces punching with the front hand

Punch #3 Specific Information

The obvious information derived from the punch is:
- it is offensive
- it is executed with the rear hand (alone)
- it is executed to short range (because of no stance rotation)
- it is executed to the high zone
- it is executed using the thrusting Method of Execution
- it is executed using linear line of travel (horizontally)

Analyzing this maneuver further exposes the following information:
- the punch is exactly like first punch - but without the block

Kick / Punch Specific Information

The obvious information derived from the maneuver is:
- the punch is executed with the front weapon
- the kick is executed with the front weapon
- the maneuver is offensive
- the maneuver is executed to long range
- the maneuver is executed using the snapping Method of Execution
- the maneuver is executed on a linear line of travel (diagonally)
- the maneuver demonstrates very minimal weight transfer to supporting leg

Analyzing this maneuver further exposes the following information:
- the kick demonstrates a new point of contact with the foot (side)
- the maneuver demonstrates execution of upper with lower zone
- the maneuver introduces execution of front with front weapon
- the maneuver demonstrates offensive with offense
- the maneuver demonstrates linear with linear motion

Transition Specific Information

The obvious information derived from the transition is:
- the maneuver is the opposite side of the inward / outward transition
- it is 90 degrees

Analyzing this sequence further exposes the following information:
- it steps back to the same direction from which it transitioned

Transition - Outward / Upward

The transition between the outward and upward block sequence is as follows:
1) draw the left foot toward the right into a right forty five degree cat stance while simultaneously retracting both arms to the right side in a 'cup and saucer' position.

The obvious information derived from this maneuver is:
- it contains the exact same information as the inward to outward transition

Analyzing this information further exposes the following information:
- compared to the inward / outward transition, the draw into the cat comes from 9:00 instead of 12:00
- compared to the inward / outward transition, the next step moves toward 6:00 instead of 9:00

© 2015 EPAKS Publications

Upward Block Sequence

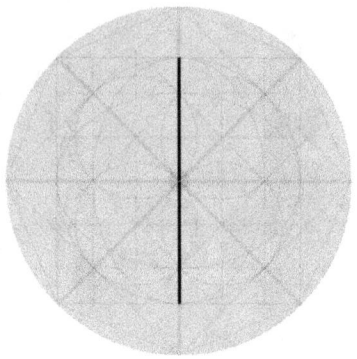

The upward block sequence is as follows:
1) step backward with the left foot into a transitory rear twist stance
2) rotate to your left into a left neutral bow, while simultaneously executing a left downward - right, inward universal block
3) shift forward into a left forward bow with a left, upward block, simultaneously with a right, forward hammer-fist
4) shift backward into a left neutral bow with left, overhead claw, simultaneously with a right, outward back-knuckle - both at head level
5) execute a left outward back-knuckle, at head level, while simultaneously retracting your right hand
6) execute a right outward back-knuckle, at head level, while simultaneously retracting your left hand
7) step backward with the right foot into a right transitory rear twist stance and repeat the above sequence on the opposite side (toward 12:00H)

Analysis of Long Form Two

The obvious information derived from this sequence is:
- it advances from the transitory (cat) position
- it utilizes the neutral bow and forward bow stances (excluding the transitional stances)
- it demonstrates execution of front with rear weapon (defensively)
- it demonstrates execution of front with rear weapon (defense with offense)
- it demonstrates execution of front and rear weapon (offensively)
- it demonstrates both sides of the sequence (opposites)
- the two sides of the sequence are execution in reverse directions

Analyzing this sequence further exposes the following information:
- it uses the power principles of torque and back-up mass
- it uses the power principles of (isolated) torque (block) with back-up mass (hammer-fist)
- it isolates the power principle of torque
- it introduces a new type of block - universal
- it introduces a new strike - hammer-fist
- it introduces a new strike - claw
- it introduces a new strike - back-knuckle
- it introduces a new method of execution - clawing
- it is executed primarily to the vertical plane
- it demonstrates triple circular strikes to match triple linear strikes of outward blocking sequence
- it demonstrates triple striking (offense) to match triple blocking (defense) of Long Form One

© 2015 EPAKS Publications

Universal Block Specific Information

The obvious information derived from the Universal Block is:
- it is the combination of an inward and downward block executed simultaneously
- it uses the thrusting Method of Execution and Hammering Method of Execution simultaneously
- the maneuver is executed with both a linear and a circular path of travel (horizontally)

Analyzing this maneuver further exposes the following information:
- the block covers both the upper zone and the middle zone
- it demonstrates defense with defense
- it demonstrates execution of front with rear arm
- it demonstrates linear with circular motion

Upward Block / Hammer-fist Specific Information

The obvious information derived from the maneuver is:
- the block is executed using circular path of travel (vertically)
- the strike is executed using circular path of travel (diagonally)
- the maneuver is executed to both the high and low zone simultaneously

Analyzing this maneuver further exposes the following information:
- the hammer-fist introduces a new striking surface of the fist (not the hand)[1]
- the hammer-fist reverses the circle of the middle-knuckle of Short Form Two
- the maneuver demonstrates defense with offense
- the maneuver demonstrates execution of front with rear weapon
- the maneuver demonstrates circular with circular motion

Claw / Back-knuckle Specific Information

The obvious information derived from the claw / back-knuckle is:
- both strikes are offensive
- both strikes demonstrate a new points of contact with the hand (finger tips - claw / back of knuckles - back-knuckle)2
- both strikes are executed to mid-range
- the claw uses the clawing Method of Execution to a vertical plane
- the claw is executed using linear line of travel (vertically)
- the claw weapon formation is new
- the claw is executed using an open hand
- the back-knuckle uses the thrusting Method of Execution
- the back-knuckle is executed using circular line of travel (diagonally)
- the back-knuckle is executed using a fist

Analyzing this maneuver further exposes the following information:
- it demonstrates offense and offense (not simultaneous)
- it demonstrates front and rear weapon (not simultaneous)
- it demonstrates linear and circular motion (not simultaneous)

© 2015 EPAKS Publications

Back-knuckle #2 Specific Information

The obvious information derived from the Back-knuckle is:
- it is offensive
- it is executed to mid-range
- it uses the snapping Method of Execution
- it is executed using a circular line of travel (vertically)
- it is executed with the front hand (opposite of previous and next back-knuckle)

Back-knuckle #3 Specific Information

The obvious information derived from the Back-knuckle is:
- it is offensive
- it is executed to mid-range
- it uses the thrusting Method of Execution
- it is executed using a circular line of travel (vertically)

Transition Specific Information

The obvious information derived from the transition is:
- it is 180 degrees

Analyzing this sequence further exposes the following information:
- the maneuver steps back to the same direction from which it transitioned

Transition - Upward / Downward

The transition between the upward and downward block sequence is as follows:
1) step your right foot to your left into a right modified reverse bow, while maintaining the position of you arms
2) immediately, rotate into a left neutral bow with a right, double factor, inside downward, block, palm up
3) without any loss of motion, settle into a left neutral bow with a left, hammering, downward block, while simultaneously retracting your right arm to a right chambered position

The obvious information derived from this maneuver is:
- it is a major departure from the previous cat transitions
- it introduces a new stance - the reverse bow

Analyzing this information further exposes the following information:
- the maneuver moves it's point of reference to a new angle ('x')

Downward Block Sequence

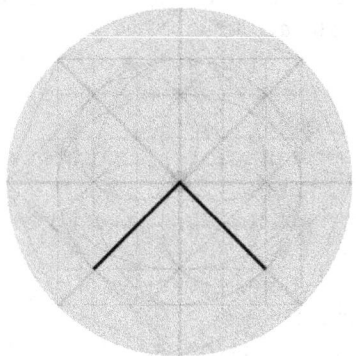

The downward block sequence is as follows:
1) settle into a left neutral bow with a left, hammering, downward block, while simultaneously retracting your right arm to a right chambered position
2) without any loss of motion from the previous move, execute a left, thrusting, inverted, vertical, roundhouse punch
3) shift forward into a left forward bow with a right, thrusting, straight punch, at solar plexus level, while simultaneously retracting your left arm to a left chambered position
4) execute a right, snapping, step through, ball kick, at groin level, with a left, thrusting straight punch, at solar plexus level, simultaneously with the retraction of your right arm to a right chambered position
5) plant your right foot forward into a modified right forward bow
6) shift into a right fighting horse with a right, thrusting, vertical punch, at rib height, while simultaneously retracting your left arm to a left chambered position
7) Repeat the sequence on the opposite side (toward 7:30H)

The obvious information derived from this sequence is:
- it utilizes the neutral bow, forward bow, and fighting horse stance
- it utilizes both the front and the rear weapon
- it demonstrates execution of front with rear weapon (offensively)
- it demonstrates execution of front with rear weapon (upper / lower)
- it demonstrates execution of front with front weapon (upper / lower)
- it demonstrates both sides of the sequence (opposites)
- the two sides of the sequence are execution at a 90 degree angle from each other

Analyzing this sequence further exposes the following information:
- it steps onto a minor angle (instead of a major angle)
- it starts the 'x' pattern
- it is only executed to the lower part of the 'x' pattern
- it introduces a new Method of Execution - round-housing
- it introduces a new strike - inverted, vertical back-knuckle strike
- it introduces a new strike - front kick
- it introduces a new type of strike - buckle
- it demonstrates the vertical punch to a new height zone (middle)
- the rotation of stances shows both the same and reverse direction of rotation in Long Form One
- the foot maneuver demonstrates the step through forward with two, simultaneous strikes
- it demonstrates execution of linear with linear
- it demonstrates execution of linear with circular
- the first (block) and second (strike) maneuver continue the same circular path of travel (vertically)

Downward Block Specific Information

The obvious information derived from the Downward Block is:
- it is defensive
- it emphasizes the power principle of torque
- it is executed using the hammering Method of Execution
- it is executed using circular path of travel (horizontally)
- it does not stop at potential point of contact

Back-knuckle Strike Specific Information

The obvious information derived from the Back-knuckle strike is:
- it is offensive
- it is executed to long range
- it is executed using circular line of travel (horizontally)
- it emphasizes the Power Principle of torque
- it is executed using the round-housing Method of Execution
- it introduces the inverted, vertical back-knuckle strike

Analyzing this maneuver further exposes the following information:
- it demonstrates the continuation of the circle of the downward block

© 2015 EPAKS Publications

Reverse Punch Specific Information

The obvious information derived from the Reverse Punch is:
- it is offensive
- it is executed to long range
- it use the thrusting Method of Execution
- it is execute using linear line of travel (horizontally)
- it emphasizes the power principle of torque

Kick / Punch Specific Information

The obvious information derived from the maneuver is:
- the kick is executed using the rear weapon
- the punch is executed using the front weapon
- the punch is executed using the thrusting Method of Execution
- the kick is executed using the snapping Method of Execution
- both strikes are offensive
- both strikes are executed to long range
- both strikes are executed using linear line of travel (horizontally)
- the maneuver demonstrates execution of middle with lower zone

Analyzing this maneuver further exposes the following information:
- the kick demonstrates a new point of contact with the foot (ball)
- the maneuver demonstrates offense with offense
- the maneuver demonstrates execution of front with rear weapon
- the maneuver demonstrates linear with linear motion
- the maneuver switches front to rear weapons

Buckle / Punch Specific Information

The obvious information derived from the Buckle / Punch is:
- the buckle is executed using circular path of travel (diagonally)
- the punch is executed using linear line of travel (horizontally)
- the punch is executed using the thrusting Method of Execution
- both strikes are offensive
- both strikes are executed to mid-range
- the maneuver emphasizes the power principle of torque

Analyzing this maneuver further exposes the following information:
- the buckle introduces a new striking surface - shin
- the punch is executed the same as the last maneuver in the inward blocking sequence, but with hand closed
- the maneuver demonstrates offense with offense
- the maneuver demonstrates execution of front with front weapon
- the maneuver demonstrates execution of middle with lower zone
- the maneuver demonstrates linear motion with circular motion

Transition Specific Information

The obvious information derived from the transition is:
- it is 225 degrees (left) and 90 degrees (right)

Half-knuckle Sequence

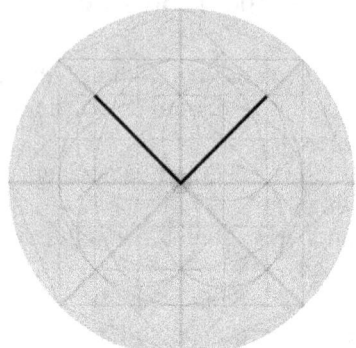

The half-knuckle sequence is as follows:
1) Execute a left, thrusting, instep (arch) kick with a left, hammering, close-fist half-knuckle strike. Without any loss of motion from the previous moves, plant your left foot forward into a left front twist.
2) Step through forward with your right foot into a right neutral bow with a right uppercut punch and without any loss of motion, execute a right, thrusting, upward horizontal forearm strike, to chin level.
3) Execute of a left, thrusting, vertical two-finger poke, at eye level.
4a) Retract of your right hand to your right upper chest region, in preparation for the next move.
4b) Execute a right, thrusting, vertical two-fingered poke, while simultaneously retracting your left hand to your left upper chest area.
5) Execute a left, thrusting, vertical two-fingered poke, while simultaneously retracting the right hand to the right upper chest area.
6) Repeat the sequence on the opposite side (toward 10:30H)

Analysis of Long Form Two

The obvious information derived from this sequence is:
- it utilizes the twist and neutral bow
- it demonstrates execution of rear with rear weapon (offensively) (upper / lower)
- it demonstrates execution with the front weapon (offensively)
- it demonstrates execution with the rear weapon (offensively)
- it demonstrates both sides of the sequence (opposites)
- it introduces the concept of threading
- the first cover is 180 degrees (without any transition)
- the two sides of the sequence are executed at a 90 degree angle from each other

Analyzing this sequence further exposes the following information:
- it steps onto a minor angle (instead of a major angle)
- it completes the 'X' pattern
- it is only executed to the upper part of the 'x' pattern
- it introduces a new kick - instep (arch) kick
- it introduces a new strike formation - half-knuckle (closed fist)
- it introduces a new strike - upward, horizontal forearm
- it introduces a new strike - vertical, two finger poke
- it demonstrates the upper-cut punch to a new height zone (high)
- the foot maneuver demonstrates the cross-over with two, simultaneous strikes

© 2015 EPAKS Publications

Half-knuckle / Instep (arch) Kick Specific Information

The obvious information derived from the Half-knuckle / Instep (arch) Kick is:
- the strikes are offensive
- the strikes emphasizes the power principle of back-up mass
- the half-knuckle is executed using the hammering Method of Execution
- the half-knuckle is executed using linear line of travel (diagonally)
- the kick is executed using the hammering Method of Execution
- the kick is executed using linear line of travel (diagonally)
- the kick demonstrates a new striking surface for the foot
- the maneuver introduces the instep (arch) kick
- the maneuver introduces the half-knuckle (closed fist)
- the foot maneuver demonstrates the cross-over with two, simultaneous strikes
- the foot maneuver demonstrates change of distance without rotation

Analyzing this maneuver further exposes the following information:
- the kick demonstrates a new point of contact with the foot (arch)
- the maneuver demonstrates offense with offense
- the maneuver demonstrates execution of rear with rear weapon
- the maneuver demonstrates linear with linear motion

Upper-cut / Upward, Horizontal Forearm Specific Information

The obvious information derived from the Upper-cut / Forearm is:
- the strikes are offensive
- the strikes are executed to mid-range
- the punch emphasizes the Power Principle of gravitational marriage
- the punch is executed using the thrusting Method of Execution
- the punch is executed using linear line of travel (vertically)
- the forearm emphasizes the Power Principle of gravitational marriage
- the forearm is executed using the thrusting Method of Execution
- the forearm is executed using linear path of travel (vertically)
- the maneuver introduces the upward, horizontal forearm strike
- the foot maneuver demonstrates change of distance without rotation

Analyzing this maneuver further exposes the following information:
- it demonstrates sophisticated motion

Vertical, Two-Finger Poke Specific Information

The obvious information derived from the Two-Finger Poke is:
- they are offensive
- they are executed to long range
- they emphasize the Power Principle of back-up mass
- they are executed using the thrusting Method of Execution
- they are executed using linear line of travel (diagonally)
- they utilize both the front and rear weapons
- the maneuver introduces the vertical, two-finger poke
- the maneuver demonstrates use of the rear hand without rotation of stance

Inside-Downward, Palm up Block Sequence

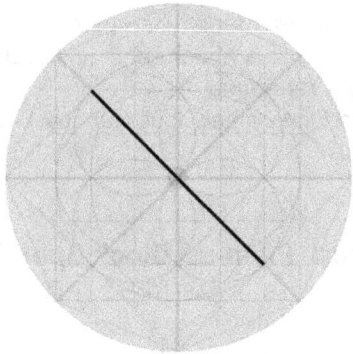

The inside-downward, palm up block sequence is as follows:
1) Step the left foot backward into a right front twist with a left, hammering, inside downward palm up block, while simultaneously retracting the right arm to a right chambered position
2) Unwind into a right neutral bow with a right, snapping vertical punch, at lower rib level, while simultaneously retracting the left arm to a left chambered position, palm up
3) Repeat the sequence on the opposite side (toward 10:30H)

The obvious information derived from this sequence is:
- it retreats
- it utilizes the twist and neutral bow stances
- it demonstrates execution with the front weapon (defensively / offensively)
- it demonstrates in-place stance rotation
- it shows both sides of the sequence (opposites)
- the two sides of the sequence are executed without change in Point of Reference

Analyzing this sequence further exposes the following information:
- it demonstrates distance then rotation - in reverse
- it steps onto a minor angle (instead of a major angle) - retreating
- it introduces a new foot maneuver - twist through (in reverse)

Inside-Downward, Palm-up Block Specific Information

The obvious information derived from the Inside-Downward Block is:
- it is defensive
- it is executed as a parrying block
- it emphasizes the power principle of back-up mass
- it uses the hammering Method of Execution
- it is executed on a linear path of travel (diagonally)

Analyzing this maneuver further exposes the following information:
- the foot maneuver (cross-over) demonstrates distance without rotation
- the foot maneuver (cross-over) enhances the execution of the block

Vertical Punch Specific Information

The obvious information derived from the Vertical Punch is:
- it is offensive
- it is executed to mid range
- it emphasizes the power principle of torque
- it uses the snapping Method of Execution
- it uses the snapping Method of Execution to a horizontal plane

Analyzing this maneuver further exposes the following information:
- the foot maneuver (unwind) demonstrates rotation without distance
- the foot maneuver (unwind) enhances the execution of the strike
- the strike is executed on a linear line of travel (horizontally)

Inside-Downward, Palm down Block Sequence

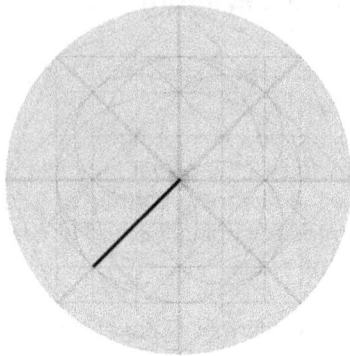

The inside-downward, palm down block sequence is as follows:
1) Step your right foot to your left into a left neutral bow with a left, hammering, inside downward palm down block, while simultaneously retracting the right arm to a right chambered position
2) Without any loss of motion, continue the circular path of your left arm until completely vertical and immediately execute a left, snapping, vertical back-knuckle thrust, to face level
3) Step backward with your left foot and repeat the sequence on the opposite side (toward 1:30H)

The obvious information derived from this sequence is:
- it retreats
- it utilizes only neutral bow stance
- it demonstrates execution with the front weapon (defensively / offensively)
- it shows both sides of the sequence (opposites)
- the two sides of the sequence are executed without change in Point of Reference

Analyzing this sequence further exposes the following information:
- the sequence steps onto a minor angle (instead of a major angle) - retreating

Inside-Downward, Palm-down Block Specific Information

The obvious information derived from the Inside-Downward Block is:
- it is defensive
- it emphasizes the power principle of torque
- it uses the thrusting Method of Execution
- it is executed on a circular path of travel (horizontally)

Analyzing this maneuver further exposes the following information:
- the foot maneuver (cover / step through) enhances the execution of the block

Vertical Back-knuckle strike Specific Information

The obvious information derived from the Vertical Back-knuckle is:
- it is offensive
- it is executed to mid range
- it emphasizes the power principle gravitational marriage
- it uses the snapping Method of Execution
- it uses the snapping Method of Execution to a diagonally plane
- it is executed on a linear line of travel (diagonally)

Analyzing this maneuver further exposes the following information:
- it extends ('degrees of' rotation) the outward back-knuckles of the Upward Block Sequence

Push-Down Block Sequence

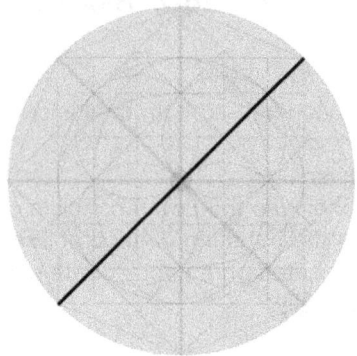

The push-down block sequence is as follows:
1) Rotate forward into a right forward bow with a left push-down block, while simultaneously retracting your right arm to a right chambered position
2a) Immediately, rotate forward into a right front twist, while allowing your left arm to cock across your body
2b) Step through forward into a left neutral bow with a left, hammering, outward, overhead elbow, at face level
2c) Without any loss of motion, settle into the left neutral bow with a left, hammering, overhead claw, at face level
3) Repeat the sequence on the opposite side (toward 1:30H)
4) Repeat the sequence on the opposite side (toward 1:30H)

The obvious information derived from this sequence is:
- it advances
- it utilizes the forward bow, twist, and neutral bow stances
- it demonstrates execution with the rear weapon (defensively)
- it demonstrates execution with the front weapon (offensively)
- it demonstrates in-place stance rotation
- it shows both sides of the sequence (opposites)
- the three sides of the sequence are execution without change in Point of Reference

Analyzing this sequence further exposes the following information:
- it demonstrates rotation then distance - forward
- it steps onto a minor angle (instead of a major angle) - advancing
- it introduces a new foot maneuver - twist through (forward)

Push-down Block Specific Information

The obvious information derived from the Push-down is:
- it is defensive
- it emphasizes the power principle of gravitational marriage
- it uses the hammering Method of Execution
- it is executed on a linear path of travel (vertically)

Analyzing this maneuver further exposes the following information:
- the stance rotation enhances the execution of the block

Stance Rotation Specific Information

The obvious information derived from the rotation is:
- the maneuver positions the intended next weapon

Analyzing this maneuver further exposes the following information:
- it completes rotation without distance

Outward, Overhead Elbow Specific Information

The obvious information derived from the Elbow is:
- it is offensive
- it is executed to mid range
- it emphasizes the power principle of gravitational marriage
- it uses the round-housing Method of Execution (vertically)
- it is executed on a circular line of travel (vertically)

Analyzing this maneuver further exposes the following information:
- the foot maneuver (step) demonstrates distance without rotation
- the foot maneuver (step) enhances the execution of the strike

Overhead, Heel-palm Specific Information

The obvious information derived from the Heel-palm is:
- it is offensive
- it is executed to mid range
- it emphasizes the power principle of gravitation marriage
- it uses the round-housing Method of Execution (vertically)
- it is executed on a circular line of travel (vertically)

Analyzing this maneuver further exposes the following information:
- it demonstrates the opposite (vertical) direction to the Downward Block Sequence of Short Form Two (horizontal)

Analysis of Long Form Two   237

Inside, Vertical Forearm Strike Sequence

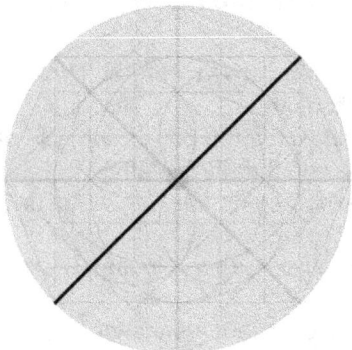

The inside, vertical forearm strike sequence is as follows:
1) Rotate forward into a left forward bow with the execution of a right, thrusting straight punch, at solar plexus level, while simultaneously cocking the left arm and fist to the left shoulder area
2) Rotate backward into a left neutral bow with a left, hammering, vertical, inside forearm strike, while simultaneously retracting the right arm to a right chambered position

The obvious information derived from this sequence is:
- it is stationary
- it utilizes the forward bow and neutral bow stances
- it demonstrates execution with the rear and front weapon (offensively)
- it demonstrates a 'degree of' in-place stance rotation
- it only shows one side of the sequence

Analyzing this sequence further exposes the following information:
- it introduces a new strike - inside, vertical forearm
- it reverses the sequence demonstrated in the Inward Block Sequence of Long Form One
- it mirrors the rotation demonstrated at the end of the Inward Block Sequence

Reverse Punch Specific Information

The obvious information derived from the Reverse Punch is:
- it is offensive
- it emphasizes the power principle of torque
- it uses the thrusting Method of Execution
- it is executed on a linear line of travel (horizontally)

Analyzing this maneuver further exposes the following information:
- the stance rotation enhances the execution of the strike

Inside, Vertical Forearm Specific Information

The obvious information derived from the Forearm is:
- it is offensive
- it emphasizes the power principle of torque
- it uses the hammering Method of Execution
- it is executed on a linear path of travel (horizontally)

Analyzing this maneuver further exposes the following information:
- the stance rotation enhances the execution of the strike

Inward, Overhead Elbow Strike Sequence

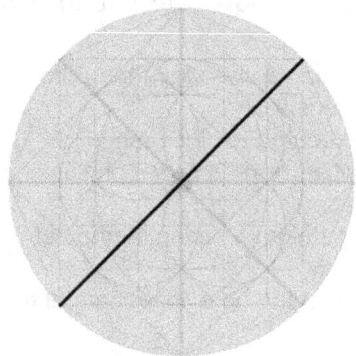

The inward, overhead elbow sequence is as follows:
1) Step through reverse into a right neutral bow with a right, hammering, inward overhead elbow, while simultaneously retracting the left arm to a left chambered position
2) Repeat the sequence on the opposite side (toward 1:30H)
3) Repeat the sequence on the opposite side (toward 1:30H)

The obvious information derived from this sequence is:
- it retreats
- it utilizes only the neutral bow stance
- it demonstrates execution with the front weapon (offensively)
- it shows both sides of the sequence (opposites)
- both sides of the sequence are execution without change of Point of Reference

Analyzing this sequence further exposes the following information:
- it steps onto a minor angle (instead of a major angle) - retreating

Inward, Overhead Elbow Specific Information

The obvious information derived from the Elbow is:
- it is offensive
- it is executed to close range
- it emphasizes the power principle of gravitational marriage
- it uses the hammering Method of Execution (vertically)
- it is executed on a linear path of travel (vertically)

Analyzing this maneuver further exposes the following information:
- it demonstrates the reverse circular path demonstrated in the Push-down Sequence

Elbow, Isolation Sequence

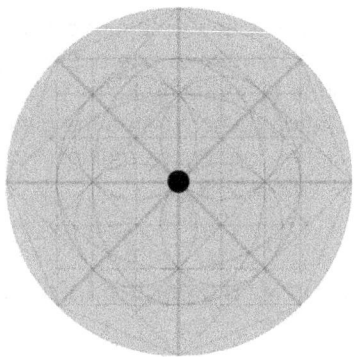

The isolation sequence is as follows:
1) Step the left foot backward into a modified, right, transitory twist, and without any loss of motion, immediately rotate into a horse stance with a right, inward, horizontal, elbow sandwich, at jaw level
2) Cock both arms across the body at chest level, palms down. Immediately, reverse the path of the previous moves, executing double, thrusting outward elbows
3) Execute a left upward elbow with a right backward elbow

The obvious information derived from this sequence is:
- it retreats (only on the first maneuver)
- it is stationary (for the isolation)
- it utilizes the twist and horse stances
- it only uses the elbow strike
- it only uses both hands (simultaneously)
- it introduces three new elbow strikes; inward, upward, back
- it demonstrates double elbow strikes
- it demonstrates offense with offense
- the transition between the first maneuver and the isolation is cocking the hands across the body

Analyzing this sequence further exposes the following information:
- it introduces a new category of strike - sandwiching
- the isolation previews one of the major themes of the next forms (Short/Long Form Three) - elbow strikes
- the isolation demonstrates the plus ('+') pattern
- the isolation introduces multiple Points of Reference (double elbow strikes)

Inward Elbow Sandwich Specific Information

The obvious information derived from the Elbow Sandwich is:
- it is offensive
- it is executed to close range
- it emphasizes the power principle of torque
- it uses the thrusting Method of Execution
- it is executed on a linear line of travel (horizontally)

Analyzing this maneuver further exposes the following information:
- the stance rotation enhances the execution of the strike
- it introduces the concept of sandwiching
- it demonstrates the opposite (horizontal) direction to the Push-down / Outward Overhead Elbow Sequences (vertical)

Outward Elbow Specific Information

The obvious information derived from the Elbow is:
- they are offensive
- they are executed to close range
- they use the thrusting Method of Execution
- they are executed on a linear line of travel (horizontally)

Analyzing this maneuver further exposes the following information:
- it demonstrates the opposite (horizontal) direction to the Push-down / Outward Overhead Elbow Sequences (vertical)
- it demonstrates the opposite (outward) direction to the previous maneuver (inward)
- it demonstrates movement in reverse directions simultaneously (side-to-side)
- the maneuver demonstrates execution of high with high zone

Upward / Back Elbow Specific Information

The obvious information derived from the maneuver is:
- they are offensive
- they are executed to close range
- the upward elbow uses the round-housing Method of Execution
- the upward elbow is executed on a circular line of travel (vertically)
- the back elbow uses the hammering Method of Execution
- the back elbow is executed on a linear line of travel (horizontally)

Analyzing this maneuver further exposes the following information:
- the upward elbow is executed in the opposite direction (upward) to the outward overhead elbows of the Push-down Sequence (downward)
- the upward elbow is executed in the opposite direction (upward) to the inward overhead elbows of the Inward, Overhead Elbow Sequence (downward)
- the back elbow introduces a new striking direction (backward)
- the upward and backward elbows go in the opposite directions to one another simultaneously (front / back)
- the maneuver demonstrates execution of high with middle zone

Form Close

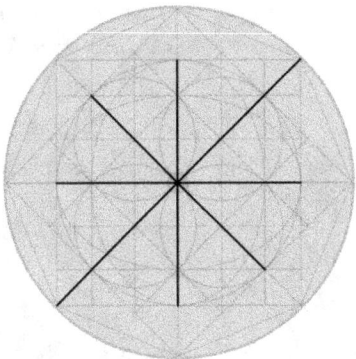

The form close maneuver is as follows:
1) Bring both arms to a meditating horse

The obvious information derived from this maneuver is:
- the maneuver has no foot maneuver (as opposed to the Short Form One and Short Form Two)

Summary

Long Form Two teaches:
1)
    The concepts that the practitioner must learn:
        a)   Long Form Two continues to expand upon the information presented in Short / Long Form One and Short Form Two
        b)   Long Form Two reverses maneuvers demonstrated in Short / Long Form One

2)
    The following new stances:
        a)   reverse bow - which introduces the following new concepts:
            i)   enhanced distance (in-place)
            ii)   Weight Distribution (40% / 60%)
            iii)   increase of distance without foot maneuver

Analysis of Long Form Two

3) The following new strikes:
   a) four, finger poke (horizontal / vertical) - which introduces the following:
      i) new weapon contact point
   b) side kick - which introduces the following:
      i) new weapon type (foot)
      ii) striking to new height zone (low)
      iii) new weapon formation (foot)
   c) hammer-fist - which introduces the following:
      i) new weapon rotation
   d) claw - which introduces the following:
      i) new weapon contact point
      ii) new weapon formation
   e) back-knuckle - which introduces the following:
      i) new weapon contact point
   f) inverted, vertical back-knuckle - which introduces the following:
      i) new weapon rotation
   g) front kick - which introduces the following:
      i) new weapon formation (foot)
      ii) new weapon contact point (foot)
   h) buckle - which introduces the following:
      i) new weapon contact point (leg)
   i) half-knuckle (closed) - which introduces the following:
      i) new weapon delivery
   j) instep (arch) kick - which introduces the following:
      i) new weapon contact point (foot)
   k) forearm (horizontal / vertical) - which introduces the following:
      i) switch of intent (defense to offense) of physically similar maneuvers
   l) two, finger poke - which introduces the following:
      i) new weapon formation
   m) vertical, back-knuckle
   n) outward, overhead elbow
   o) inward, overhead elbow
   p) inward elbow

© 2015 EPAKS Publications

         i)   new weapon contact point (elbow)
    q)   upward elbow
    r)   back elbow

4)
   The following new blocks:
      a)   universal block - which introduces the following:
         i)   defense with both front and rear weapons simultaneously
         ii) defense to multiple height zones simultaneously (middle / low)

5)
   The following new foot maneuvers:
      a)   crossover
         i)   front
         ii) rear
      b)   twist through
         i)   distance / rotation
         ii) rotation / distance

6)
   The following new Methods of Execution:
      a)   Poking
      b)   Clawing
      c)   Round-housing

7)
   Reinforces previously introduced concepts:
      a)   closed environment
      b)   transitional maneuvers
      c)   power principle isolation
      d)   'degrees of'
      e)   line of sight
      f)   two-in-one timing
      g)   isolation maneuvers

Analysis of Long Form Two

8)
   Does not reinforce previous introduced concepts:
   a)   realistic positioning
   b)   covering / checking
   c)   'nip the tip'

9)
   The following new (major) concepts:
   a)   sandwiching
   b)   threading (contouring)

Long Form Two falls into the category of a dictionary form. As such, it continues the following elements of the dictionary forms.

1)
   The blocking sequence:
   a)   In
   b)   Out
   c)   Up
   d)   Down
   e)   extends the sequence with:
       i)   universal block
       ii)   inside, downward, palm up block
       ii)   inside, downward, palm down block
       ii)   push down block

2)
   The form starts from the meditating horse stance

Long Form Two has a number of other elements it teaches / expands upon:

© 2015 EPAKS Publications

1)
    It is specified as follows:
        a)   a predominantly advancing form
        b)   two-in-one timing
        c)   power principle isolation
        d)   intersection position
        e)   delivery of multiple maneuvers simultaneously
            i)   defense / defense
            ii)   offense / offense
            iii) defense / offense

2)
    An enhancement of stance rotation reasons:
        a)   power generation (extended)
        b)   reach of rear weapon (extended)
        c)   positioning of future weapon

3)
    An enhancement of the ways two-in-one timing can be demonstrated

4)
    Defense with offense simultaneously

5)
    Defense and offense with the same hand

6)
    Double factors:
        a)   retreating
        b)   advancing

7)
    Switching rear hand to front hand and front hand to rear hand both for defense and offense

	Analysis of Long Form Two	251

8) An exposure of foot maneuver elements - distance / rotation:
    a)   change of distance with rotation (step through)
    b)   change of distance without rotation (cross over)
    c)   change of distance then rotation (twist through)
    d)   change of rotation then distance (twist through)
    e)   change of rotation without distance (cover without step - i.e. Point of Reference change)

Advanced Analysis

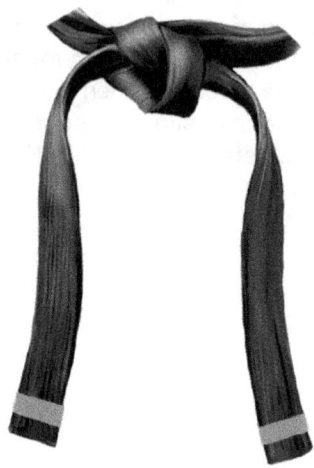

This section will cover the analysis of Long Form Two from an advanced perspective. Before continuing forward into this section, it is advised that the reader be very comfortable with the majority of information presented in the Beginning / Intermediate Analysis section and its methodology of analysis. It is the purpose of this section to expose the reader to information that is usually not openly presented by an instructor until later in a practitioner's training, or frequently only eluded to at some point during a review of the form with an instructor; or not at all. One may ask - why not at all? To be perfectly frank, some of the information contained in the forms was designed by SGM Parker to be self-exposed information. That is: information the practitioner was expected to deduce for them-self after being taught how to analyze the motion contained in American Kenpo forms - i.e. after the information and methodology of analysis presented in the Beginner / Intermediate Analysis section became common knowledge. The scenario for how this succession of information was supposed to work is as follows:

Analysis of Long Form Two

The instructor was to teach form 'x' to the student. This consisted of all the maneuvers along with some information about the maneuvers and how they generally fit into the American Kenpo system. Then, through repeated review, the instructor was to expose more information and also allude to the fact that their was still yet more information which needed to be uncovered by the student. At which point the student was then instructed to reflect further upon the form and ask questions to the instructor (and possibly other students) about the information deduced through this self-analysis. Through this process it was intended that the instructor would guide the student into self-exposing more and more information about the form - until all (or mostly all) of the information was exposed. And, ultimately the student became self-dependent - and completely able to think and deduce information on their own.

One may then further ask - if this is supposed to be mainly self-exposed information, why is this type of information illustrated in this section? Again to be perfectly frank, the above scenario didn't always completely work as intended - for numerous reasons. Most of which are self-evident to any serious, long term practitioner of American Kenpo. In the end, the final result was that, in general, less and less information was passed down to each generation further from SGM Parker. And, to make matters worse, the practitioners were not even aware of the fact that there was more information contained in the forms than what they were exposed to by their instructor. Therefore, this section can be used by instructors and advanced practitioners to reclaim, re-acquaint, refresh, and / or learn the 'lost' or 'hidden' information contained in the form.

As recommended in the Beginning / Intermediate Analysis section, the information presented in this section should be examined through numerous passes over a long period of time. Through this practice, the reader will often uncover new, overlooked information that was not readily apparent from a previous review. And, through repeated exposure and contemplation, the information presented will become easier and easier to absorb, while simultaneously improving self-discovery of information contained in the form.

Walk-Through Analysis

As stated in the Beginning / Intermediate section, the design of the lower four (4) American Kenpo forms (aka the 'dictionary' forms) is to start with the information presented in Short Form One and build upon it with each progressive form. One of the best ways to illustrate how this is accomplished is to step through the form and explain the information exposed from each maneuver - exposing how it compounds the information from the previous forms. Through this approach the reader will not only be exposed to some of the less known information presented in both forms but more importantly be exposed to constructing a thought pattern for comparing and contrasting information presented throughout the American Kenpo system. The importance of using this thought pattern for advanced analysis cannot be over emphasized. By analyzing American Kenpo through this specific methodology, one can begin to learn how to think properly about the composition of information contained therein and ultimately learn to self-expose more aspects of the design of American Kenpo, beyond what is presented in this guide. Or as SGM Parker put it: "learn to think for yourself."

Analysis of Long Form Two

Form Overview Analysis

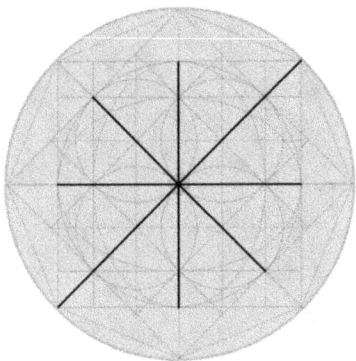

An overview of this form exposes the following themes:
- category completion of simultaneous front / rear weapon combination
- physical analysis of rotation and distance (foot maneuvers, offense, defense)
- closed environment
- reverses of the ones (i.e. Short Form One / Long Form One)

An analysis overview of this form exposes that the form introduces:
- new weapon formation: finger strikes, knuckle strikes, claws, elbows
- new points of contact on the foot: side of foot, ball of foot, instep arch
- new Methods of Execution: poking, raking, round-housing, hooking
- new foot maneuver timings

Inward Block Sequence

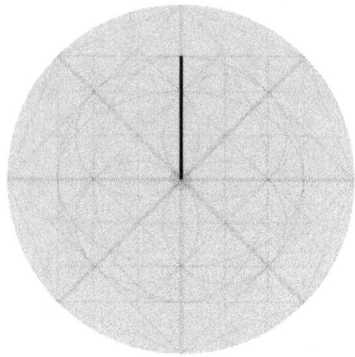

The inward block sequence is as follows:
1) step forward into a right neutral bow while delivering a hammering, right, inward block to the front while drawing the left hand to a left chambered position, in a fist, at the your left side
2) slightly settle into stance with the execution of a right, hammering outward hand-sword to the front at neck level
3) continue the previous motion of your right hand until it draws to your right side, palm-up and in a fist, while simultaneously rotating to your right into a right forward bow with a left, thrusting, horizontal, four finger poke at eye level
4) rotate to your left, returning to a right neutral bow with a right, forward, thrusting, vertical, four finger spear hand at rib level, while simultaneously retracting your left hand into a left chambered position, hand open and palm up
5) step through forward into a left neutral bow, repeating the above steps on the left side

An analysis of this sequence exposes the following information:
- it utilizes both two-in-one timing and one-in-one timing
- elements of the sequence isolate the power principle of torque (but not back-up mass)
- there is no transitional maneuver between the first and second side
- the block / hand-sword demonstrates full 'degree of' opening the hand
- up to the third strike, it replicates Long Form One, but with an insert strike (hand-sword) and stepping forward
- the final (finger poke) strike stance rotation reverses the motion of the previous (finger poke) strike
- the first finger poke is horizontal (based upon its potential target - the eyes)
- the second finger poke is vertical (based upon the positioning of the previous finger poke)
- some positioning in the sequence does NOT allow for Economy of Motion - but rather extended Path of Travel

Inward Block Specific Information

An analysis of this specific maneuver exposes the following information:
- the block is delivered with the side of the weapon (arm)
- the block is executed with right arm first - i.e. the strong side

Right / Left Inward Block Specific Information

An analysis of these specific maneuvers exposes the following information:
- the Method of Execution of the block is hammering due to the Point of Origin of the arm during the meditating horse
- the retraction of the rear arm to a chambered position places the practitioner in 'non-realistic' position - i.e. the rear hand is positioned for Path of Travel of the next left handed maneuver - not for protecting the body

Hand-sword Specific Information

An analysis of this specific maneuver exposes the following information:
- the strike is executed from Point of Origin of the completion of the block
- the strike has a Line of Sight to its potential target
- the settle with the hand-sword demonstrates the concept of Body English
- the settle introduces a small degree of Gravitational Marriage into the sequence
- the positioning of the rear hand does not allow for direct Line of Sight to any potential target to the front

Horizontal, Four Finger Poke Specific Information

An analysis of this specific maneuver exposes the following information:
- the strike is executed using one-in-one timing
- the strike is executed from Point of Origin, but not Line of Sight
- the shift forward causes the practitioner to slightly Close the Gap
- the strike also employs the power principle of back-up mass
- the opposite arm is retracted creating a posture that is not covered (checked)
- the forward bow demonstrates a Brace Angle
- the forward bow dramatically increases the range of the rear arm
- the strike borrows momentum (force) from the previous maneuver

Vertical, Four Finger Poke Specific Information

An analysis of this specific maneuver exposes the following information:
- the strike is executed using one-in-one timing
- the strike has a Line of Sight to its potential target
- the shift back to the Neutral Bow causes the practitioner to slightly Open the Gap
- the opposite arm is retracted creating posture that is not covered (checked)
- the strike relies upon Body Alignment
- the previous maneuver prepares (cocks) this maneuver

Transition - Inward / Outward

The transition between the inward and outward block sequence is as follows:
1) draw the left foot toward the right into a right 45 degree cat stance while simultaneously retracting both arms to the right side in a 'cup and saucer' position.

An analysis of this maneuver exposes the following information:
- the hand positioning cocks both the right and left hands simultaneously (to the same side of the body)
- the intersection position of the cat (lower) is opposite of the intersection position of the blocks (upper)

Outward Block Sequence

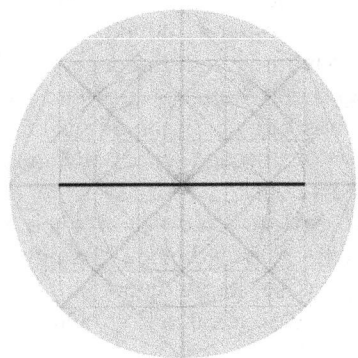

The outward block sequence is as follows:
1) step to the left with the left foot with the execution of both a left vertical outward block and a right ninety degree straight punch
2) execute a left straight thrust punch, at head level, while simultaneously retracting your right arm to your right upper chest area
3) execute a right straight thrust punch, at head level, while simultaneously retracting your left arm to your left shoulder area
4) execute a left, snapping, vertical punch, at head level, simultaneously with a left, snapping, side kick, at shin level
5) draw the right foot toward the left into a right forty five degree cat stance while simultaneously retracting both arms to the left side in a 'cup and saucer' position
6) step to the right with the right foot, repeating the above sequence on the right side

An analysis of this sequence exposes the following information:
- it utilizes two-in-one timing (simultaneously)
- it utilizes one-in-one timing
- it demonstrates both the direction of the punch (straight) and the block (outward) simultaneously
- it demonstrates both the use of the side of the weapon (block) and tip of the weapon (knuckles) simultaneously
- it's movements are directed to the horizontal plane (opposite of upward block / hammer-fist sequence)
- the right offset horse demonstrates the opposite side executed in Long Form One (and same for left side)
- it demonstrates the reverse triple sequence (rear, front, rear) to Long Form One (front, rear, front)

Outward Block / Punch Specific Information

An analysis of this specific maneuver exposes the following information:
- the block is delivered with the opposite side of the weapon (arm) as the inward block
- the block utilizes isolated torque
- the strike is not properly aligned with the body (like a reverse punch)

Punch #2 Specific Information

An analysis of this specific maneuver exposes the following information:
- the strike is executed using isolated back-up mass
- the strike rotation (horizontal) is not proper for its executed height zone
- the strike is executed from a non-cocked Point of Origin

Punch #3 Specific Information

An analysis of this specific maneuver exposes the following information:
- the strike is not properly aligned with the body (like a reverse punch)
- the strike is executed using isolated back-up mass

Kick / Punch Specific Information

An analysis of this specific maneuver exposes the following information:
- the striking surface of the kick matches the striking surface of the hand-sword
- the punch is executed using an opposite rotation (vertical) to the other punches in the sequence (horizontal)
- the punch rotation (vertical) is proper for its executed height zone
- the maneuver demonstrates the use of the two closest available weapons to potential targets
- the maneuver demonstrates no rotation, cocking, or adjustments of either strike (optimal prior positioning)
- the maneuver demonstrates vertical weapon (punch) rotation with horizontal weapon rotation (kick)
- the maneuver demonstrates the reverse weight transfer (minimal) of a forward bow
- the maneuver starts the upper weapon with lower weapon category (front with front)
- the linear line of travel shows the opposite (upward) direction to the Half-knuckle sequence (downward)

Upward Block Sequence

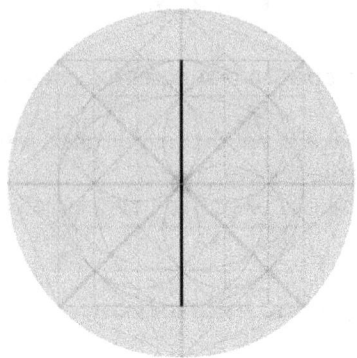

The upward block sequence is as follows:
1) step backward with the left foot into a transitory rear twist stance
2) rotate to your left into a left neutral bow, while simultaneously executing a left downward - right, inward universal block
3) shift forward into a left forward bow with a left, upward block, simultaneously with a right, forward hammer-fist
4) shift backward into a left neutral bow with left, overhead claw, simultaneously with a right, outward back-knuckle - both at head level
5) execute a left outward back-knuckle, at head level, while simultaneously retracting your right hand
6) execute a right outward back-knuckle, at head level, while simultaneously retracting your left hand
7) step backward with the right foot into a right transitory rear twist stance and repeat the above sequence on the right side

Analysis of Long Form Two | 265

An analysis of this sequence exposes the following information:
- it utilizes two-in-one timing (simultaneously)
- it utilizes one-in-one timing
- it demonstrates both forward movement (hammer-fist) with upward movement (block)
- it demonstrates orbital switching
- it demonstrates the reverse triple sequence (rear, front, rear) to Long Form One (front, rear, front)
- it demonstrates the figure 8 within a single sequence (instead of with combined sequences)
- it's movements are directed to the vertical plane (opposite of outward block / punch sequence)
- it never steps onto the upper part of the '+' pattern - only faces the 12:00 direction

Universal Block Specific Information

An analysis of this maneuver exposes the following information:
- the block is executed from a neutral bow - unlike the modified forward bow of Long Form One, rear hand inward block
- the block is executed from a neutral bow - exposing the rule: front hand - neutral bow, rear hand - forward bow, both hands - either
- it achieves the same main goal of the triple block sequence in Long Form One, but with two-in-one timing

Upward Block / Hammer-fist Specific Information

An analysis of this maneuver exposes the following information:
- the block utilizes isolated torque
- the upward block is executed from a forward bow (but with the front hand - unlike Short / Long Form One)
- the hammer-fist rotation continues 'degree of rotation' concept
- the hammer-fist introduces the concept Orbital Switch

Claw / Back-knuckle Specific Information

An analysis of this maneuver exposes the following information:
- the two-in-one timing is similar to the inward block sequence (but with both hands and offense / offense)
- the claw is executed on a vertical plane - the opposite (horizontal) plane of the four-finger strike
- the claw continues the concept of 'degrees of open' of a weapon[3]
- the claw introduces isolated gravitational marriage
- the stance rotation is the reverse to the inward block sequence

Back-knuckle #2 Specific Information

An analysis of this maneuver exposes the following information:
- the strike is executed using one-in-one timing

Back-knuckle #3 Specific Information

An analysis of this maneuver exposes the following information:
- the strike is executed using one-in-one timing
- the strike positions the weapon for the next maneuver (on both sides)

Transition Specific Information

An analysis of this maneuver exposes the following information:
- the maneuver steps into the unknown

Transition - Upward / Downward

The transition between the upward and downward block sequence is as follows:
1) step your right foot to your left into a right modified reverse bow, while maintaining the position of you arms
2) immediately, rotate into a left neutral bow with a right, double factor, inside downward, block, palm
3) without any loss of motion, settle into a left neutral bow with a left, hammering, downward block, while simultaneously retracting your right arm to a right chambered position

An analysis of this maneuver exposes the following information:
- the maneuver completes the stepping sequence of the first downward blocks of Short / Long Form One - Short Form Two

Downward Block Sequence

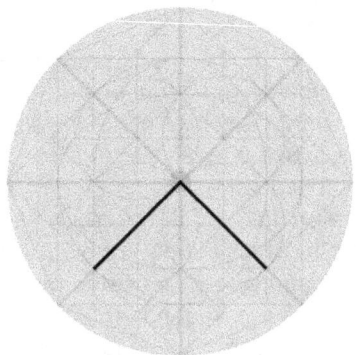

The downward block sequence is as follows:
1) settle into a left neutral bow with a left, hammering, downward block, while simultaneously retracting your right arm to a right chambered position
2) without any loss of motion from the previous move, execute a left, thrusting, inverted, vertical, roundhouse punch
3) shift forward into a left forward bow with a right, thrusting, straight punch, at solar plexus level, while simultaneously retracting your left arm to a left chambered position
4) execute a right, snapping, step through, ball kick, at groin level, with a left, thrusting straight punch, at solar plexus level, simultaneously with the retraction of your right arm to a right chambered position
5) plant your right foot forward into a modified right forward bow
6) shift into a right fighting horse with a right, thrusting, vertical punch, at rib height, while simultaneously retracting your left arm to a left chambered position

An analysis of this sequence exposes the following information:
- the step through transitions the rear hand to the front hand
- the downward block/punch maneuver demonstrates the up-side-down execution of the inward block/hand-sword maneuver of the inward block sequence
- it uses two-in-one timing
- it uses one-in-one timing
- it reverses (left / right) the block sequence - in relation to Short / Long Form One (right / left)
- it demonstrates sophisticated motion utilizing the first (block) and second (strike) maneuvers
- the sophisticated motion is demonstrated in the beginning of the sequence
- the first two maneuvers of both sides of the sequence combined complete a circular path (vertically)

Downward Block Specific Information

An analysis of this maneuver exposes the following information:
- the draw of the rear hand is to a non-realistic position
- the positioning of the hand prior to execution (in side #1) negates the need to cock weapon with double-factor block

Back-knuckle Strike Information

An analysis of this maneuver exposes the following information:
- the strike rotation continues 'degree of rotation' concept
- the strike is executed using two-in-one timing
- the strike introduces the concept Orbital Adjustment

Reverse Punch Specific Information

An analysis of this maneuver exposes the following information:
- the strike is executed using one-in-one timing
- the strike repeats the maneuver demonstrated in Long Form One on to the minor angle ('x')

Kick / Punch Specific Information

An analysis of this maneuver exposes the following information:
- the maneuver continues the upper with lower category (front with back)
- the maneuver demonstrates the opposite weapon rotation of the final maneuver of the outward block sequence (horizontal vs vertical)

Buckle / Punch Specific Information

An analysis of this maneuver exposes the following information:
- the buckle reverses the Pivot Point of the outward block
- the buckle introduces a specialized Method of Execution
- settling into stance during the buckle execution emphasizes the power principle torque
- the maneuver demonstrates using the rotation of stance for offense with lower body

Transition Specific Information

An analysis of this maneuver exposes the following information:
- the double factor demonstrates a degree of cup and saucer with only the cocked arm in cup and saucer position

Half-knuckle Sequence

The half-knuckle sequence is as follows:
1) Execute a left, thrusting, instep (arch) kick with a left, hammering, close-fist half-knuckle strike. Without any loss of motion from the previous moves, plant your left foot forward into a left front twist.
2) Step through forward with your right foot into a right neutral bow with a right uppercut punch and without any loss of motion, execute a right, thrusting, upward horizontal forearm strike, to chin level.
3) Execute of a left, thrusting, vertical two-finger poke, at eye level.
4a) Retract of your right hand to your right upper chest region, in preparation for the next move.
4b) Execute a right, thrusting, vertical two-fingered poke, while simultaneously retracting your left hand to your left upper chest area.
5) Execute a left, thrusting, vertical two-fingered poke, while simultaneously retracting the right hand to the right upper chest area.
6) Repeat the sequence on the opposite side (toward 10:30H)

An analysis of this sequence exposes the following information:
- it demonstrates distance without rotation
- it demonstrates front hand converted into the rear hand with the switch in Point of Reference
- it uses two-in-one timing
- it uses one-in-one timing
- it demonstrates sophisticated motion
- the sophisticated motion is demonstrated in the middle of the sequence

Half-knuckle / Instep (arch) Kick Specific Information

An analysis of this maneuver exposes the following information:
- the rear weapons do not have direct line-of-sight to intended targets
- cover is done without foot maneuver - only switch in Point of Reference
- maneuver is executed using two-in-one timing
- the maneuver switches rear weapons to front weapons after foot maneuver execution
- the maneuver begins execution as a circular line of travel and completes on a linear line of travel
- the linear line of travel shows the opposite (downward) direction to the Outward block sequence (upward)

© 2015 EPAKS Publications

Upper-cut / Upward, Horizontal Forearm Specific Information

An analysis of this maneuver exposes the following information:
- the foot maneuver with the upper-cut adds a degree of back-up mass to the strike
- the forearm is used for a new intent (offense)
- the forearm demonstrates the opposite (vertical) direction to the Inside, Vertical Forearm Sequence (horizontal)
- maneuver is executed using two-in-one timing
- the rotation after the execution of the upper-cut adds a degree of torque to the forearm strike

Vertical, Two-Finger Poke Specific Information

An analysis of this maneuver exposes the following information:
- maneuver is executed using one-in-one timing
- the maneuver demonstrates converting a strike (offense) into a pressing check (defense) - i.e. changing intent

Inside-Downward, Palm up Block Sequence

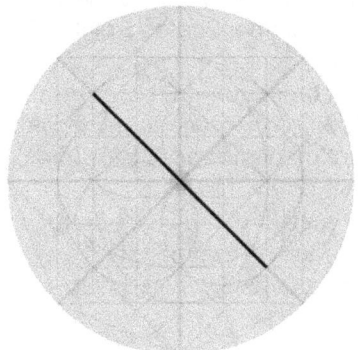

The inside-downward, palm up block sequence is as follows:
1) Step the left foot backward into a right front twist with a left, hammering, inside downward palm up block, while simultaneously retracting the right arm to a right chambered position
2) Unwind into a right neutral bow with a right, snapping vertical punch, at lower rib level, while simultaneously retracting the left arm to a left chambered position, palm up
3) Repeat the sequence on the opposite side (toward 10:30H)

An analysis of this sequence exposes the following information:
- it alters the inside-downward palm-down, palm-up, push-down sequence of Long Form One
- it uses one-in-one timing
- it introduces retreating on the minor angle ('x')
- it demonstrates the same maneuver as the end of the Downward Block sequence but stepping in reverse.
- it demonstrates the equivalent of a step through, separating the two major components- distance and rotation
- it covers both the upper left and lower right parts of the minor angles ('x')
- it does not demonstrate the reverse punch of Long Form One on to the minor angle ('x')

Inside-Downward, Palm up Block Specific Information

An analysis of this maneuver exposes the following information:
- the block demonstrates Point of Origin from the previous sequence
- the foot maneuver adds a small degree of gravitational marriage to the block
- the foot maneuver adds a degree of back-up mass "in front of" the blocking weapon
- the execution of the block starts as the front hand but finishes as the rear hand
- it introduces a new type of block category - parrying blocks

Vertical Punch Specific Information

An analysis of this maneuver exposes the following information:
- the foot maneuver (unwind) expands the 'degree of' stance rotation of the Inward Block sequence

Inside-Downward, Palm down Block Sequence

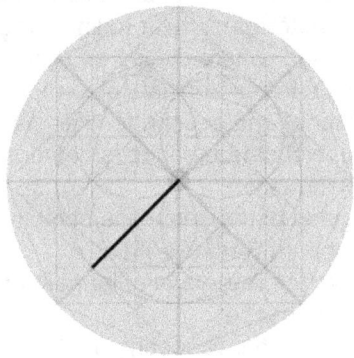

The inside-downward, palm down block sequence is as follows:
1) Step your right foot to your left into a left neutral bow with a left, hammering, inside downward palm down block, while simultaneously retracting the right arm to a right chambered position
2) Without any loss of motion, continue the circular path of your left arm until completely vertical and immediately execute a left, snapping, vertical back-knuckle thrust, to face level
3) Step backward with your left foot and repeat the sequence on the opposite side (toward 1:30H)

An analysis of this sequence exposes the following information:
- the sequence uses one-in-one timing
- it demonstrates circular to linear motion with the same hand (where circles end-lines begin)
- it demonstrates sophisticated motion utilizing the first (block) and second (strike) maneuvers
- the sophisticated motion is demonstrated is the entire sequence
- both sides of the sequence combined complete a circular path (vertically)
- it shows the reverse circular path of the Downward Block sequence
- it demonstrates retreating on the minor angle ('x')
- it covers only the lower left part of the minor angles ('x')
- it uses two-in-one timing

Inside-Downward, Palm down Block Specific Information

An analysis of this maneuver exposes the following information:
- the (first) block demonstrates Point of Origin from the previous sequence

Vertical Back-knuckle Specific Information

An analysis of this maneuver exposes the following information:
- combined with the previous maneuver demonstrates sophisticated motion

Push-Down Block Sequence

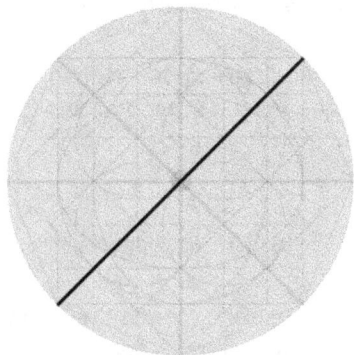

The push-down block sequence is as follows:
1) Rotate forward into a right forward bow with a left push-down block, while simultaneously retracting your right arm to a right chambered position
2a) Immediately, rotate forward into a right front twist, while allowing your left arm to cock across your body
2b) Step through forward into a left neutral bow with a left, hammering, outward, overhead elbow, at face level
2c) Without any loss of motion, settle into the left neutral bow with a left, hammering, overhead claw, at face level
3) Repeat the sequence on the opposite side (toward 1:30H)
4) Repeat the sequence on the opposite side (toward 1:30H)

An analysis of this sequence exposes the following information:
- the sequence uses one-in-one timing
- the sequence uses two-in-one timing
- the sequence demonstrates a sophisticated maneuver
- the sophisticated motion is demonstrated at the end of the sequence
- it covers both the lower left and upper right parts of the minor angles ('x')
- it travels on the opposite (perpendicular, overlapping) angle of the Inside, Downward Palm up Sequence

Push-down Block Specific Information

An analysis of this maneuver exposes the following information:
- the rotation of the stance allows for proper positioning of the block

Stance Rotation Specific Information

An analysis of this maneuver exposes the following information:
- the maneuver reverses demonstrates the 'degree of' stance rotation of the Inside-downward, palm up Block sequence

Outward, Overhead Elbow Specific Information

An analysis of this maneuver exposes the following information:
- the foot maneuver (step) adds a degree of back-up mass to the strike

Overhead, Heel-palm Specific Information

An analysis of this maneuver exposes the following information:
- the maneuver demonstrates sophisticated motion (with the elbow strike)

Inside, Vertical Forearm Strike Sequence

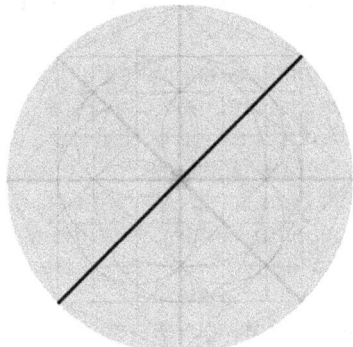

The inside, vertical forearm strike sequence is as follows:
1) Rotate forward into a left forward bow with the execution of a right, thrusting straight punch, at solar plexus level, while simultaneously cocking the left arm and fist to the left shoulder area
2) Rotate backward into a left neutral bow with a left, hammering, vertical, inside forearm strike, while simultaneously retracting the right arm to a right chambered position

An analysis of this sequence exposes the following information:
- the sequence uses one-in-one timing
- the sequence highlights the concept of intent

Reverse Punch Specific Information

An analysis of this maneuver exposes the following information:
- the strike is executed using one-in-one timing
- the strike repeats the maneuver demonstrated in Long Form One on to the minor angle ('x')

Inside, Vertical Forearm Specific Information

An analysis of this maneuver exposes the following information:
- the strike is executed using one-in-one timing
- the strike has a Line of Sight to its potential target
- the maneuver highlights the concept of intent
- the shift back to the Neutral Bow causes the practitioner to slightly Open the Gap
- the opposite arm is retracted creating posture that is not covered (checked)
- the previous maneuver prepares (cocks) this maneuver
- it demonstrates the opposite (horizontal) direction to the Half-knuckle Sequence (vertical)

Inward, Overhead Elbow Strike Sequence

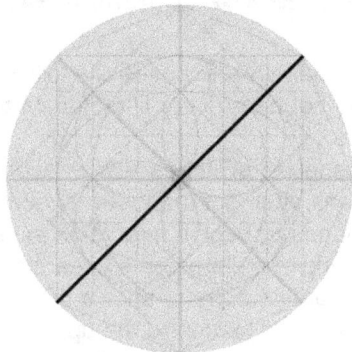

The inward, overhead elbow sequence is as follows:
1) Step through reverse into a right neutral bow with a right, hammering, inward overhead elbow, while simultaneously retracting the left arm to a left chambered position
2) Repeat the sequence on the opposite side (toward 1:30H)
3) Repeat the sequence on the opposite side (toward 1:30H)

An analysis of this sequence exposes the following information:
- it uses one-in-one timing
- it demonstrates retreating on the minor angle ('x')
- it travels on the opposite (perpendicular, overlapping) angle of the Inside, Downward Palm up Sequence
- it reverses the direction traveled by the Push-down Sequence

Inward, Overhead Elbow Specific Information

An analysis of this maneuver exposes the following information:
- it does not have direct line-of-sight to intended targets
- the maneuver switches rear weapons to front weapons after foot maneuver execution
- the maneuver begins execution as a circular line of travel and completes on a linear line of travel
- the linear line of travel shows the opposite (downward) direction to the upper-cut in the Half-knuckle Sequence (upward)
- settling into stance during the execution emphasizes the power principle gravitational marriage
- part of the executing arm travels outside the Outer Rim

Elbow, Isolation Sequence

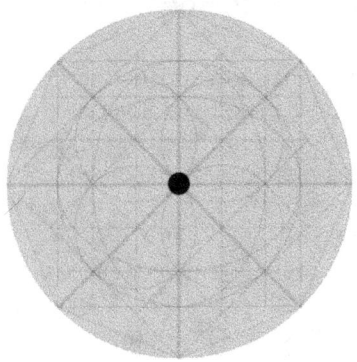

The isolation sequence is as follows:
1) Step the left foot backward into a modified, right, transitory twist, and without any loss of motion, immediately rotate into a horse stance with a right, inward, horizontal, elbow sandwich, at jaw level
2) Cock both arms across the body at chest level, palms down. Immediately, reverse the path of the previous moves, executing double, thrusting outward elbows
3) Execute a left upward elbow with a right backward elbow

An analysis of this sequence exposes the following information:
- the sequence uses two-in-one timing
- it introduces double cocking of weapons
- the isolation fills in missing information of the next form (Short Form Three)
- the isolation demonstrates the opposite tip (elbow) the weapons (punches) demonstrated in the isolation of Long Form One

© 2015 EPAKS Publications

Inward Elbow Sandwich Specific Information

An analysis of this maneuver exposes the following information:
- the sandwiching hand does not travel in a path that enhances the sandwiching maneuver
- the foot maneuver is executed to the opposite (backward) direction to the step (forward) into the isolation of Long Form One
- the foot maneuver demonstrates distance then rotation into the isolation stance - in contrast to the step with rotation maneuver of Long Form One

Outward Elbow Specific Information

An analysis of this maneuver exposes the following information:
- the previous maneuver (double cocking) allows for full path of travel
- it demonstrates the reverse line of travel of the 9:00 and 3:00 straight punches of the isolation of Long Form One
- it demonstrates the double maneuver to the (single) outward elbow of Long Form One

Upward / Back Elbow Specific Information

An analysis of this maneuver exposes the following information:
- the upward elbow demonstrates the opposite (bottom half) of the circle previously demonstrated in the Push-down / Inward Overhead Elbow Sequences (top half)
- the upward elbow demonstrates the short range to the upper-cuts in the isolation of Long Form One
- the back elbow has an extremely similar appearance to the chamber motion, but has a different intent
- the back elbow demonstrates the reverse line to the 12:00 straight punches in the isolation of Long Form One

Form Close

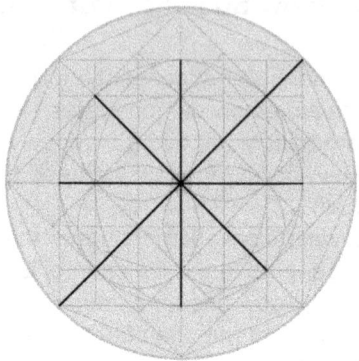

The form close maneuver is as follows:
1) Bring both arms to a meditating horse

An analysis of this maneuver exposes the following information:
- the maneuver demonstrates obtaining the meditating horse by moving both hands in reverse directions (up / down) simultaneously

Summary

Long Form Two teaches:
1)
    Most of the concepts introduced in Short / Long Form One and Short Form Two are applicable to this form

2)
    Theme stance:
        a)   Twist stance

3)
    The following new strikes:
- a) four, finger poke (horizontal / vertical) - which demonstrates the following:
  - i) open handed weapon using tip as contact point
  - ii) degree of hand rotation
- b) side kick - which demonstrates the following:
  - i) execution with offense (in same direction / time)
  - ii) execution with foot maneuver (without stance rotation)
  - iii) offensive weapon contact without full (proper) stance
  - iv) executed without retraction of weapon
- c) hammer-fist - which introduces the following:
  - i) degree of hand rotation
  - ii) same weapon formation / different weapon contact point
- d) claw - which demonstrates the following:
  - i) new Method of Execution
  - ii) degree of hand opening
  - iii) execution with offense (not simultaneous)
- e) back-knuckle - which demonstrates the following:
  - i) no stance rotation with strike
- f) inverted, vertical back-knuckle - which demonstrates the following:
  - i) degree of hand rotation
  - ii) execution with defense (not simultaneous)
  - iii) no stance rotation with strike
- g) front kick - which demonstrates the following:
  - i) execution with foot maneuver (with stance rotation)
  - ii) execution with offense (simultaneous)
  - iii) advance with offense (multiple)
  - iv) offensive weapon contact without full (proper) stance
  - v) executed without retraction of weapon
- h) buckle - which demonstrates the following:

- i) new category of offensive weapon
- ii) execution with offense (simultaneous)
- iii) new stance rotation rationale

i) half-knuckle (closed) - which demonstrates the following:
- i) execution with foot maneuver (without stance rotation)
- ii) execution with offense (simultaneous)
- iii) advance with offense (multiple)
- iv) same weapon contact point / different weapon formation
- v) offensive weapon contact without full (proper) stance

j) instep (arch) kick - which demonstrates the following:
- i) execution with foot maneuver (without stance rotation)
- ii) execution with offense (simultaneous)
- iii) advance with offense (multiple)
- iv) offensive weapon contact without full (proper) stance
- v) executed without retraction of weapon

k) forearm (horizontal / vertical) - which demonstrates the following:
- i) execution with offense (not simultaneous)
- ii) new (offensive) weapon Point of Contact
- iii) no stance rotation with strike
- iv) sophisticated maneuver

l) two, finger poke - which demonstrates the following:
- i) same weapon type / different number of contact points
- ii) no stance rotation with strike

m) vertical, back-knuckle
- i) degree of hand rotation
- ii) execution with defense (not simultaneous)
- iii) no stance rotation with strike

n) outward, overhead elbow
- i) execution with foot maneuver (without stance rotation)

ii) sophisticated maneuver
- o) inward, overhead elbow
  - i) execution with foot maneuver (with stance rotation)
  - ii) strike enhanced with settle into stance
- p) inward elbow
  - i) strike enhanced with rotation into stance
  - ii) new weapon delivery category - sandwiching
- q) upward elbow
  - i) execution with offense (simultaneous) (in opposite direction)
  - ii) multiple Points of Reference
- r) back elbow
  - i) execution with offense (simultaneous) (in opposite direction)
  - ii) multiple Points of Reference

4) The following new blocks:
   - a) universal block - which demonstrates the following:
     - i) new type of blocking category (double)

5)
    The following new stances:
        a)   reverse bow - which demonstrates the following:
            i)   increased distance from Point of Reference

6)
    The following new foot maneuvers:
        a)   crossover - which demonstrates the following:
            i)   distance without rotation
        b)   twist through - which demonstrates the following:
            i)   distance then rotation
            ii)   rotation then distance

7)
    Sequences:
        a)   inward block sequence - which demonstrates the following:
            i)   power generation from forward bow to neutral bow
        b)   outward block sequence - which demonstrates the following:
            i)   closest weapon to closest target
            ii)   minimal weight transfer with final maneuver
        c)   upward block sequence - which demonstrates the following:
            i)   inserts into in / out / up / down pattern
            ii)   introduces claw / back-knuckle category
        d)   downward block sequence - which demonstrates the following:
            i)   introduces continuation of the blocking circular motion
            ii)   introduces moving lower body pivot points
        e)   half-knuckle sequence - which demonstrates the following:
            i)   introduces perceived intent
            ii)   introduces threading (vertical-vertical / vertical-horizontal)
            iii)   introduces sophisticated maneuvers
            iv)   execution of new weapon while maintaining position of previous weapon

- f) inside-downward, palm up block sequence - which demonstrate the following:
  - i) blocking from Point of Origin
  - ii) degree of stance rotation
- g) inside-downward, palm down block sequence - which demonstrate the following:
  - i) expands continuation of the blocking circular motion
  - ii) sophisticated maneuvers
  - iii) manipulation of pivot points
- h) push-down block sequence - which demonstrate the following:
  - i) change of stance rotation rationale
  - ii) degree of stance rotation
  - iii) positional cocking
  - iv) sophisticated maneuvers
- i) inside, vertical forearm sequence - which demonstrate the following:
  - i) perceived intent highlighting
  - ii) sequence order reversing
  - iii) positional cocking (not chambered)
- j) inward, overhead elbow sequence - which demonstrate the following:
  - i) return to form origin
- k) elbow, isolation sequence - which demonstrate the following:
  - i) Point of Origin cocking
  - ii) multiple Points of Reference
  - iii) preview of things to come
  - iv) new elbow types
  - v) continuation of elbow category

8)
The following new (major) concepts:
- a) sophisticated maneuvers
- b) positional cocking

Analysis of Long Form Two

Long Form Two falls into the category of a dictionary form. As such, it maintains the following elements of the dictionary forms.

1)
    Each dictionary form changes the foot pattern on the first downward block.

Long Form Two has a number of other elements it teaches / expands upon:

1)
    Category Completion:
        a)   striking with arm / hand major contact points mostly completed

Reverse / Opposite Analysis

This section will cover the analysis of Long Form Two from the perspective of reverses and opposites. Since one of the major purposes of an American Kenpo form is to demonstrate reverses and opposites, a section on just this information is warranted. But, before continuing forward into this section an overview of what constitutes a reverse as opposed to an opposite is needed.

Reverse

Reverses tend to be more physically oriented and precise than an opposite. This typically manifests itself in a form in a much more limited way than an opposite. A reverse is typically directly related to physical direction and/or sequence order.

Examples of reverse directions are:
- travel on a 12:00 / 6:00 path vs travel on a 6:00 / 12:00 path
- movement directly forward vs directly backward
- clockwise rotation vs counter-clockwise rotation

Sequence order deals with multiple maneuvers. Examples of reverse sequence order are:
- block / punch vs punch / block (i.e. 1 / 2 vs 2 / 1)
- block / punch / kick / vs kick / punch / block (i.e. 1 / 2 / 3 vs 3 / 2 / 1)

Things to keep in mind when determining whether something is a reverse are:
- reverses are more precise in nature than opposites
- reverses tend to be physical not conceptual
- all reverse are opposites, but not all opposites are reverses

Examples of things that may appear to be reverses, but under closer scrutiny clearly aren't are:
- travel on a 12:00 / 6:00 path vs travel on a 1:30 / 7:30 path
- diagonally upward vs straight ahead travel
- 1 / 2 / 3 vs 1 / 3 / 2 sequence change
- block / punch vs punch / strike

Opposite

Opposites tend to be more conceptually oriented than a reverse. This typically manifests itself in a form in a very broad way and can be derived from any number of perspectives. Something that is not determined to be an opposite from one perspective may be determined to be, if looked at from another perspective. For example; a two-finger poke is not an opposite of a four-finger poke, by itself. But if one poke is oriented (rotated) vertically and the other is oriented (rotated) horizontally, or if one poke is from the left hand and other poke is from the right hand - they would qualify as opposites. This would be from the perspective of plane orientation or body side, rather than from the perspective of point(s) of contact or opening / closing of a weapon.

Examples of opposite categories are:
- Side - left vs right / top vs bottom
- Intention - defense vs offense
- (general) Direction - in vs out / up vs down / forward vs backward
- Contact Point - top vs bottom / front vs back / any opposite side
- Orientation - palm up vs palm down
- Plane - horizontal vs vertical
- Weapon Configuration - open vs closed
- Weapon Range - close vs far
- Travel Surface Exposure - Path of Travel (length) vs Line of Travel (tip)
- Sophistication - simple vs sophisticated
- Weapon Hardness - hard (contact point) vs soft (contact point)
- Travel Path - circle vs line
- Method of Execution - snapping vs thrusting / hammering vs thrusting

Things to keep in mind when determining whether something is an opposite is:
- opposites must be diametrically opposed (i.e. extremes of one another)
- 'degrees of' are not opposites (i.e. fully closed vs partially open)
- all reverses are opposites and can coexist in both categories
- always look at the comparison from different perspectives

Examples of things that may appear to be opposites, but under closer scrutiny clearly aren't are:
- 'degrees of' - such as: rotation / open
- Zone - top vs middle / middle vs bottom
- Number of contact points (with fingers - i.e. 1 vs 4)
- Method of Execution - whipping vs snapping

| 300 | The Official EPAKS Guide to Long Form Two |

Notes

The analysis in this section does not illustrate the perspective from which the determination of reverse / opposite was derived. That information is purposely left up to the reader to resolve.

The analysis in this section is limited to only the information contained in Short / Long Form Two and Short / Long Form One. It does not include information from future forms.

Analysis

Note: Due to the large number of potential opposites in certain instances, some areas may highlight only major opposites and / or consolidate opposites.

* - indicates basic consolidated
** - indicates section consolidated

Stances

Right Neutral Bow
    Reverses
        None
    Opposites
        Left Neutral Bow
        Twist Stance*
        Horse
        Left Stance*

Left Neutral Bow
    Reverses
        None
    Opposites
        Right Neutral Bow
        Twist Stance*
        Horse
        Right Stance*

Right Forward Bow
    Reverses
        Left Reverse Bow
    Opposites
        Left Forward Bow
        Twist Stance*
        Horse
        Left Stance*

Left Forward Bow
   Reverses
      Left Reverse Bow
   Opposites
      Right Forward Bow
      Twist Stance*
      Horse
      Right Stance*

Left Horse (Offset)
   Reverses
      None
   Opposites
      Right Horse (Offset)
      Twist Stance*
      Horse
      Right Stance*

Right Horse (Offset)
   Reverses
      None
   Opposites
      Left Horse (Offset)
      Twist Stance*
      Horse
      Left Stance*

Left 45 degree Cat
   Reverses
      Left 45 degree Reverse Cat
   Opposites
      Right 45 degree Cat
      Twist Stance*
      Horse
      Right Stance*

Right 45 degree Cat
    Reverses
        Right 45 degree Reverse Cat
    Opposites
        Left 45 degree Cat
        Twist Stance*
        Horse
        Left Stance*

Left Rear 45 degree Cat
    Reverses
        Left 45 degree Cat
    Opposites
        Right 45 degree Cat
        Twist Stance*
        Horse
        Right Stance*

Right Rear 45 degree Cat
    Reverses
        Right 45 degree Cat
    Opposites
        Left 45 degree Cat
        Twist Stance*
        Horse
        Left Stance*

Left Reverse Bow
    Reverses
        Left Forward Bow
    Opposites
        Right Forward Bow
        Twist Stance*
        Horse
        Right Stance*

Left Front Twist
  Reverses
    Left Rear Twist
  Opposites
    Right Front Twist
    Horse
    Right Stance*

Right Front Twist
  Reverses
    Right Rear Twist
  Opposites
    Left Front Twist
    Horse
    Right Stance*

Horse
  Reverses
    None
  Opposites
    Horse (Offset)
    Twist Stance*
    Stance (excluding Attention)*

Blocks

Right Hammering Inward Block
    Reverses
        Inward Block (stepping backward)
        Left Inside-Downward, Palm Up Block
    Opposites
        Rear Hand / Front Hand Block
        Left Block*
        Left Inward Block
        Thrusting Inward Block
        Vertical Outward Block
        Extended Outward Block
        (Outside) Downward Block
        Inside-Downward Block
        Universal Block (Downward / Inward) Block
        Push-down Block
        Strike*
        Punch*
        Hand-sword
        Hammer-fist
        Back-knuckle*
        Middle-knuckle
        Heel-palm
        Half-knuckle*
        Poke*
        Claw*
        Forearm*
        Elbow*
        Buckle
        Kick*
        Thrusting / Snapping / Raking / Clawing Method of
            Execution

Left Thrusting Inward Block
    Reverses
        Inward Block (stepping backward)
        Right Inside-Downward, Palm Up Block
    Opposites
        Rear Hand / Front Hand Block
        Right Block*
        Right Inward Block
        Hammering Inward Block
        Vertical Outward Block
        Extended Outward Block
        (Outside) Downward Block
        Inside-Downward Block*
        Universal Block (Downward / Inward) Block
        Push-down Block
        Strike*
        Punch*
        Hand-sword
        Hammer-fist
        Back-knuckle*
        Middle-knuckle
        Heel-palm
        Half-knuckle*
        Poke*
        Claw*
        Forearm*
        Elbow*
        Buckle
        Kick*
        Hammering / Snapping / Raking / Clawing Method of
            Execution

Left Vertical Outward Block
    Reverses
        Right Vertical Outward Block
        Left Covering Inward Block
        Left Inside-Downward, Palm Down Block
        Left Middle-knuckle strike[4]
    Opposites
        Rear Hand / Front Hand Block*
        Right Block*
        Inward Block*
        Extended Outward Block
        Universal Block (Downward / Inward) Block
        (Outside) Downward Block
        Inside-Downward Block*
        Push-down Block
        Strike*
        Punch*
        Hand-sword
        Hammer-fist
        Back-knuckle*
        Middle-knuckle
        Heel-palm
        Half-knuckle*
        Poke*
        Claw*
        Forearm*
        Elbow*
        Buckle
        Kick*
        Hammering / Snapping / Raking / Clawing Method of Execution

Right Vertical Outward Block
    Reverses
        Left Vertical Outward Block
        Right Covering Inward Block
        Right Inside-Downward, Palm Down Block
        Right Middle-knuckle Strike[4]
    Opposites
        Rear Hand / Front Hand Block
        Left Block*
        Inward Block
        Extended Outward Block
        Universal Block (Downward / Inward) Block
        (Outside) Downward Block
        Inside-Downward Block*
        Push-down Block
        Strike*
        Punch*
        Hand-sword
        Hammer-fist
        Back-knuckle*
        Middle-knuckle
        Heel-palm
        Half-knuckle*
        Poke*
        Claw*
        Forearm*
        Elbow*
        Buckle
        Kick*
        Hammering / Snapping / Raking / Clawing Method of
            Execution

Universal Block (Left Downward / Right Inward) Block
    Reverses
        None
    Opposites
        Universal Block (Right Downward / Left Inward)
            Block
        Inward Block
        Upward Block
        Vertical Outward Block
        Extended Outward Block
        (Outside) Downward Block
        Inside-Downward Block*
        Push-down Block
        Strike*
        Punch*
        Hand-sword
        Hammer-fist
        Back-knuckle*
        Middle-knuckle
        Heel-palm
        Half-knuckle*
        Poke*
        Claw*
        Forearm*
        Elbow*
        Buckle
        Kick*
        Snapping / Raking / Clawing Method of Execution

Universal Block (Right Downward / Left Inward) Block
    Reverses
        None
    Opposites
        Universal Block (Left Downward / Right Inward) Block
        Inward Block
        Upward Block
        Vertical Outward Block
        Extended Outward Block
        (Outside) Downward Block
        Inside-Downward Block*
        Push-down Block
        Strike*
        Punch*
        Hand-sword
        Hammer-fist
        Back-knuckle*
        Middle-knuckle
        Heel-palm
        Half-knuckle*
        Poke*
        Claw*
        Forearm*
        Elbow*
        Buckle
        Kick*
        Snapping / Raking / Clawing Method of Execution

Left Upward Block
    Reverses
        Push-Down Block
        Inward, Overhead Elbow
    Opposites
        Rear Hand / Front Hand Block*
        Right Block*
        Right Upward Block
        Vertical Outward Block
        Extended Outward Block
        (Outside) Downward Block
        Inside-Downward Block*
        Push-down Block
        Universal Block (Downward / Inward) Block
        Strike*
        Punch*
        Hand-sword
        Hammer-fist
        Back-knuckle*
        Middle-knuckle
        Heel-palm
        Half-knuckle*
        Poke*
        Claw*
        Forearm*
        Elbow*
        Buckle
        Kick*
        Hammering / Snapping / Raking / Clawing Method of Execution

Right Upward Block
    Reverses
        Push-Down Block
        Inward, Overhead Elbow
    Opposites
        Rear Hand / Front Hand Block*
        Left Block*
        Left Upward Block
        Vertical Outward Block
        Extended Outward Block
        (Outside) Downward Block
        Inside-Downward Block*
        Push-down Block
        Universal Block (Downward / Inward) Block
        Strike*
        Punch*
        Hand-sword
        Hammer-fist
        Back-knuckle*
        Middle-knuckle
        Heel-palm
        Half-knuckle*
        Poke*
        Claw*
        Forearm*
        Elbow*
        Buckle
        Kick*
        Hammering / Snapping / Raking / Clawing Method of Execution

Left (Outside) Downward Block
    Reverses
        Left Inside Downward Block (Palm Down)
        Right Outside Downward Block
        Right Vertical Outward Block
    Opposites
        Rear Hand / Front Hand Block*
        Right Block*
        Inward Block
        Upward Block
        Vertical Outward Block
        Extended Outward Block
        Universal Block (Downward / Inward) Block
        Inside-Downward Block*
        Push-down Block
        Strike*
        Punch*
        Hand-sword
        Hammer-fist
        Back-knuckle*
        Middle-knuckle
        Heel-palm
        Half-knuckle*
        Poke*
        Claw*
        Forearm*
        Elbow*
        Buckle
        Kick*
        Thrusting / Snapping / Raking / Clawing Method of Execution

© 2015 EPAKS Publications

Right (Outside) Downward Block
    Reverses
        Right Inside Downward Block (Palm Down)
        Left Outside Downward Block
        Left Vertical Outward Block
    Opposites
        Rear Hand / Front Hand Block*
        Left Block*
        Inward Block
        Upward Block
        Vertical Outward Block
        Extended Outward Block
        Universal Block (Downward / Inward) Block
        Inside-Downward Block*
        Push-down Block
        Strike*
        Punch*
        Hand-sword
        Hammer-fist
        Back-knuckle*
        Middle-knuckle
        Heel-palm
        Half-knuckle*
        Poke*
        Claw*
        Forearm*
        Elbow*
        Buckle
        Kick*
        Thrusting / Snapping / Raking / Clawing Method of Execution

Analysis of Long Form Two — 315

Left Inside-Downward, Palm Up Block
   Reverses
      Right Inward Block
   Opposites
      Right Inside-Downward, Palm Up Block
      Inside-Downward, Palm Down Block
      Rear Hand / Front Hand Block*
      Right Block*
      Inward Block
      Vertical Outward Block
      Extended Outward Block
      Universal Block (Downward / Inward) Block
      Upward Block
      (Outside) Downward Block
      Push-down Block
      Strike*
      Punch*
      Hand-sword
      Hammer-fist
      Back-knuckle*
      Middle-knuckle
      Heel-palm
      Half-knuckle*
      Poke*
      Claw*
      Forearm*
      Elbow*
      Buckle
      Kick*
      Thrusting / Snapping / Raking / Clawing Method of Execution

Right Inside-Downward, Palm Up Block
    Reverses
        Left Inward Block
    Opposites
        Left Inside-Downward, Palm Up Block
        Inside-Downward, Palm Down Block
        Rear Hand / Front Hand Block
        Left Block*
        Inward Block
        Vertical Outward Block
        Extended Outward Block
        Universal Block (Downward / Inward) Block
        Upward Block
        (Outside) Downward Block
        Push-down Block
        Strike*
        Punch*
        Hand-sword
        Hammer-fist
        Back-knuckle*
        Middle-knuckle
        Heel-palm
        Half-knuckle*
        Poke*
        Claw*
        Forearm*
        Elbow*
        Buckle
        Kick*
        Thrusting / Snapping / Raking / Clawing Method of Execution

Left Inside-Downward, Palm Down Block
   Reverses
      Right Covering Inward Block
      Left Vertical Outward Block
      Left (Outside) Downward Block
      Right Inside-Downward, Palm Down Block
   Opposites
      Right Inside-Downward, Palm Down Block
      Rear Hand / Front Hand Block*
      Right Block*
      Inward Block
      Vertical Outward Block
      Extended Outward Block
      Universal Block (Downward / Inward) Block
      Upward Block
      (Outside) Downward Block
      Inside-Downward, Palm Up Block
      Push-down Block
      Strike*
      Punch*
      Hand-sword
      Hammer-fist
      Back-knuckle*
      Middle-knuckle
      Heel-palm
      Half-knuckle*
      Poke*
      Claw*
      Forearm*
      Elbow*
      Buckle
      Kick*
      Thrusting / Snapping / Raking / Clawing Method of Execution

Right Inside-Downward, Palm Down Block
    Reverses
        Left Covering Inward Block
        Right Vertical Outward Block
        Right (Outside) Downward Block
        Left Inside-Downward, Palm Down Block
    Opposites
        Left Inside-Downward, Palm Down Block
        Rear Hand / Front Hand Block*
        Left Block*
        Inward Block
        Vertical Outward Block
        Extended Outward Block
        Universal Block (Downward / Inward) Block
        Upward Block
        (Outside) Downward Block
        Inside-Downward, Palm Up Block
        Push-down Block
        Strike*
        Punch*
        Hand-sword
        Hammer-fist
        Back-knuckle*
        Middle-knuckle
        Heel-palm
        Half-knuckle*
        Poke*
        Claw*
        Forearm*
        Elbow*
        Buckle
        Kick*
        Thrusting / Snapping / Raking / Clawing Method of Execution

Left Push-down Block
   Reverses
      Upward Block
      Uppercut Punch
      Upward Elbow
   Opposites
      Right Push-down Block
      Rear Hand / Front Hand Block
      Right Block*
      Inward Block
      Vertical Outward Block
      Extended Outward Block
      Upward Block
      Universal Block (Downward / Inward) Block
      (Outside) Downward Block
      Inside-Downward Block*
      Strike*
      Punch*
      Hand-sword
      Hammer-fist
      Back-knuckle*
      Middle-knuckle
      Heel-palm
      Half-knuckle*
      Poke*
      Claw*
      Forearm*
      Elbow*
      Buckle
      Kick*
      Thrusting / Snapping / Raking / Clawing Method of
          Execution

Right Push-down Block
    Reverses
        Upward Block
        Uppercut Punch
        Upward Elbow
    Opposites
        Left Push-down Block
        Rear Hand / Front Hand Block*
        Left Block*
        Inward Block
        Vertical Outward Block
        Extended Outward Block
        Upward Block
        Universal Block (Downward / Inward) Block
        (Outside) Downward Block
        Inside-Downward Block*
        Strike*
        Punch*
        Hand-sword
        Hammer-fist
        Back-knuckle*
        Middle-knuckle
        Heel-palm
        Half-knuckle*
        Poke*
        Claw*
        Forearm*
        Elbow*
        Buckle
        Kick*
        Thrusting / Snapping / Raking / Clawing Method of Execution

Strikes (upper body)

Right Hand-sword
    Reverses
        None
    Opposites
        Left Hand-sword
        Left Strike*
        Punch*
        Hammer-fist
        Back-knuckle*
        Middle-knuckle
        Half-knuckle*
        Poke*
        Claw*
        Heel-palm
        Left Inward, Vertical Forearm
        Elbow*
        Buckle
        Kick*
        Block*
        Inward Block
        Vertical Outward Block
        Upward Block
        Outside Downward Block
        Inside Downward Block*
        Extended Outward Block
        Universal Block (Downward / Inward) Block
        Push-Down Block
        Thrusting / Snapping / Raking / Clawing Method of
            Execution

Left Hand-sword
   Reverses
      None
   Opposites
      Right Hand-sword
      Right Strike*
      Punch*
      Hammer-fist
      Back-knuckle*
      Middle-knuckle
      Half-knuckle*
      Poke*
      Claw*
      Heel-palm
      Left Inward, Vertical Forearm
      Elbow*
      Buckle
      Kick*
      Block*
      Inward Block
      Vertical Outward Block
      Upward Block
      Outside Downward Block
      Inside Downward Block*
      Extended Outward Block
      Universal Block (Downward / Inward) Block
      Push-Down Block
      Thrusting / Snapping / Raking / Clawing Method of
          Execution

Analysis of Long Form Two

Left Horizontal, Four Finger Poke
    Reverses
        Right Back Elbow
    Opposites
        Right Horizontal, Four Finger Poke
        Vertical, Four Finger Poke
        Vertical, Two Finger Poke
        Right Strike*
        Punch*
        Hammer-fist
        Back-knuckle*
        Middle-knuckle
        Half-knuckle (closed)
        Claw*
        Heel-palm
        Hand-sword
        Left Inward, Vertical Forearm
        Upward, Horizontal Forearm
        Elbow*
        Buckle
        Kick*
        Block*
        Inward Block
        Vertical Outward Block
        Upward Block
        Outside Downward Block
        Inside Downward Block*
        Extended Outward Block
        Universal Block (Downward / Inward) Block
        Push-Down Block
        Hammering / Snapping / Raking / Clawing Method of Execution

Right Horizontal, Four Finger Poke
    Reverses
        Right Back Elbow
    Opposites
        Left Horizontal, Four Finger Poke
        Vertical, Four Finger Poke
        Vertical, Two Finger Poke
        Left Strike*
        Punch*
        Hammer-fist
        Back-knuckle*
        Middle-knuckle
        Half-knuckle (closed)
        Claw*
        Heel-palm
        Hand-sword
        Left Inward, Vertical Forearm
        Upward, Horizontal Forearm
        Elbow*
        Buckle
        Kick*
        Block*
        Inward Block
        Vertical Outward Block
        Upward Block
        Outside Downward Block
        Inside Downward Block*
        Extended Outward Block
        Universal Block (Downward / Inward) Block
        Push-Down Block
        Hammering / Snapping / Raking / Clawing Method of Execution

Right Vertical, Four Finger Poke
    Reverses
        Right Back Elbow
    Opposites
        Left Vertical, Four Finger Poke
        Horizontal, Four Finger Poke
        Left Strike*
        Punch*
        Hammer-fist
        Back-knuckle*
        Middle-knuckle
        Half-knuckle*
        Claw*
        Heel-palm
        Hand-sword
        Left Inward, Vertical Forearm
        Upward, Horizontal Forearm
        Elbow*
        Buckle
        Kick*
        Block*
        Inward Block
        Vertical Outward Block
        Upward Block
        Outside Downward Block
        Inside Downward Block*
        Extended Outward Block
        Universal Block (Downward / Inward) Block
        Push-Down Block
        Hammering / Snapping / Raking / Clawing Method of
            Execution

Left Vertical, Four Finger Poke
    Reverses
        Right Back Elbow
    Opposites
        Right Vertical, Four Finger Poke
        Horizontal, Four Finger Poke
        Right Strike*
        Punch*
        Hammer-fist
        Back-knuckle*
        Middle-knuckle
        Half-knuckle*
        Claw*
        Heel-palm
        Hand-sword
        Left Inward, Vertical Forearm
        Upward, Horizontal Forearm
        Elbow*
        Buckle
        Kick*
        Block*
        Inward Block
        Vertical Outward Block
        Upward Block
        Outside Downward Block
        Inside Downward Block*
        Extended Outward Block
        Universal Block (Downward / Inward) Block
        Push-Down Block
        Hammering / Snapping / Raking / Clawing Method of
            Execution

Analysis of Long Form Two

Left Straight Punch
    Reverses (excluding 45 degree)
        Outward Elbow
        Back Elbow
    Opposites
        Right Straight Punch (includes all degrees)
        Vertical Punch
        Uppercut
        Ball Kick
        Right Strike*
        Poke*
        Hand-sword
        Heel-palm
        Middle-knuckle*
        Half-knuckle* (excluding Left open)
        Forearm*
        Elbow*
        Buckle
        Kick*
        Block*
        Inward Block
        Vertical Outward Block
        Upward Block
        Outside Downward Block
        Inside Downward Block*
        Extended Outward Block
        Universal Block (Downward / Inward) Block
        Push-Down Block
        Hammering / Snapping / Raking / Clawing Method of
            Execution

© 2015 EPAKS Publications

Right Straight Punch
    Reverses (excluding 45 degree)
        Outward Elbow
        Back Elbow
    Opposites
        Left Straight Punch (includes all degrees)
        Vertical Punch
        Uppercut
        Ball Kick
        Left Strike*
        Poke*
        Hand-sword
        Heel-palm
        Middle-knuckle
        Half-knuckle* (excluding Right open)
        Forearm*
        Elbow*
        Buckle
        Kick*
        Block*
        Inward Block
        Vertical Outward Block
        Upward Block
        Outside Downward Block
        Inside Downward Block*
        Extended Outward Block
        Universal Block (Downward / Inward) Block
        Push-Down Block
        Hammering / Snapping / Raking / Clawing Method of Execution

Analysis of Long Form Two

Left Vertical Punch
  Reverses
    Right Outward Elbow
  Opposites
    Right Vertical Punch
    Straight Punch
    Inverted Back-knuckle
    Uppercut
    Right Strike*
    Back-knuckle*
    Hammer-fist
    Middle-knuckle
    Horizontal, Four Finger Poke
    Hand-sword
    Heel-palm
    Half-knuckle*
    Forearm*
    Elbow*
    Buckle
    Kick*
    Block*
    Inward Block
    Vertical Outward Block
    Upward Block
    Outside Downward Block
    Inside Downward Block*
    Extended Outward Block
    Universal Block (Downward / Inward) Block
    Push-Down Block
    Hammering / Snapping / Raking / Clawing Method of Execution

Right Vertical Punch
    Reverses
        Left Outward Elbow
    Opposites
        Left Vertical Punch
        Straight Punch
        Inverted Back-knuckle
        Uppercut
        Left Strike*
        Back-knuckle*
        Hammer-fist
        Middle-knuckle
        Horizontal, Four Finger Poke
        Hand-sword
        Heel-palm
        Half-knuckle*
        Forearm*
        Elbow*
        Buckle
        Kick*
        Block*
        Inward Block
        Vertical Outward Block
        Upward Block
        Outside Downward Block
        Inside Downward Block*
        Extended Outward Block
        Universal Block (Downward / Inward) Block
        Push-Down Block
        Hammering / Snapping / Raking / Clawing Method of
            Execution

Right Hammer-fist
   Reverses
      Middle-knuckle
   Opposites
      Left Hammer-fist
      Hand-sword
      Left Strike*
      Punch*
      Back-knuckle*
      Poke*
      Heel-palm
      Half-knuckle*
      Forearm*
      Elbow*
      Buckle
      Kick*
      Block*
      Inward Block
      Vertical Outward Block
      Upward Block
      Outside Downward Block
      Inside Downward Block*
      Extended Outward Block
      Universal Block (Downward / Inward) Block
      Push-Down Block
      Hammering / Snapping / Raking / Clawing Method of Execution

Left Hammer-fist
    Reverses
        Middle-knuckle
    Opposites
        Right Hammer-fist
        Hand-sword
        Right Strike*
        Punch*
        Back-knuckle*
        Poke*
        Heel-palm
        Half-knuckle*
        Forearm*
        Elbow*
        Buckle
        Kick*
        Block*
        Inward Block
        Vertical Outward Block
        Upward Block
        Outside Downward Block
        Inside Downward Block*
        Extended Outward Block
        Universal Block (Downward / Inward) Block
        Push-Down Block
        Hammering / Snapping / Raking / Clawing Method of Execution

Analysis of Long Form Two

    Left Downward Claw
        Reverses
            Uppercut
            Left Upward Elbow
        Opposites
            Right Downward Claw
            Right Strike*
            Poke*
            Punch*
            Heel-palm
            Left Forearm*
            Outward Elbow
            Right Back Elbow
            Hand-sword
            Forearm*
            Middle-knuckle
            Hammer-fist
            Back-knuckle*
            Outward Overhead Elbow
            Inward Overhead Elbow
            Right Inward Elbow
            Buckle
            Kick*
            Block*
            Inward Block
            Vertical Outward Block
            Upward Block
            Outside Downward Block
            Inside Downward Block*
            Extended Outward Block
            Universal Block (Downward / Inward) Block
            Push-Down Block
            Hammering / Thrusting / Snapping / Raking Method
                of Execution

© 2015 EPAKS Publications

Right Downward Claw
    Reverses
        Uppercut
        Left Upward Elbow
    Opposites
        Left Downward Claw
        Left Strike*
        Poke*
        Punch*
        Heel-palm
        Left Forearm*
        Outward Elbow
        Right Back Elbow
        Hand-sword
        Forearm*
        Middle-knuckle
        Hammer-fist
        Back-knuckle*
        Outward Overhead Elbow
        Inward Overhead Elbow
        Right Inward Elbow
        Buckle
        Kick*
        Block*
        Inward Block
        Vertical Outward Block
        Upward Block
        Outside Downward Block
        Inside Downward Block*
        Extended Outward Block
        Universal Block (Downward / Inward) Block
        Push-Down Block
        Hammering / Thrusting / Snapping / Raking Method
            of Execution

Right Outward Back-knuckle
    Reverses
        Left Outward Back-knuckle
        Right Inverted Back-knuckle
        Right Inward Elbow
    Opposites
        Left Outward Back-knuckle
        Left Inverted Back-knuckle
        Vertical Back-knuckle
        Left Upward Elbow
        Left Strike*
        Half-knuckle*
        Poke*
        Punch*
        Heel-palm
        Outward Elbow
        Right Back Elbow
        Hand-sword
        Outward Overhead Elbow
        Forearm*
        Inward Overhead Elbow
        Buckle
        Kick*
        Middle-knuckle
        Hammer-fist
        Block*
        Inward Block
        Vertical Outward Block
        Upward Block
        Outside Downward Block
        Inside Downward Block*
        Extended Outward Block
        Universal Block (Downward / Inward) Block
        Push-Down Block
        Hammering / Snapping / Raking / Clawing Method of
            Execution

Left Outward Back-knuckle
    Reverses
        Right Outward Back-knuckle
        Left Inverted Back-knuckle
    Opposites
        Right Outward Back-knuckle
        Right Inverted Back-knuckle
        Vertical Back-knuckle
        Right Inward Elbow
        Left Upward Elbow
        Right Strike*
        Half-knuckle*
        Poke*
        Punch*
        Heel-palm
        Outward Elbow
        Right Back Elbow
        Hand-sword
        Outward Overhead Elbow
        Forearm*
        Inward Overhead Elbow
        Buckle
        Kick*
        Middle-knuckle
        Hammer-fist
        Block*
        Inward Block
        Vertical Outward Block
        Upward Block
        Outside Downward Block
        Inside Downward Block*
        Extended Outward Block
        Universal Block (Downward / Inward) Block
        Push-Down Block
        Hammering / Snapping / Raking / Clawing Method of
            Execution

Left Inverted, Vertical Back-knuckle
   Reverses
      Right Inverted, Vertical Back-knuckle
   Opposites
      Right Inverted, Vertical Back-knuckle
      Outward Back-knuckle
      Vertical Back-knuckle
      Right Inward Elbow
      Left Upward Elbow
      Right Strike*
      Middle-knuckle
      Poke*
      Punch*
      Heel-palm
      Outward Elbow
      Right Back Elbow
      Hand-sword
      Outward Overhead Elbow
      Forearm*
      Inward Overhead Elbow
      Buckle
      Kick*
      Hammer-fist
      Block*
      Inward Block
      Vertical Outward Block
      Upward Block
      Outside Downward Block
      Inside Downward Block*
      Extended Outward Block
      Universal Block (Downward / Inward) Block
      Push-Down Block
      Hammering / Snapping / Raking / Clawing Method of Execution

Right Inverted, Vertical Back-knuckle
    Reverses
        Left Inverted, Vertical Back-knuckle
    Opposites
        Left Inverted, Vertical Back-knuckle
        Outward Back-knuckle
        Vertical Back-knuckle
        Right Inward Elbow
        Left Upward Elbow
        Left Strike*
        Middle-knuckle
        Poke*
        Punch*
        Heel-palm
        Outward Elbow
        Right Back Elbow
        Hand-sword
        Outward Overhead Elbow
        Forearm*
        Inward Overhead Elbow
        Buckle
        Kick*
        Hammer-fist
        Block*
        Inward Block
        Vertical Outward Block
        Upward Block
        Outside Downward Block
        Inside Downward Block*
        Extended Outward Block
        Universal Block (Downward / Inward) Block
        Push-Down Block
        Hammering / Snapping / Raking / Clawing Method of
            Execution

Analysis of Long Form Two

Left Half-knuckle
   Reverses
      None
   Opposites
      Right Half-knuckle*
      Back-knuckle*
      Right Strike*
      Right Inward Elbow
      Left Upward Elbow
      Poke*
      Punch*
      Heel-palm
      Outward Elbow
      Right Back Elbow
      Outward Overhead Elbow
      Inward Overhead Elbow
      Hand-sword
      Hammer-fist
      Forearm*
      Buckle
      Kick*
      Block*
      Inward Block
      Vertical Outward Block
      Upward Block
      Outside Downward Block
      Inside Downward Block*
      Extended Outward Block
      Universal Block (Downward / Inward) Block
      Push-Down Block
      Thrusting / Snapping / Raking / Clawing Method of Execution

Right Half-knuckle
    Reverses
        None
    Opposites
        Left Half-knuckle*
        Back-knuckle*
        Left Strike*
        Right Inward Elbow
        Left Upward Elbow
        Poke*
        Punch*
        Heel-palm
        Outward Elbow
        Right Back Elbow
        Outward Overhead Elbow
        Inward Overhead Elbow
        Hand-sword
        Hammer-fist
        Forearm*
        Buckle
        Kick*
        Block*
        Inward Block
        Vertical Outward Block
        Upward Block
        Outside Downward Block
        Inside Downward Block*
        Extended Outward Block
        Universal Block (Downward / Inward) Block
        Push-Down Block
        Thrusting / Snapping / Raking / Clawing Method of Execution

Right Uppercut Punch
   Reverses
      Inward Elbow
   Opposites
      Left Uppercut Punch
      Straight Punch
      Vertical Punch
      Ball Kick
      Left Strike*
      Poke*
      Hand-sword
      Heel-palm
      Middle-knuckle
      Half-knuckle*
      Forearm*
      Elbow*
      Buckle
      Kick*
      Block*
      Inward Block
      Vertical Outward Block
      Upward Block
      Outside Downward Block
      Inside Downward Block*
      Extended Outward Block
      Universal Block (Downward / Inward) Block
      Push-Down Block
      Hammering / Snapping / Raking / Clawing Method of Execution

Left Uppercut Punch
    Reverses
        Inward Elbow
    Opposites
        Right Uppercut Punch
        Straight Punch
        Vertical Punch
        Ball Kick
        Right Strike*
        Poke*
        Hand-sword
        Heel-palm
        Middle-knuckle
        Half-knuckle*
        Forearm*
        Elbow
        Buckle
        Kick*
        Block*
        Inward Block
        Vertical Outward Block
        Upward Block
        Outside Downward Block
        Inside Downward Block*
        Extended Outward Block
        Universal Block (Downward / Inward) Block
        Push-Down Block
        Hammering / Snapping / Raking / Clawing Method of
            Execution

Right Upward, Horizontal Forearm
   Reverses
      None
   Opposites
      Left Upward, Horizontal Forearm
      Buckle
      Inward Block
      Right Strike*
      Hand-sword
      Heel-palm
      Back-knuckle*
      Middle-knuckle
      Half-knuckle*
      Hammer-fist
      Poke*
      Punch*
      Outward Elbow
      Outward Overhead Elbow
      Inward Overhead Elbow
      Right Inward Elbow
      Left Upward Elbow
      Right Back Elbow
      Kick*
      Block*
      Vertical Outward Block
      Universal Block (Downward / Inward) Block
      Upward Block
      Outside Downward Block
      Inside Downward Block*
      Extended Outward Block
      Push-Down Block
      Hammering / Snapping / Raking / Clawing Method of
          Execution

Left Upward, Horizontal Forearm
    Reverses
        None
    Opposites
        Right Upward, Horizontal Forearm
        Buckle
        Inward Block
        Left Strike*
        Hand-sword
        Heel-palm
        Back-knuckle*
        Middle-knuckle
        Half-knuckle*
        Hammer-fist
        Poke*
        Punch*
        Outward Elbow
        Outward Overhead Elbow
        Inward Overhead Elbow
        Right Inward Elbow
        Left Upward Elbow
        Right Back Elbow
        Kick
        Block*
        Vertical Outward Block
        Universal Block (Downward / Inward) Block
        Upward Block
        Outside Downward Block
        Inside Downward Block*
        Extended Outward Block
        Push-Down Block
        Hammering / Snapping / Raking / Clawing Method of Execution

Analysis of Long Form Two — 345

Left Vertical, Two Finger Poke
    Reverses
        None
    Opposites
        Right Vertical, Two Finger Poke
        Right Vertical, Four Finger Poke
        Horizontal, Four Finger Poke
        Right Strike*
        Punch*
        Hammer-fist
        Back-knuckle*
        Middle-knuckle
        Half-knuckle*
        Claw*
        Heel-palm
        Hand-sword
        Left Inward, Vertical Forearm
        Upward, Horizontal Forearm
        Elbow*
        Buckle
        Kick*
        Block*
        Inward Block
        Vertical Outward Block
        Upward Block
        Outside Downward Block
        Inside Downward Block*
        Extended Outward Block
        Universal Block (Downward / Inward) Block
        Push-Down Block
        Hammering / Thrusting / Raking / Clawing Method of Execution

Right Vertical, Two Finger Poke
  Reverses
    None
  Opposites
    Left Vertical, Two Finger Poke
    Left Vertical, Four Finger Poke
    Horizontal, Four Finger Poke
    Left Strike*
    Punch*
    Hammer-fist
    Back-knuckle*
    Middle-knuckle
    Half-knuckle*
    Claw*
    Heel-palm
    Hand-sword
    Left Inward, Vertical Forearm
    Upward, Horizontal Forearm
    Elbow*
    Buckle
    Kick*
    Block*
    Inward Block
    Vertical Outward Block
    Upward Block
    Outside Downward Block
    Inside Downward Block*
    Extended Outward Block
    Universal Block (Downward / Inward) Block
    Push-Down Block
    Hammering / Thrusting / Raking / Clawing Method of Execution

Left Vertical, Back-knuckle
- Reverses
    - None
- Opposites
    - Right Vertical, Back-knuckle
    - Inverted Back-knuckle
    - Outward Back-knuckle
    - Left Upward Elbow
    - Right Strike*
    - Half-knuckle*
    - Poke*
    - Punch*
    - Heel-palm
    - Outward Elbow
    - Right Back Elbow
    - Hand-sword
    - Outward Overhead Elbow
    - Forearm*
    - Inward Overhead Elbow
    - Right Inward Elbow
    - Buckle
    - Kick*
    - Middle-knuckle
    - Hammer-fist
    - Block*
    - Inward Block
    - Vertical Outward Block
    - Upward Block
    - Outside Downward Block
    - Inside Downward Block*
    - Extended Outward Block
    - Universal Block (Downward / Inward) Block
    - Push-Down Block
    - Hammering / Thrusting / Raking / Clawing Method of Execution

Right Vertical, Back-knuckle
   Reverses
      None
   Opposites
      Left Vertical, Back-knuckle
      Inverted Back-knuckle
      Outward Back-knuckle
      Left Upward Elbow
      Left Strike*
      Half-knuckle*
      Poke*
      Punch*
      Heel-palm
      Outward Elbow
      Right Back Elbow
      Hand-sword
      Outward Overhead Elbow
      Forearm*
      Inward Overhead Elbow
      Right Inward Elbow
      Buckle
      Kick*
      Middle-knuckle
      Hammer-fist
      Block*
      Inward Block
      Vertical Outward Block
      Upward Block
      Outside Downward Block
      Inside Downward Block*
      Extended Outward Block
      Universal Block (Downward / Inward) Block
      Push-Down Block
      Hammering / Thrusting / Raking / Clawing Method of
          Execution

Left Outward Overhead Elbow
    Reverses
        Left Inward, Overhead Elbow
    Opposites
        Right Outward Overhead Elbow
        Right Inward Overhead Elbow
        Right Elbow*
        Right Strike*
        Poke*
        Punch*
        Heel-palm
        Right Inward Elbow
        Left Upward Elbow
        Outward Elbow
        Right Back Elbow
        Back-knuckle*
        Hand-sword
        Hammer-fist
        Forearm*
        Buckle
        Kick*
        Block*
        Inward Block
        Vertical Outward Block
        Upward Block
        Outside Downward Block
        Inside Downward Block*
        Extended Outward Block
        Universal Block (Downward / Inward) Block
        Push-Down Block
        Thrusting / Snapping / Raking / Clawing Method of
            Execution

Right Outward Overhead Elbow
    Reverses
        Right Inward Overhead Elbow
    Opposites
        Left Outward Overhead Elbow
        Inward Overhead Elbow
        Left Elbow*
        Left Strike*
        Poke*
        Punch*
        Heel-palm
        Right Inward Elbow
        Left Upward Elbow
        Outward Elbow
        Right Back Elbow
        Back-knuckle*
        Hand-sword
        Hammer-fist
        Forearm*
        Buckle
        Kick*
        Block*
        Inward Block
        Vertical Outward Block
        Upward Block
        Outside Downward Block
        Inside Downward Block*
        Extended Outward Block
        Universal Block (Downward / Inward) Block
        Push-Down Block
        Thrusting / Snapping / Raking / Clawing Method of Execution

Analysis of Long Form Two

    Left Inward, Vertical Forearm
        Reverses
            Right Inside Downward, Palm up Block
        Opposites
            Upward, Vertical Forearm
            Buckle
            Inward Block
            Right Strike*
            Hand-sword
            Heel-palm
            Back-knuckle*
            Middle-knuckle
            Half-knuckle*
            Hammer-fist
            Poke*
            Punch*
            Outward Elbow
            Outward Overhead Elbow
            Inward Overhead Elbow
            Right Inward Elbow
            Left Upward Elbow
            Right Back Elbow
            Kick*
            Block*
            Vertical Outward Block
            Universal Block (Downward / Inward) Block
            Upward Block
            Outside Downward Block
            Inside Downward Block*
            Extended Outward Block
            Push-Down Block
            Hammering / Snapping / Raking / Clawing Method of
                  Execution

Left Inward Overhead Elbow
    Reverses
        Left Outward Overhead Elbow
        Left Upward Elbow
    Opposites
        Right Inward Overhead Elbow
        Right Outward Overhead Elbow
        Right Elbow*
        Right Strike*
        Poke*
        Punch*
        Heel-palm
        Right Inward Elbow
        Outward Elbow
        Right Back Elbow
        Back-knuckle*
        Hand-sword
        Hammer-fist
        Forearm*
        Buckle
        Kick*
        Block*
        Inward Block
        Vertical Outward Block
        Upward Block
        Outside Downward Block
        Inside Downward Block*
        Extended Outward Block
        Universal Block (Downward / Inward) Block
        Push-Down Block
        Thrusting / Snapping / Raking / Clawing Method of
            Execution

Analysis of Long Form Two — 353

Right Inward Overhead Elbow
    Reverses
        Right Outward Overhead Elbow
        Left Upward Elbow
    Opposites
        Left Inward Overhead Elbow
        Right Outward Overhead Elbow
        Left Strike*
        Poke*
        Punch*
        Heel-palm
        Right Inward Elbow
        Left Upward Elbow
        Outward Elbow
        Right Back Elbow
        Back-knuckle*
        Hand-sword
        Hammer-fist
        Forearm*
        Buckle
        Kick*
        Block*
        Inward Block
        Vertical Outward Block
        Upward Block
        Outside Downward Block
        Inside Downward Block*
        Extended Outward Block
        Universal Block (Downward / Inward) Block
        Push-Down Block
        Thrusting / Snapping / Raking / Clawing Method of
            Execution

Right Inward Elbow (Sandwich)
   Reverses
      Right Outward Back-knuckle
      Left Inverted Back-knuckle
   Opposites
      Outward Elbow
      Left Upward Elbow
      Right Back Elbow
      Outward Overhead Elbow
      Inward Overhead Elbow
      Left Strike*
      Left Outward Back-knuckle
      Right Inverted Back-knuckle
      Vertical Back-knuckle
      Half-knuckle*
      Poke*
      Punch*
      Heel-palm
      Hand-sword
      Forearm*
      Buckle
      Kick*
      Middle-knuckle
      Hammer-fist
      Block*
      Inward Block
      Vertical Outward Block
      Upward Block
      Outside Downward Block
      Inside Downward Block*
      Extended Outward Block
      Universal Block (Downward / Inward) Block
      Push-Down Block
      Hammering / Snapping / Raking / Clawing Method of Execution

Left Outward Elbow
   Reverses
      Right Outward Elbow
      Left Straight Punch (only 90 degree)
   Opposites
      Right Outward Elbow
      Right Inward Elbow
      Left Upward Elbow
      Right Back Elbow
      Straight Punch (includes all degrees)
      Right Strike*
      Vertical Punch
      Heel-palm
      Uppercut
      Poke*
      Hand-sword
      Middle-knuckle*
      Half-knuckle
      Forearm*
      Back-knuckle*
      Buckle
      Kick*
      Block*
      Inward Block
      Vertical Outward Block
      Upward Block
      Outside Downward Block
      Inside Downward Block*
      Extended Outward Block
      Universal Block (Downward / Inward) Block
      Push-Down Block
      Hammering / Snapping / Raking / Clawing Method of
          Execution

© 2015 EPAKS Publications

Right Outward Elbow
- Reverses
  - Left Outward Elbow
  - Right Straight Punch (only 90 degree)
- Opposites
  - Left Outward Elbow
  - Right Inward Elbow
  - Left Upward Elbow
  - Straight Punch (includes all degrees)
  - Left Strike*
  - Vertical Punch
  - Heel-palm
  - Uppercut
  - Poke*
  - Hand-sword
  - Middle-knuckle
  - Half-knuckle*
  - Forearm*
  - Back-knuckle*
  - Buckle
  - Kick*
  - Block*
  - Inward Block
  - Vertical Outward Block
  - Upward Block
  - Outside Downward Block
  - Inside Downward Block*
  - Extended Outward Block
  - Universal Block (Downward / Inward) Block
  - Push-Down Block
  - Hammering / Snapping / Raking / Clawing Method of Execution

Left Upward Elbow
- Reverses
    - Push-down
    - Inward Overhead Elbow
- Opposites
    - Outward Elbow
    - Right Inward Elbow
    - Right Back Elbow
    - Right Strike*
    - Punch*
    - Heel-palm
    - Poke*
    - Hand-sword
    - Middle-knuckle
    - Half-knuckle*
    - Forearm*
    - Back-knuckle*
    - Buckle
    - Kick*
    - Block*
    - Inward Block
    - Vertical Outward Block
    - Upward Block
    - Outside Downward Block
    - Inside Downward Block*
    - Extended Outward Block
    - Universal Block (Downward / Inward) Block
    - Push-Down Block
    - Hammering / Snapping / Raking / Clawing Method of Execution

© 2015 EPAKS Publications

Right Back Elbow
    Reverses
        Straight Punch (excluding 45 and 90 degree)
        Ball Kick
    Opposites
        Left Outward Elbow
        Straight Punch (includes all degrees)
        Vertical Punch
        Uppercut
        Right Strike*
        Poke*
        Heel-palm
        Hand-sword
        Middle-knuckle*
        Half-knuckle* (excluding right closed)
        Forearm*
        Inward Overhead Elbow
        Outward Overhead Elbow
        Left Upward Elbow
        Buckle
        Side Kick
        Instep (arch) Kick
        Block*
        Inward Block
        Vertical Outward Block
        Upward Block
        Outside Downward Block
        Inside Downward Block*
        Extended Outward Block
        Universal Block (Downward / Inward) Block
        Push-Down Block
        Thrusting / Snapping / Raking / Clawing Method of
            Execution

Strikes (lower body)
Left Side Kick
    Reverses
        Left Instep (arch) Kick
        Left (90 degree) Straight Punch
        Right Outward Elbow
    Opposites
        Right Side Kick
        Front Kick
        Instep (arch) Kick
        Right Kick*
        Buckle
        Punch*
        Hand-sword
        Hammer-fist
        Back-knuckle*
        Middle-knuckle
        Heel-palm
        Half-knuckle*
        Poke*
        Claw*
        Forearm*
        Elbow
        Block*
        Inward Block
        Vertical Outward Block
        Extended Outward Block
        Universal Block (Downward / Inward) Block
        Upward Block
        (Outside) Downward Block
        Inside-Downward Block*
        Push-down Block
        Hammering / Snapping / Raking / Clawing Method of
            Execution

Right Side Kick
   Reverses
      Right Instep (arch) Kick
      Right (90 degree) Straight Punch
      Left Outward Elbow
   Opposites
      Left Side Kick
      Front Kick
      Instep (arch) Kick
      Left Kick*
      Buckle
      Punch*
      Hand-sword
      Hammer-fist
      Back-knuckle*
      Middle-knuckle
      Heel-palm
      Half-knuckle*
      Poke*
      Claw*
      Forearm*
      Elbow*
      Block*
      Inward Block
      Vertical Outward Block
      Extended Outward Block
      Universal Block (Downward / Inward) Block
      Upward Block
      (Outside) Downward Block
      Inside-Downward Block*
      Push-down Block
      Hammering / Snapping / Raking / Clawing Method of Execution

Right Front Kick
   Reverses
      Right Back Elbow
   Opposites
      Left Front Kick
      Side Kick
      Instep (arch) Kick
      Left Kick*
      Buckle
      Punch*
      Hand-sword
      Hammer-fist
      Back-knuckle*
      Middle-knuckle
      Heel-palm
      Half-knuckle*
      Poke*
      Claw*
      Forearm*
      Elbow*
      Block*
      Inward Block
      Vertical Outward Block
      Extended Outward Block
      Universal Block (Downward / Inward) Block
      Upward Block
      (Outside) Downward Block
      Inside-Downward Block*
      Push-down Block
      Hammering / Snapping / Raking / Clawing Method of Execution

    Left Front Kick
        Reverses
            Right Back Elbow
        Opposites
            Right Front Kick
            Side Kick
            Instep (arch) Kick
            Right Kick*
            Buckle
            Punch*
            Hand-sword
            Hammer-fist
            Back-knuckle*
            Middle-knuckle
            Heel-palm
            Half-knuckle*
            Poke*
            Claw*
            Forearm*
            Elbow*
            Block*
            Inward Block
            Vertical Outward Block
            Extended Outward Block
            Universal Block (Downward / Inward) Block
            Upward Block
            (Outside) Downward Block
            Inside-Downward Block*
            Push-down Block
            Hammering / Snapping / Raking / Clawing Method of
                Execution

Analysis of Long Form Two

Right Buckle
    Reverses
        None
    Opposites
        Left Buckle
        Forearm*
        Left Strike*
        Side Kick
        Front (ball) Kick
        Instep (arch) Kick
        Hand-sword
        Hammer-fist
        Heel-palm
        Back-knuckle*
        Middle-knuckle
        Half-knuckle*
        Poke*
        Punch*
        Outward Elbow
        Right Back Elbow
        Right Inward Elbow
        Left Upward Elbow
        Outward Overhead Elbow
        Inward Overhead Elbow
        Block*
        Inward Block
        Vertical Outward Block
        Upward Block
        Outside Downward Block
        Inside Downward Block*
        Extended Outward Block
        Universal Block (Downward / Inward) Block
        Push-Down Block
        Hammering / Snapping / Raking / Clawing Method of
            Execution

Left Buckle
    Reverses
        None
    Opposites
        Right Buckle
        Forearm*
        Right Strike*
        Side Kick
        Front (ball) Kick
        Instep (arch) Kick
        Hand-sword
        Hammer-fist
        Heel-palm
        Back-knuckle*
        Middle-knuckle
        Half-knuckle*
        Poke*
        Punch*
        Outward Elbow
        Right Back Elbow
        Right Inward Elbow
        Left Upward Elbow
        Outward Overhead Elbow
        Inward Overhead Elbow
        Block*
        Inward Block
        Vertical Outward Block
        Upward Block
        Outside Downward Block
        Inside Downward Block*
        Extended Outward Block
        Universal Block (Downward / Inward) Block
        Push-Down Block
        Hammering / Snapping / Raking / Clawing Method of
            Execution

Left Instep (arch) Kick
   Reverses
      Left Side Kick
      Right (90 degree) Straight Punch
      Left Outward Elbow
   Opposites
      Right Instep (arch) Kick
      Side Kick
      Front Kick
      Right Kick*
      Buckle
      Punch*
      Hand-sword
      Hammer-fist
      Back-knuckle*
      Middle-knuckle
      Heel-palm
      Half-knuckle*
      Poke*
      Claw*
      Forearm*
      Elbow*
      Block*
      Inward Block
      Vertical Outward Block
      Extended Outward Block
      Universal Block (Downward / Inward) Block
      Upward Block
      (Outside) Downward Block
      Inside-Downward Block*
      Push-down Block
      Hammering / Snapping / Raking / Clawing Method of
          Execution

Right Instep (arch) Kick
    Reverses
        Right Side Kick
        Left (90 degree) Straight Punch
        Right Outward Elbow
    Opposites
        Left Instep (arch) Kick
        Side Kick
        Front Kick
        Left Kick*
        Buckle
        Punch*
        Hand-sword
        Hammer-fist
        Back-knuckle*
        Middle-knuckle
        Heel-palm
        Half-knuckle*
        Poke*
        Claw*
        Forearm*
        Elbow*
        Block*
        Inward Block
        Vertical Outward Block
        Extended Outward Block
        Universal Block (Downward / Inward) Block
        Upward Block
        (Outside) Downward Block
        Inside-Downward Block*
        Push-down Block
        Hammering / Snapping / Raking / Clawing Method of Execution

Foot Maneuvers
Right Step Through Forward
    Reverses
        Right Step Through Reverse
    Opposites
        Left Step Through Reverse
        Left Step Through Forward
        Cover*
        45 Degree Cover
        180 Degree Cover
        225 Degree Cover

Left Step Through Forward
    Reverses
        Left Step Through Reverse
    Opposites
        Right Step Through Reverse
        Right Step Through Forward
        Cover*
        45 Degree Cover
        180 Degree Cover
        225 Degree Cover

Right 90 Degree Cover
    Reverses
        Left 90 Degree Cover
    Opposites
        Left 90 Degree Cover
        Left Cover*
        45 Degree Cover
        180 Degree Cover
        225 Degree Cover
        Step Through Forward / Reverse

Left 90 Degree Cover
    Reverses
        Right 90 Degree Cover
    Opposites
        Right 90 Degree Cover
        Right Cover*
        45 Degree Cover
        180 Degree Cover
        225 Degree Cover
        Step Through Forward / Reverse

Left 180 Degree Cover
    Reverses
        Right 180 Degree Cover
    Opposites
        Right Cover*
        Right 180 Degree Cover
        45 Degree Cover
        90 Degree Cover
        225 Degree Cover
        Step Through Forward / Reverse

Right 180 Degree Cover
    Reverses
        Left 180 Degree Cover
    Opposites
        Left Cover*
        Left 180 Degree Cover
        45 Degree Cover
        90 Degree Cover
        225 Degree Cover
        Step Through Forward / Reverse

Left 225 Degree Cover
    Reverses
        None
    Opposites
        Right Cover*
        45 Degree Cover
        90 Degree Cover
        180 Degree Cover
        Step Through Forward / Reverse

Left 45 Degree Cover
    Reverses
        None
    Opposites
        Left Cover*
        90 Degree Cover
        180 Degree Cover
        225 Degree Cover
        Step Through Forward / Reverse

Sequence Analysis

Inward Block Sequence
    Reverses
        Inward Block (Short Form One)
        Inward Block Sequence (Long Form One)
        Inside, Vertical Forearm Sequence
    Opposites**
        Inward Block (Short Form One)
        Inward Block Sequence (Long Form One)
        Outward Block Sequence*
        Upward Block Sequence*
        Downward Block Sequence*
        Extended Outward Block Sequence

Outward Block Sequence
    Reverses
        Outward Block Sequence (Short / Long Form One)
        Upward Block Sequence (Long Form Two)
    Opposites**
        Outward Block (Short Form One)
        Inward Block Sequence*
        Upward Block Sequence (Short / Long Form Two)
        Downward Block Sequence*

Upward Block Sequence
    Reverses
        Upward Block Sequence (Short / Long Form One)
        Upward Block Sequence (Short Form Two)
        Outward Block Sequence (Long Form Two)
    Opposites**
        Inward Block (Short Form One)
        Downward Block Sequence*
        Outward Block Sequence*
        Half-knuckle Sequence (Long Form Two)
        Push-down Sequence

Analysis of Long Form Two 371

Downward Block Sequence
   Reverses
      Downward Block Sequence (Short / Long Form One)
      Downward Block Sequence (Short Form Two)
      Inside-Downward, Palm down Sequence
   Opposites**
      Inward Block (Short Form One)
      Inward Block Sequence (Long Form One)
      Outward Block (Short Form One)
      Outward Block Sequence*
      Upward Block (Short Form One)
      Upward Block Sequence*
      Extended Outward Block Sequence
      Push-down Sequence

Half-knuckle Sequence
   Reverses
      Outward Block Sequence (Long Form Two)
      Short Form One*
      Inside-Downward, Palm up Sequence
      Inside, Vertical Forearm Sequence
      Inward, Overhead Elbow Sequence
   Opposites**
      Upward Block Sequence (Long Form Two)
      Downward Block Sequence (Long Form Two)
      Extended Outward Block Sequence
      Short Form One*
      Triple Block Sequence*

Inside-Downward, Palm up Sequence
    Reverses
        Downward Block Sequence (Long Form Two)
        Half-knuckle Sequence (Long Form Two)
        Inside, Vertical Forearm Sequence
        Push-down Sequence
        Inward Block Sequence (Long Form One)
        Downward Block Sequence (Long Form One)
        Isolation (Long Form One)
        Downward Block Sequence (Short Form Two)
    Opposites**
        Downward Block Sequence (Long Form Two)
        Inside-Downward, Palm down Sequence
        (Left) Upward Block Sequence (Long Form One)
        Short Form Two*
        Inward Block Sequence (Short / Long Form Two)*
        Extended Outward Block Sequence

Inside-Downward, Palm down Sequence
    Reverses
        Push-down Sequence
        Downward Block Sequence*
        Isolation (Long Form One)
        (Left) Upward Block Sequence (Long Form One)
        Short Form Two*
    Opposites**
        Outward Block Sequence*
        Half-knuckle Sequence (Long Form Two)
        Inside-Downward, Palm up Sequence (Long Form Two)

Push-down Sequence
   Reverses
      Inside-Downward Sequence*
      Inside, Vertical Forearm Sequence
      Inward, Overhead Elbow Sequence
      Upward Block Sequence*
   Opposites**
      Downward Block Sequence (Long Form Two)
      Half-knuckle Sequence (Long Form Two)
      Short Form One*
      Block / Punch Sequences (Long Form One)*

Inside, Vertical Forearm Sequence
   Reverses
      Inward Block Sequence (Long Form One)
   Opposites**
      Short Form One*
      Right Inward Bock Sequence (Long Form One)
      Triple Block Sequence (Long Form One)*
      Upward Block Sequence (Long Form Two)
      Downward Block Sequence (Long Form Two)
      Half-knuckle Sequence (Long Form Two)
      Inside-downward, Palm-up Block Sequence

Inward, Overhead Elbow Sequence
   Reverses
      Push-down Sequence
   Opposites**
      Short Form One*
      Left Upward Block Sequence (Long Form One)
      Triple Block Sequence (Long Form One)*
      Isolation (Long Form One)
      Short Form Two*
      Upward Block Sequence (Short Form Two)
      Downward Block Sequence (Short Form Two)
      Half-knuckle Sequence*
      Isolation (Long Form Two)

© 2015 EPAKS Publications

Elbow, Isolation Sequence
    Reverses
        Isolation (Long Form One)
    Opposites**
        Short Form One*
        Triple Block Sequence (Long Form One)*
        Outward Block Sequence (Long Form Two)
        Upward Block Sequence (Long Form Two)
        Downward Block Sequence (Long Form Two)
        Push-down Sequence
        Inward, Overhead Elbow Sequence

Principles / Rules / Theories / Concepts / Definitions Analysis

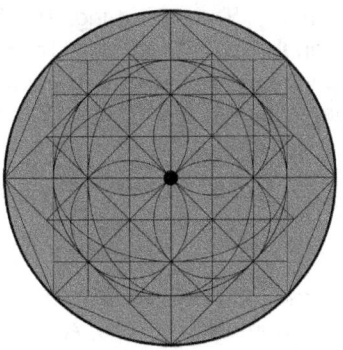

Dictionary

Advance, Aim, Align, Alter, Amplify, Analogy, Anchor, Angle, Apex, Attacker, Attention, Attitude, Available, Back, Balance, Ball, Base, Basic, Block, Bob, Bounce, Bow, Break, Breathe, Category, Center-line, Chamber, Check, Chop, Circle, Clock, Cock, Concentration, Concept, Conscious, Contact, Contour, Control, Coordination, Counter, Cover, Defense, Deflect, Degree, Deliver, Depth, Deviate, Diagonal, Dictionary, Dimension, Direct, Direction, Disharmony, Distance, Downward, Embryonic, Environment, Execute, Exhale, Focus, Force, Form, Forward, Front, Gap, Gauge, Guide, Hammer, Hard, Harm, Harmony, Height, Hide, Hidden, Hinge, Horizontal, Hurt, Idea, Inhale, Inside, Intent, Intentional, Intercept, Intersect, Intersection, Inward, Isolation, Kata, Kiai, Lever, Leverage, Line, Mace, Major, Maneuver, Mechanical, Meditation, Meet, Method, Minor, Minus, Motion, Move, Mumble, Neutral, Obscure, Offense, Opponent, Opposite, Outer, Outward, Path, Penetration, Pivot, Plane, Plant, Plus, Position, Posture, Power, Practice, Practitioner, Prevent, Primitive, Principle, Pronounce, Proportional, Protect, Punch, Range, Rank, Read, Rear, Rearrange, Redirect, Regulate, Relax, Retract, Reverse, Rhythm, Rotate, Rule, Salutation, Saying, Scan, School, Sensei, Set, Settle, Shape,

Shift, Side, Signify, Simultaneous, Slide, Snap, Soft, Solidify, Sophisticated, Space, Speed, Square, Stable, Stationary, Step, Strike, Student, Studio, Style, Subconscious, Survey, Switch, Sword, Symmetrical, Sync, Synchronize, System, Tactic, Tailor, Target, Telegraph, Theory, Thrust, Timing, Tip, Torque, Touch, Tournament, Traditional, Train, Transitory, Travel, Triangle, Turn, Unify, Unuseful, Upward, Use, Useless, Velocity, Vertical, Viewpoint, Weapon, Width, With, X, Yield, Zone

Terms

8 Major Angles of Attack, 8 Major Angles of Balance, 8 Major Angles of Defense, Accumulated Force, Alphabet of Motion, Analogy of Dictionary / Encyclopedia / Appendix, Anatomical Positioning, Anatomical Weak Point, Angle Alignment, Angle of Attack, Angle of Avoidance, Angle of Balance, Angle of Cancellation, Angle of Closure, Angle of Contact, Angle of Cover, Angle of Defense, Angle of Deflection, Angle of Delivery, Angle of Departure, Angle of Deviation, Angle of Efficiency, Angle of Entry, Angle of Execution, Angle of Incidence, Angle of Obscurity, Angle of Prevention, Angle of Protection, Angle of Retraction, Angle of Return, Angle of Travel, Area Check, Area Cover, Articulation of Motion, Associated Moves, Axis of Rotation, Back-up Mass, Body Alignment, Body English, Body Harmony, Body Fusion, Body Mechanics, Body Momentum, Body Rotation, Body Settle, Brace Angle, Break the Heel, Broken Rhythm, Category Completion, Center of Gravity, Center of Mass, Chambered Position, Changing the Guard, Chicken Wing, Circular Confinement, Circular Rotation, Clock Principle, Close the Gap, Close the Gate, Close the Line, Close Range, Close Range Weapon, Cocking Check, Colliding Forces, Compact Unit, Completed Path of Travel, Conceptual Box, Contact Deviation, Contact Penetration, Contour Confinement, Contour Guidance, Corrective Adjustment, Cover Step, Cup and Saucer, Defensive Check, Defensive Defense, Defensive Reaction, Degree of Attack, Degree of Contact, Degree of Intent, Degree of Rotation, Delayed Movement, Depth of Action, Depth Penetration, Depth Perception, Depth Zone, Diagonal Plane,

© 2015 EPAKS Publications

Analysis of Long Form Two — 377

Dictionary Form, Dimensional Zone, Direct Gravitational Marriage, Direct Opposites, Directional Change, Directional Harmony, Directional Movement, Directional Switch, Disharmony of Travel, Disharmony of Force, Disrupted Rhythm, Double Factor, Economy of Motion, Environmental Awareness, Environmental Condition, Establish your Base, Explosive Action, Field of View, Fighting Stance, Filling the Gap, Fluid Movement, Form Indicator, Forward Back-up Mass, Frozen Motion, Full Beat Timing, Gauging Leg, General Rule, Geometric Angle, Geometric Line, Geometric Path, Gravitational Marriage, Half-fist, Hand-sword, Harmonious Movement, Harmonized Power, Heel-Knee Alignment, Heel-Toe Alignment, Height Zone, Horizontal Plane, Horizontal Punch, Horizontal Zone, Horizontal Zone of Attack, Horizontal Zone of Defense, Horizontal Zone of Protection, In Sync, In-Place, Intercepting Forces, Intersecting Action, Intersecting Forces, Invisible Box, Jet Lag, Line of Action, Line of Attack, Line of Defense, Line of Delivery, Line of Execution, Line of Sight, Line of Travel, Lock-Out, Long Form, Long Range, Long Range Weapon, Lower Case, Maintain the Gap, Margin for Error, Marriage of Gravity, Marriage with Gravity, Medium Range, Medium Range Weapon, Mental Distraction, Mental Harmony, Method of Attack, Method of Defense, Method of Delivery, Method of Execution, Method of Travel, Mirror Image, Motion Analysis, Movement of Punctuation, Natural Defenses, Natural Weapon, Neutral Zone of Defense, Obscure Zone, Offensive Offense, Open Ended Triangle, Open the Gap, Open the Gate, Open the Line, Opposing Forces, Opposite Motion, Optimum Angle of Incidence, Outer Rim, Over Reach, Over Rotate, Path of Action, Path of Attack, Path of Defense, Path of Delivery, Path of Entry, Path of Execution, Path of Retraction, Path of Travel, Penetration Point, Peripheral Assessment, Peripheral Awareness, Peripheral Registering, Peripheral Scan, Peripheral Vision, Physical Harmony, Physical Preparedness, Physical Speed, Pivot Point, Pivoting Axis, Placement of Target, Point of Cancellation, Point of Contact, Point of Impact, Point of Origin, Point of Pivot, Point of Reference, Position of Readiness, Positional Alignment, Positional Check, Positional Cock, Positional Cover, Positioned Block, Positioned Check, Positioned Cover, Postural Position, Power Principle, Prolonged Exposure, Proportional Dimension, Proportional Execution,

© 2015 EPAKS Publications

Protective Measure, Ready Position, Reference Point, Residual Torque, Return Motion, Reverse Motion, Reverse Punch, Rotating Axis, Rotating Force, Rotational Velocity, Scenic Route, Self-correcting, Settle into Balance, Short Form, Short Range, Short Range Weapon, Solidify your Base, Stabilize your Base, Stages of Range, Step Back, Surface Contact, Target Area, Target Availability, Target Placement, Toe-Heel Alignment, Toe-Toe Alignment, Toe-Toe Heel-Heel Alignment, Total Harmony, Total Mental Harmony, Total Physical Harmony, Transitional Move, Universal Pattern, Upper Case, Useless, V Step, Vertical Plane, Visual Interpretation, Vital Area, Vital Target, Wasted Motion, Weapon Alignment, Weapon Availability, Weight Distribution, Width Zone, Zone of Confinement, Zone of Obscurity, Zone of Protection

Chapter 10 - Improving Your Execution of Long Form Two

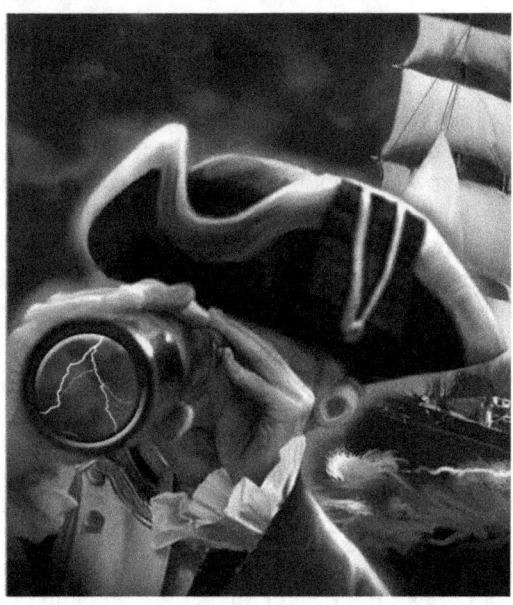

There is a lot of subtle and often overlooked execution information that can be learned from Long Form Two. The vast majority of this information is absorbed through perfecting the form through practice and through feedback from an instructor. Often this feedback and 'perfecting' is minute and absorbed through repetition and repeated correction. Also, this information is often absorbed over a long period of time, over a large number of practice sessions, and gets almost to the point that the information is absorbed subconsciously. To quote an often used phrase - 'One cannot fool experience'.

Also, perfecting the execution of the other American Kenpo forms can help improve the execution of Long Form Two. Therefore, it is not recommended that the practitioner preclude the practice of the other forms for this one. The diverse movements of the other forms can and will help to improve the execution of the maneuvers of this form.

Even though Long Form Two is still considered a relatively basic form, the skilled eye can easily discern differences between practiced and knowledgeable executions, from those that are more primitive and/or less experienced. Pace, timing, coordination, elimination of wasted motion, settling, power, and smooth execution are only some of the factors that comprise a properly executed form.

Occasionally, a practitioner will attempt to hide or compensate for inexperience with enthusiasm and/or over acting. This is most often done for competition. The purpose of this practice is to try to convince a panel of judges to grant a higher score by having them overlook other shortcomings in the form. This tactic often works and is why some competitors employ this strategy. While this practice may be of use for competition, it should not be used to dismiss or bypass the overall refinement and improvement process of the form - which is sometimes done.

All too often, execution emphasis is used as a substitution for proper execution. And, sometimes it is used to purposely distort proper execution. Each element is important for proper execution of a form. And, one element should not be used to compromise or diminish the other.

As mentioned earlier in this guide, changing a form for competition is fairly common and is not discouraged. But, it is discouraged that a personal modification to a form make its way back to the standard execution of a form. In other words, the practitioner should be able to distinguish between and execute the form both the standard way and with their own personal modifications.

Improving Your Execution of Long Form Two

Regardless of its origin, each execution error falls into one of three types: 1) movements / methods that the practitioner was not aware they were doing and were never corrected; 2) movements / methods that the practitioner is aware of and currently working on to correct; 3) movements / methods that the practitioner is aware of and not motivated (for whatever reason) to correct. This chapter is designed to help with the first two and to discourage and/or help eliminate the third.

What follows is a fairly comprehensive overview of the most common and egregious errors / mistakes that should be eliminated from the proper execution of Long Form Two. These problems are typically found and corrected by a qualified instructor, but can also be corrected by self-analysis. The information presented in this chapter can be used as a sort of checklist of items to look for when attempting to find / fix problems with form execution.

One common way to self correct problems of form execution is to video the execution of the form and review the video, looking for errors and areas of improvement. This practice goes all the way back to SGM Parker who often filmed himself and others and used these films both as reference and for improving execution of material. Today it is relatively easy and commonplace to video one's self. One can often find it an eye-opening experience to see them-self from a third person's perspective. This is because viewing one's self on a video is often very different from what one imagines it to be. A final point about this exercise - it is good practice to have multiple people view and give recommendations about the same video. Often, different individuals viewing the same video will find different items of correction. This is due to the different experiences and perspectives of each individual. These differences of observation can be used to make the corrections of the form more comprehensive.

General Errors

a) improper coordination:
   i) major block is not timed with the settle into stance
   ii) dual motion is not executed at the same time
   iii) settle / rotation into stance is not timed with strike

b) not turning head to new direction prior to foot maneuver

c) not looking straight ahead – i.e. looking up, down or wondering eyes

d) improper breathing:
   i) holding breath
   ii) breathing in during execution of major blocks and/or strikes

e) improper execution:
   i) not obeying Economy of Motion principle

Timing

Timing is a general term that encompasses a number of more specific terms that refer to time as it relates to execution of maneuvers. These terms include coordination, pace, speed, and synchronization to name a few. Timing is an extremely important concept when it comes to proper execution of a form. Coordination is characterized as the timing of multiple motions into a single maneuver such that they are synchronized as intended. Pace is the general speed at which a form is executed. Speed can refer to overall speed or speed related to a single or multiple maneuvers - and can sometimes be used interchangeably with pace. Synchronization refers to coordination of multiple movements into a single harmonious maneuver - and can sometimes be used interchangeably with coordination. As one can clearly see, the definitions of terms related to timing have specific definitions, but can often be used interchangeably with other similar terms.

Timing is demonstrated throughout the form in a number of ways:

- by timing foot maneuvers with blocks, strikes, and re-positioning
- by timing settle in stance with blocks and strikes
- by timing rotation in stance with blocks and strikes
- by timing minor movements within major movements without adversely effecting the major movement
- by timing weapon formation with weapon delivery
- by timing breathing with overall maneuver execution
- by timing the overall execution (pace) of the form
- by timing the execution (speed) of individual maneuvers

Each of these forms of timing are intended to coordinate the lower with the upper body in such a way as to create harmonious and fluid maneuvers which complete their travel in-sync with one another at an effective and synchronized manner. With experience and practice, one can easily discern correctly timed maneuvers from incorrectly timed maneuvers.

Gaze

The look on a practitioner's face and specifically the look in their eyes can heavily influence the perception of how a form is perceived. It is said that the eyes are the window to the soul. One can use this adage to their advantage to manipulate the viewer's perception of one's performance. This along with the practitioner's attitude can go a long way to overcoming other short-falls that may occur in their form execution.

During the execution of Long Form Two, the practitioner should always keep their gaze at eye level and parallel to the floor. This practice helps in maintaining a straight back and well balanced stance. Also, it is a general rule to always look into the direction one is intending to step before executing the foot maneuver. This should be done by not only shifting the eyes, but also turning the head.

Breathing

Breathing is an important part of the execution of any maneuver in American Kenpo. Long Form Two is no exception. One must learn the importance of breath and how it effects their performance.

One bad habit that numerous beginner to intermediate students sometimes pick up is the holding of their breath during the execution of maneuvers. This should be corrected by having the practitioner concentrate on smooth and relaxed breathing. The only emphasis in one's breath should be at the anticipated point of contact of the block and/or strike. This emphasis of breath should be for the purpose of helping to focus one's energy. Holding one's breath can lead to Constipated Motion - i.e. motion that is not fluid and/or smooth, but rather staccato and/or stiff in nature.

Improving Your Execution of Long Form Two

The kiai is a form of focusing one's breath by creating an audible sound with the breath through tightening of the abdominal muscles, thus forcing the breath to exhale. Some instructors teach using kiais to help students focus their breath with their maneuvers. Although Long Form Two does not specifically contain any kiais in it's standard execution, it is not an incorrect nor bad teaching tool. On the contrary, it can be used to help a student correct breathing issues, along with teaching the purpose of tightening muscles in anticipation of absorbing an oncoming strike to the body. It can also be used as an 'attention getter' when executing a form in competition.

Stance Errors

Stances are the base of our execution. Stances can be loosely defined as frozen motion. Without properly articulated stances, the execution of Long Form Two can never be perfected. The most commonly overlooked item among stances is proper positioning. Positioning includes a large number of elements. These include foot/leg alignments, body alignments, arm/hand alignments, and neck/head alignments. One should become comfortable with the knowledge of proper alignments and dimensions of the stances and proper positioning of the upper body in relation to the intended stance. Even though the upper body positioning is not directly related to the stance when analyzing the stance as a basic, the upper body positioning becomes extremely important when analyzed in relation to the execution of the form. The proper dimensions and alignments of each of the stances is highlighted in detail in SGM Parker's book, "Infinite Insights into Kenpo - book #2 (Physical Analyzation I)."

Improving Your Execution of Long Form Two

Long Form Two exposes seven stances during it's execution, depending upon how the form is executed (not including the salutation): the Meditating Horse, Neutral Bow, 45 degree Cat, Offset Horse, Forward Bow, Reverse Bow, and Twist.

It is very common for the practitioner to start out with proper alignments, but quickly lose the alignments once any foot maneuvers are executed. One good exercise for drawing attention to the stances is to perform the entire form without the use of the upper body - rather execute the entire form with both hands on hips or in chamber. This exercise allows the practitioner to pay exclusive attention to the stances and foot maneuvers without having to split their attention on proper upper body maneuver execution.

General Stance Errors

a) improper alignments / dimensions:
   i) improper stance width (too narrow / wide)
   ii) improper stance depth (too close / far)
   iii) improper stance height (knees not bent enough or too much)

b) improper rotation:
   i) improper upper body rotation (over / under rotation)
   ii) improper hip rotation (over / under rotation)
   iii) improper foot rotation (over / under rotation - for either or both feet)

c) improper weight distribution:
   i) improper center of mass over feet:
      1) positioned to far forward / backward
      2) positioned to far toward toes / heels
   ii) leaning in stance:
      1) leaning forward / backward
      2) leaning side-to-side

d) improper positioning:
   i) head not facing correct direction
   i) muscles not relaxed:
      1) shoulders not relaxed (hunched)
      2) overall muscles not relaxed (too tense)
   ii) improper arm/hand positioning
   iii) improper foot positioning

Note: Typically arm/hand and head positioning is not considered part of stance analysis. But, because one of the key goals of American Kenpo forms is the proper coordination between the upper and lower body, these are mentioned here and in the other relevant sections of this chapter.

Note: Certain general errors that are more commonly seen for a specific type of stance (such as improper alignments) may be repeated in that stance's section. This is to call attention to the error and how common it is for that specific type of stance.

Improving Your Execution of Long Form Two

Meditating Horse

a) proper alignments:
    i)   width = feet slightly wider than shoulders
    ii)   depth = toe/toe - heel/heel
    iii)   height = bend of knees such that shins are vertical

b) proper rotation:
    i)   feet = directly forward or pointing slightly inward
    ii)   body = directly forward

c) proper weight distribution:
    i)   50% / 50% between feet
    ii)   weight pressed to the outer edges of feet

d) proper positioning:
    i)   hands positioned at chest to chin level
    ii)   back vertical

Comments

i) Common errors:
    1)   not having the toes point directly ahead (or slightly inward)
    2)   not bending the knees properly
    3)   not having both elbows point downward at a 45 degree angle
    4)   not keeping the back up straight

ii) If one wishes to delay before the execution of the form, the Meditating Horse can be used for this purpose. It is common practice to indicate a delay by closing one's eyes and/or bow the head (but this is not a requirement).

© 2015 EPAKS Publications

Example of proper Meditating Horse

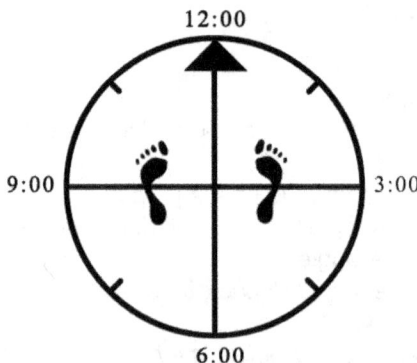

Example of proper Meditating Horse

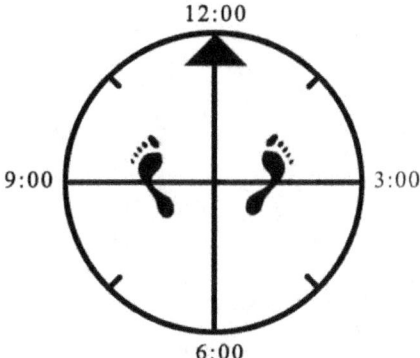

Example of improper foot rotation (both - not pointing directly forward or slightly inward) for Horse

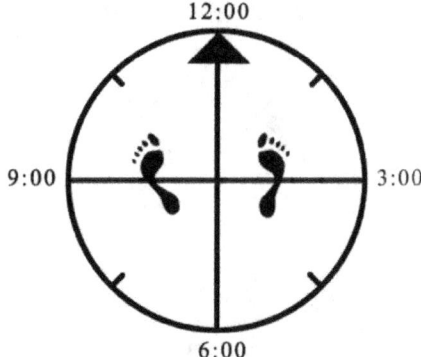

Example improper rotation of one foot (left - not pointing directly forward or slightly inward) for Horse

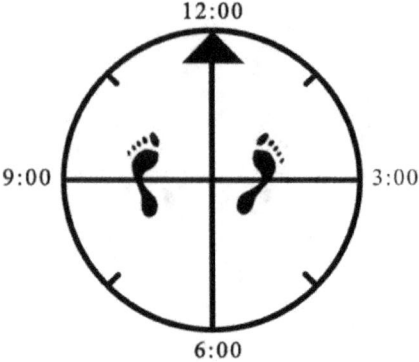

Example improper rotation of one foot
(right - not pointing directly forward or
slightly inward) for Horse

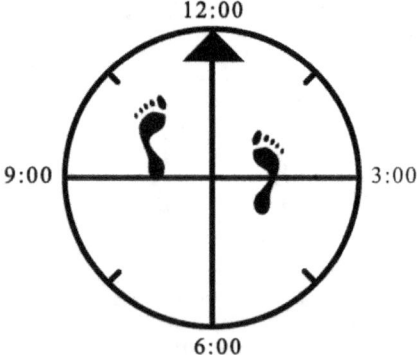

Example of improper depth alignment
(toe-toe / heel - heel) for Horse

Improving Your Execution of Long Form Two

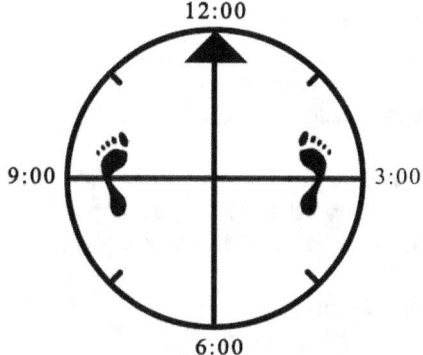

Example of improper width alignment (well beyond shoulder width / too wide) for Horse

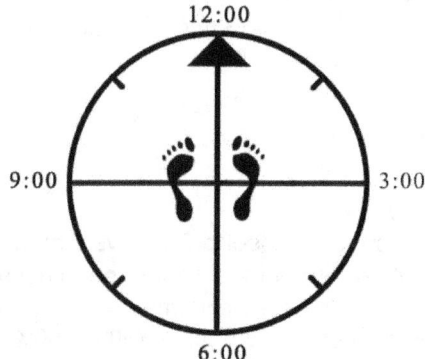

Example of improper width (narrower than shoulder width / too narrow) for Horse

Neutral Bow

a) proper alignments:
    i)   width = toe/heel
    ii)   depth = heel/knee
    iii)   height = slight bend of knees

b) proper rotation:
    i)   feet = forward at 45 degree angle
    ii)   body = forward at 45 degree angle

c) proper weight distribution:
    i)   50% / 50% between feet

d) proper positioning:
    i)   back vertical

Form Specific

a) improper positioning:
    i)   minor hand not covering / improper positioning of cover - when required

Comments

a) Common errors:
    i)   not having both feet point forward at 45 degree angle
    ii)   not having the proper width (toe / heel alignment) or depth (heel / knee alignment)
    iii)   uneven weight distribution (50% / 50%)
    iv)   not keeping the back up straight
    v)   not keeping the shoulders relaxed
    vi)   not keeping the knees bent (i.e. too straight - causing the stance to be to high)

b) One common way to ensure proper rotation of the feet and body in a Neutral Bow is to have the feet/body point to the corners (minor angles) when facing the major angles (12:00/3:00/6:00/9:00) and the walls (major angles) when facing the minor angles (1:30/4:30/7:30/10:30)

Example of proper Neutral Bow (right)

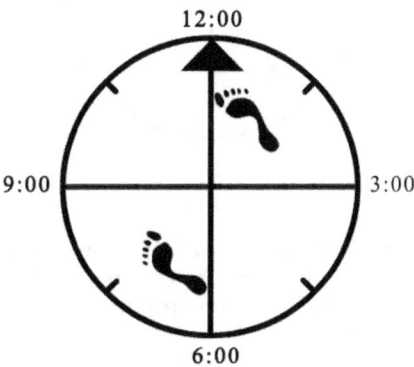

Example of proper Neutral Bow (right)

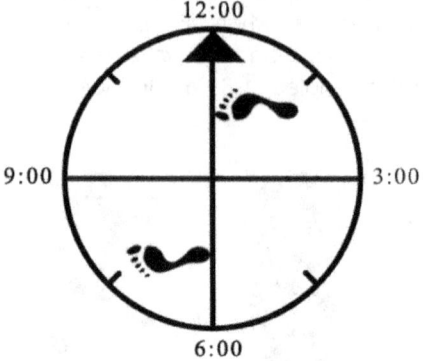

Example of improper foot rotation (both - not pointing forward at 45 degree angle) for Neutral Bow (right)

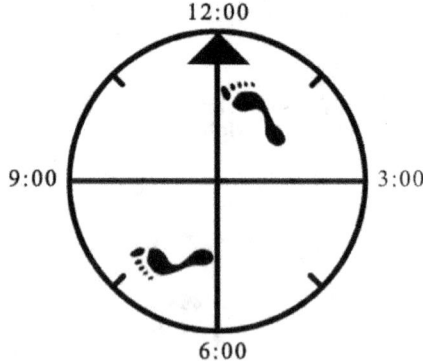

Example of improper foot rotation (rear - not pointing forward at 45 degree angle) for Neutral Bow (right)

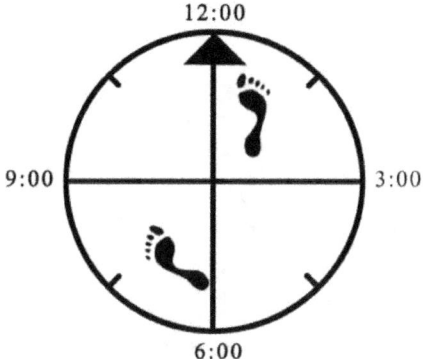

Example of improper foot rotation (front - not pointing forward at 45 degree angle) for Neutral Bow (right)

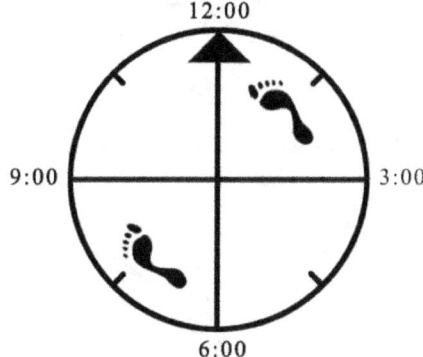

Example of improper width alignment (toe - heel / too wide) for Neutral Bow (right)

© 2015 EPAKS Publications

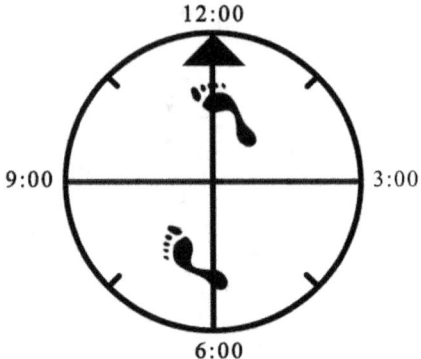

Example of improper width alignment (toe - heel / too narrow) for Neutral Bow (right)

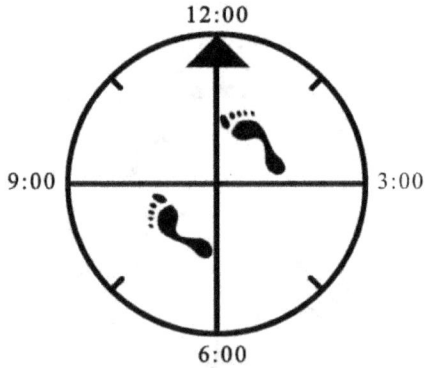

Example of improper depth alignment (heel - knee / too shallow) for Neutral Bow (right)

Improving Your Execution of Long Form Two

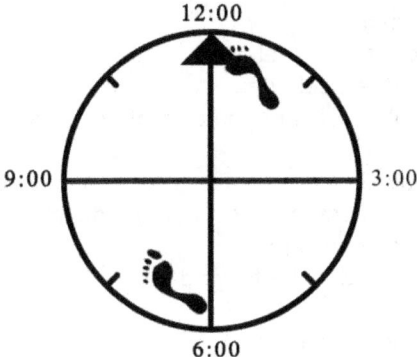

Example of improper depth alignment (heel - knee / too deep) for Neutral Bow (right)

Forward Bow

a) proper alignments:
   i) width = toe/heel
   ii) depth = heel/knee
   iii) height = slight bend of front knee - rear leg straight

b) proper rotation:
   i) feet = front foot forward at 45 degree angle - rear foot directly forward
   ii) body = directly forward

c) proper weight distribution:
   i) 60% / 40%

d) proper positioning:
   i) back vertical

Form Specific

a) improper positioning:
   i) no full rotation forward - on snapping strikes
   ii) not maintaining both feet flat

Comments

a) Common errors:
   i) not having front foot point forward at 45 degree angle
   ii) not having rear foot point directly forward
   iii) not having the proper width (toe / heel alignment) or depth (heel / knee alignment)
   iv) uneven weight distribution (60% / 40%)
   v) not keeping the back up straight
   vi) not keeping the rear foot flat
   vii) not rotating the body to point directly forward (either under rotating or over rotating)

Improving Your Execution of Long Form Two

Example of proper Forward Bow (right)

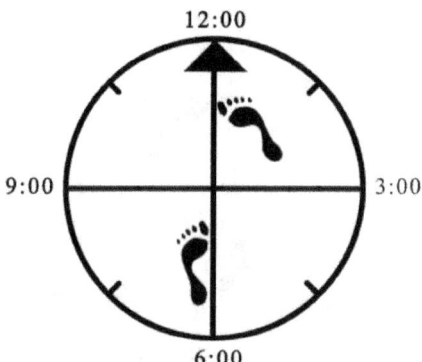

Example of proper Forward Bow (right)

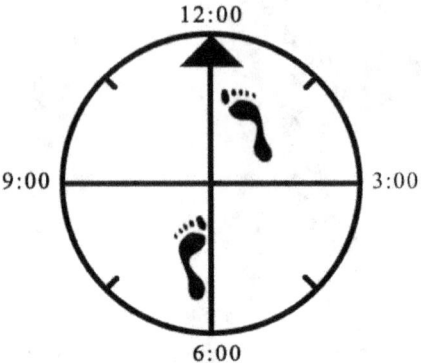

Example of improper foot rotation (front - not pointing forward at 45 degree angle) for Forward Bow (right)

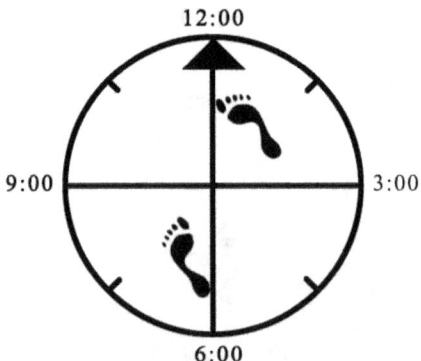

Example of improper foot rotation (rear - not pointing directly forward) for Forward Bow (right)

Improving Your Execution of Long Form Two

Example of improper foot placement (rear - heel not planted) for Forward Bow (right)

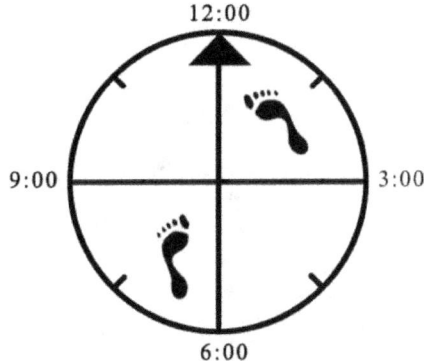

Example of improper width alignment (toe - heel / too wide) for Forward Bow (right)

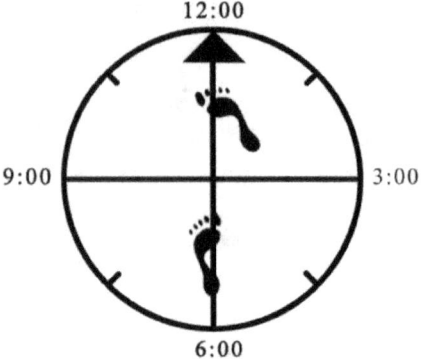

Example of improper width alignment (toe - heel / too narrow) for Forward Bow (right)

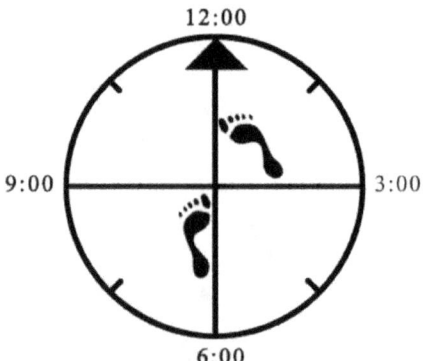

Example of improper depth alignment (heel - knee / too shallow) for Forward Bow (right)

Improving Your Execution of Long Form Two

Example of improper depth alignment (heel - knee / too deep) for Forward Bow (right)

45 Degree Cat

a) proper alignments:
   i) width = toe/heel
   ii) depth = front foot 1 1/2 length of foot from rear foot
   iii) height = bend of rear leg such that front shin is vertical over front toes

b) proper rotation:
   i) feet = front - directly forward / rear - forward at 45 degree angle
   ii) body = forward at 45 degree angle

c) proper weight distribution:
   i) 10% / 90% - weight and positioning primarily over rear foot

d) proper positioning:
   i) back vertical
   ii) front foot on ball

Form Specific

a) improper positioning:
   i) 'cup and saucer' improper positioning - when required

Improving Your Execution of Long Form Two | 409

b) proper execution:
  i) stance is typically held for a short period of time to emphasis its importance in the form (i.e. slightly longer than a typical transition maneuver)

Comments

1) Common errors:
   i) not having the front foot point forward
   ii) not having the proper width (toe / heel alignment) or depth (front vertical shin)
   iii) uneven weight distribution (10% / 90%)
   iv) not keeping the back up straight
   v) not keeping the rear leg bent

b) It is very common to not draw the feet to the proper positioning (depth and rotation) when immediately transitioning to the next move

Example of proper 45 degree Cat (left)

© 2015 EPAKS Publications

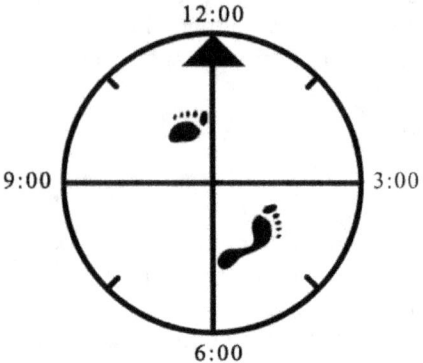

Example of proper 45 degree Cat (left)

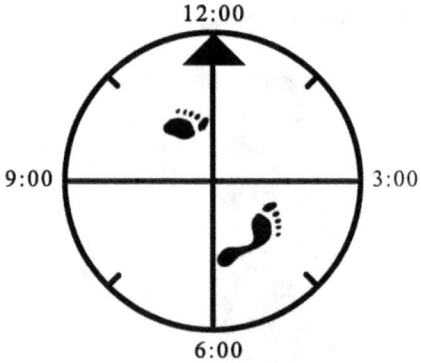

Example of improper foot rotation (front - not facing directly forward) for 45 degree Cat (left)

Improving Your Execution of Long Form Two

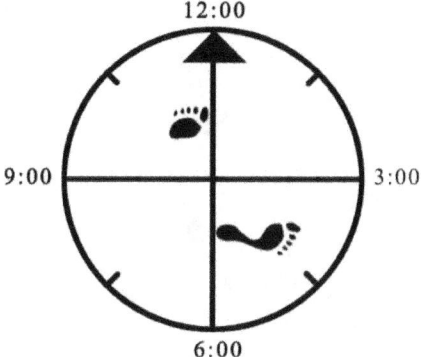

Example of improper foot rotation (rear - not facing forward at 45 degree angle) for 45 degree Cat (left)

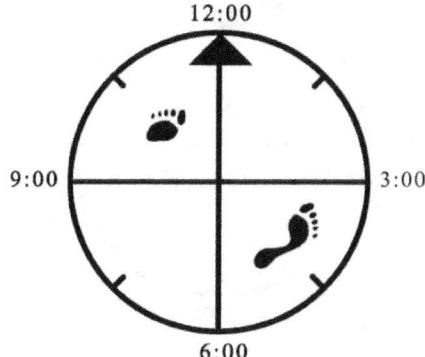

Example of improper width alignment (toe - heel / too wide) for 45 degree Cat (left)

© 2015 EPAKS Publications

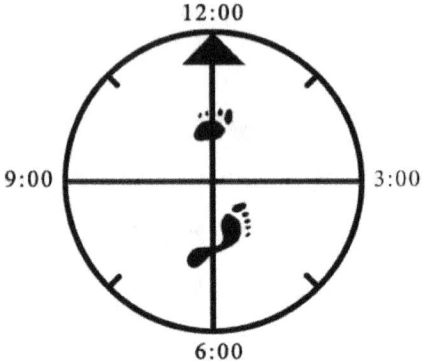

Example of improper width alignment (toe - heel / too narrow) for 45 degree Cat (left)

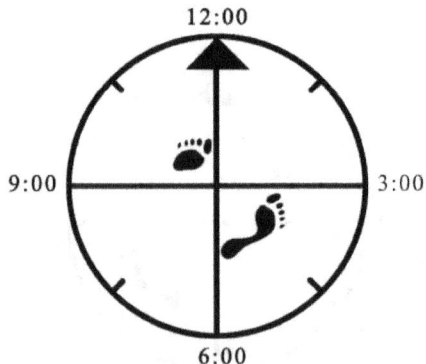

Example of improper depth alignment (1.5 "feet" / too shallow) for 45 degree Cat (left)

Improving Your Execution of Long Form Two

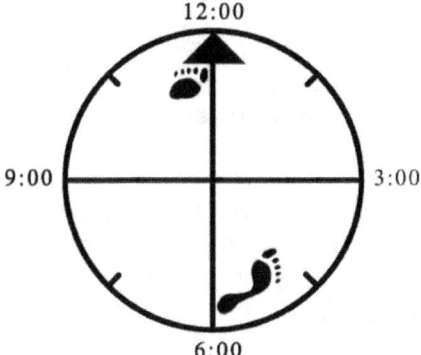

Example of improper depth alignment (1.5 "feet" / too deep) for 45 degree Cat (left)

Offset Horse

a) proper alignments:
   i) width = feet slightly wider than shoulders
   ii) depth = toe/heel
   iii) height = bend of knees such that shins are vertical

b) proper rotation:
   i) feet = directly forward or pointing slightly inward (perpendicular to Point of Reference)
   ii) body = directly forward (perpendicular to Point of Reference)

c) proper weight distribution:
   i) 50% / 50% between feet
   ii) weight pressed to the outer edges of feet

d) proper positioning:
   i) back vertical
   ii) both feet placed completely flat

Form Specific

a) improper execution:
   i) over rotation when transitioning into stance

Note: The offset Horse is used to isolate the power principle of Back-up mass and as such any rotation with the execution of the block / strike should be eliminated.

Comments

a) Common errors:
   i) turning into a Forward Bow or Neutral Bow
   ii) over rotation of the upper body toward the intended target(s)
   iii) not keeping the back up straight

© 2015 EPAKS Publications

Improving Your Execution of Long Form Two | 415

Example of proper offset Horse (right)

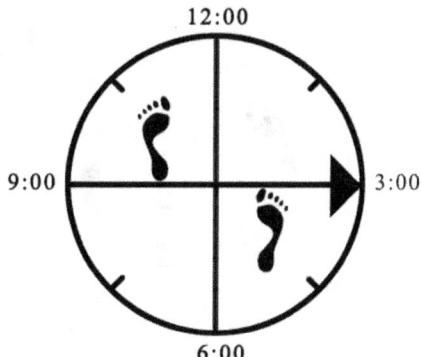

Example of proper offset Horse (right)

© 2015 EPAKS Publications

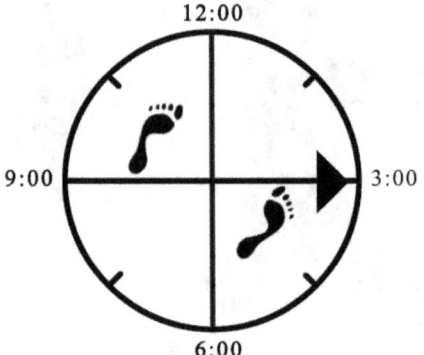

Example of improper foot rotation (both - not pointing directly to side) for offset Horse (right)

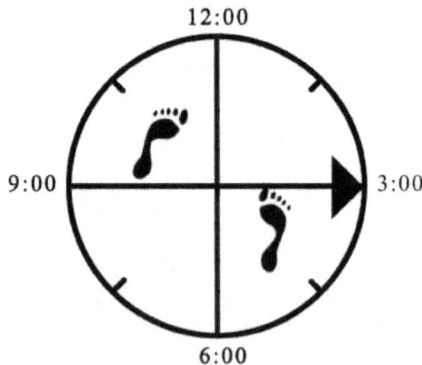

Example of improper foot rotation (rear - not pointing directly to side) for offset Horse (right)

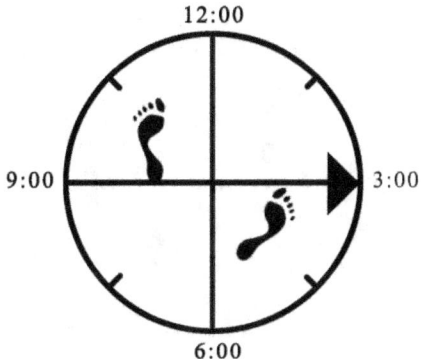

Example of improper foot rotation (front - not pointing directly to side) for offset Horse (right)

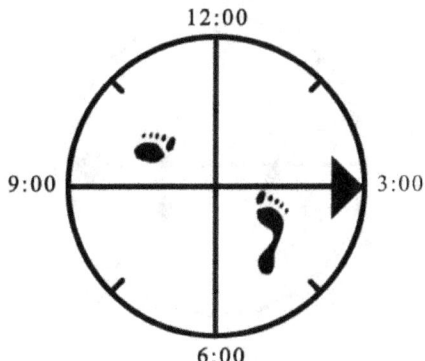

Example of improper foot positioning (rear - lifted heel and rotated) for offset Horse (right)

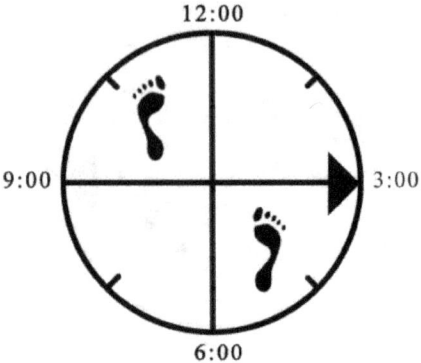

Example of improper width alignment (toe - heel / too wide) for offset Horse (right)

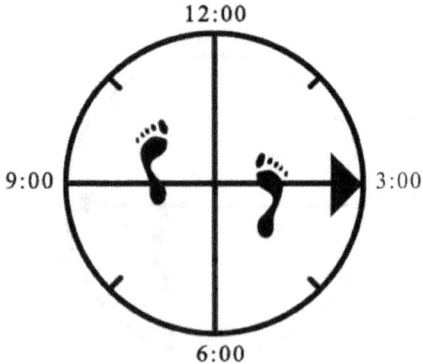

Example of improper width alignment (toe - heel / too narrow) for offset Horse (right)

Improving Your Execution of Long Form Two

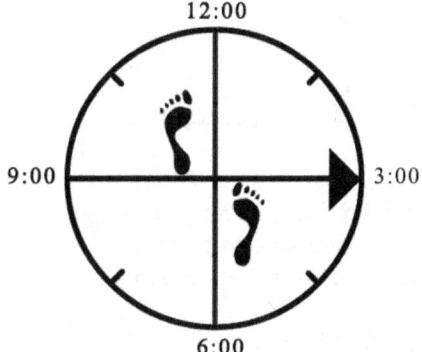

Example of improper depth alignment (heel - knee / too shallow) for offset Horse (right)

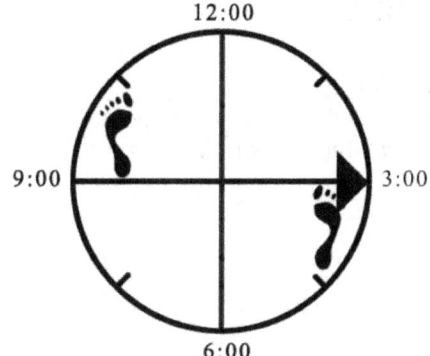

Example of improper depth alignment (heel - knee / too deep) for offset Horse (right)

© 2015 EPAKS Publications

Reverse Bow

a) proper alignments:
    i)   width = toe/heel
    ii)   depth = heel/knee
    iii)   height = front leg straight - slight bend of rear knee

b) proper rotation:
    i)   feet = front foot directly backward - rear foot backward at 45 degree angle
    ii)   body = backward at 45 degree angle

c) proper weight distribution:
    i)   40% / 60% between feet

d) proper positioning:
    i)   back vertical

Form Specific

a) improper positioning:
    i)   no full rotation backward - on step
    ii)   not maintaining both feet flat

Comments

a) Common errors:
    i)   not having front foot point directly backward
    ii)   not having rear foot point backward at a 45 degree angle
    iii)   not having the proper width (toe / heel alignment) or depth (heel / knee alignment)
    iv)   uneven weight distribution (40% / 60%)
    v)   not keeping the back up straight
    vi)   not keeping the front foot flat
    vii) not rotating the body to point backward at a 45 degree angle (either under rotating or over rotating)

Example of proper Reverse Bow (left)

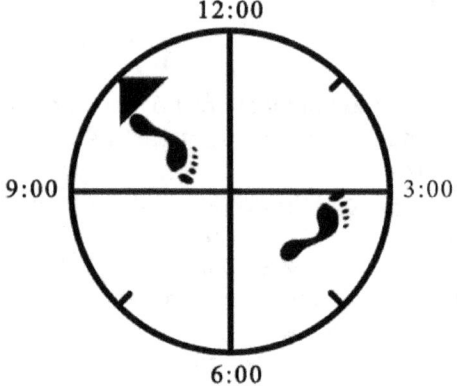

Example of proper Reverse Bow

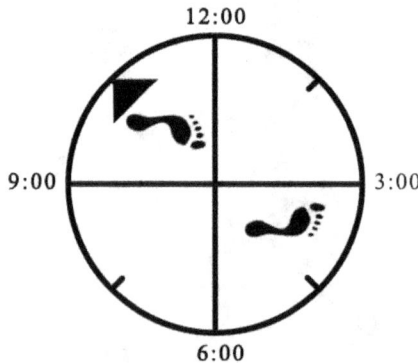

Example of improper foot rotation (both)
for Reverse Bow (left)

Improving Your Execution of Long Form Two

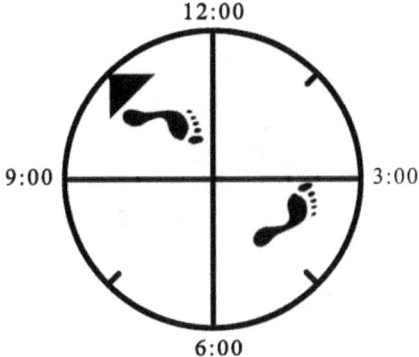

Example of improper foot rotation (front - not facing directly away) for Reverse Bow (left)

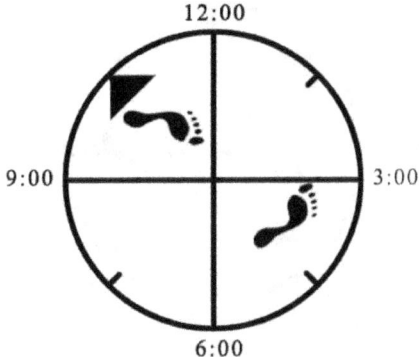

Example of improper foot rotation (rear - not pointing backward at 45 degree angle) for Reverse Bow (left)

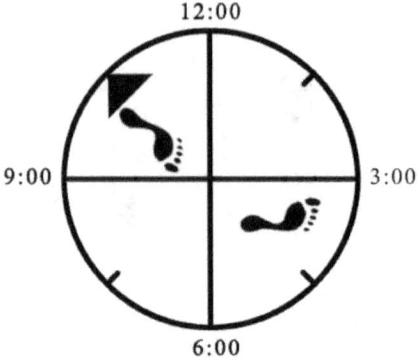

Example of improper foot positioning (front - heel not planted) for Reverse Bow (left)

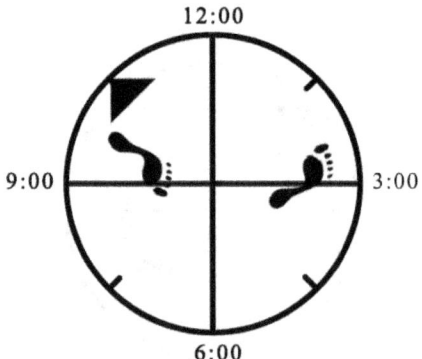

Example of improper width alignment (toe - heel / too wide) for Reverse Bow (left)

Improving Your Execution of Long Form Two — 425

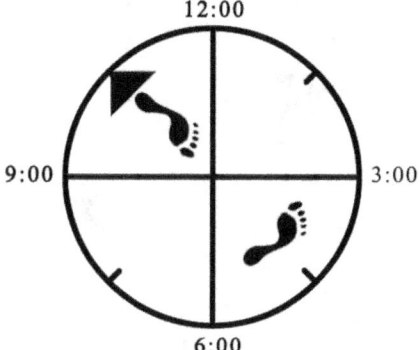

Example of improper width alignment (toe - heel / too narrow) for Reverse Bow (left)

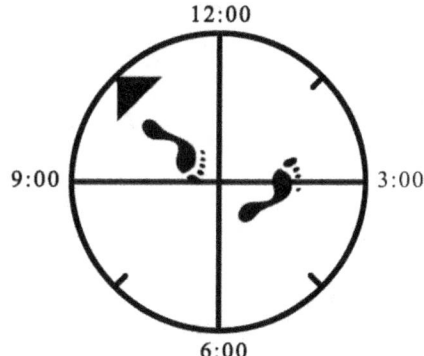

Example of improper depth alignment (knee - heel / too shallow) for Reverse Bow (left)

© 2015 EPAKS Publications

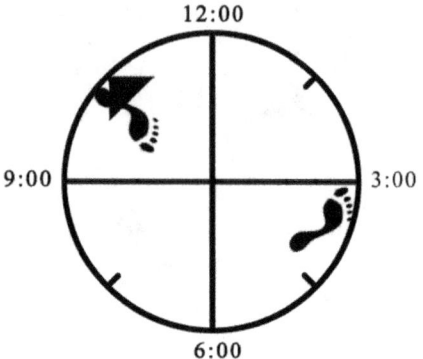

**Example of improper depth alignment
(knee - heel / too deep) for Reverse Bow
(left)**

Twist

a) proper alignments:
   i) width = toe/heel
   ii) depth = front foot 1 1/2 length of foot from rear foot
   iii) height = bend of supporting leg such that the opposite knee is at calf level of the supporting leg

b) proper rotation:
   i) feet = front - directly backward / rear - backward at 45 degree angle
   ii) body = backward at 45 degree angle

c) proper weight distribution:
   i) 10% / 90% - weight and positioning primarily over rear foot

d) proper positioning:
   i) back vertical
   ii) front foot on ball

Form Specific

a) improper positioning:
   i) 'cup and saucer' improper positioning - when required

Comments

a) Common errors:
   i) not having the front foot point backward
   ii) not having the proper width (toe / heel alignment) or depth (front foot 1 1/2 length of foot from rear foot)
   iii) uneven weight distribution (10% / 90%)
   iv) not keeping the back up straight
   v) not having the knees properly bent

b) It is very common to not draw the feet to the proper positioning (depth and rotation)

Example of proper Twist (front / right)

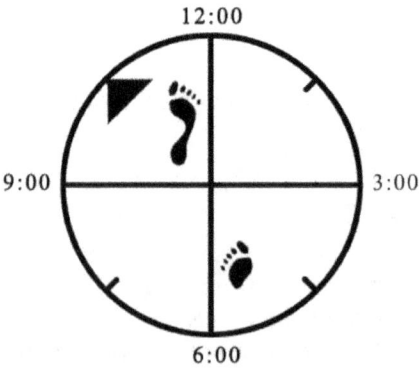

Example of proper Twist (front / right)

Improving Your Execution of Long Form Two | 429

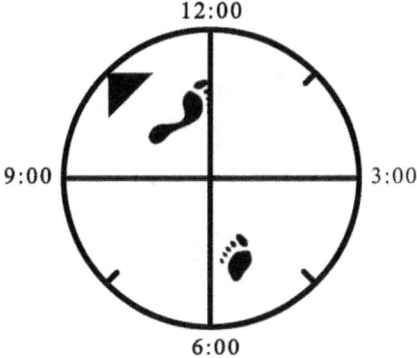

Example of improper foot rotation (front - not facing forward at 45 degree angle) for Twist (front / right)

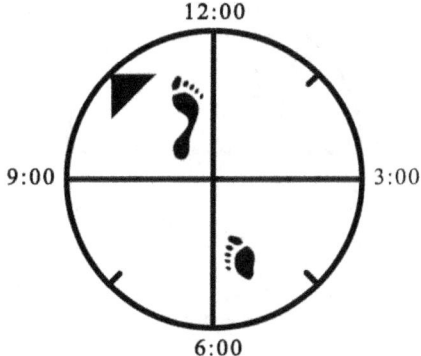

Example of improper foot rotation (rear - not facing directly forward) for Twist (front / right)

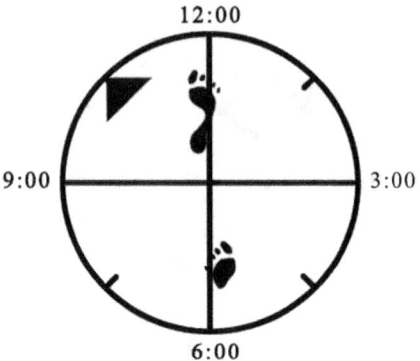

Example of improper width alignment (heel - toe / too wide) for Twist (front / right)

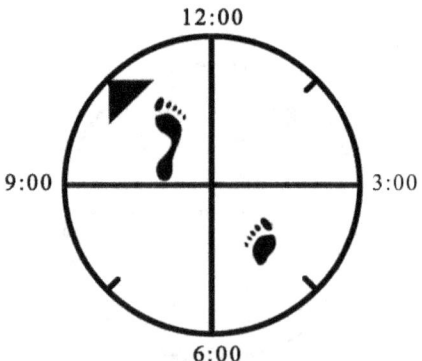

Example of improper width alignment (heel - toe / too narrow) for Twist (front / right)

Improving Your Execution of Long Form Two

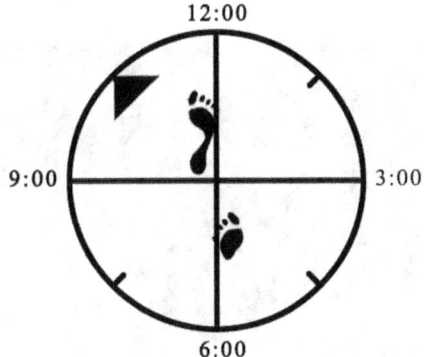

Example of improper depth alignment (heel - knee / too shallow) for Twist (front / right)

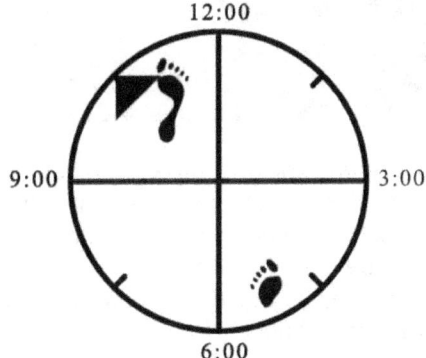

Example of improper depth alignment (heel - knee / too deep) for Twist (front / right)

Foot Maneuver Errors

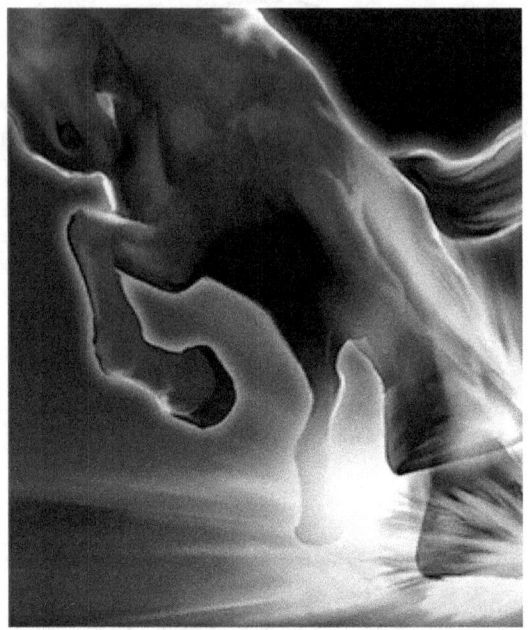

Foot maneuvers are basically the movement between stances. The improper execution of foot maneuvers can introduce a number of complexities of not only the movement itself, but also effect the new stance that is obtained at the end of the foot maneuver. The section on stance correction gives further highlights into this information.

There are a number of common errors exhibited while executing foot maneuvers. Bobbing is one of the most common problems demonstrated by many beginning practitioners. Transitions between stances should be fluid while also maintaining the same height level, unless specifically demonstrating a change in height.

Improving Your Execution of Long Form Two 433

Another common foot maneuver error is extraneous motions, i.e. breaking the principle of Economy of Motion. This problem is exhibited in many forms, the most common of which are: moving the feet prior to actually executing the foot maneuver (extremely common), breaking the heel (lifting the heel) during step through maneuvers, pivoting on the heel of the foot, and/or Jet Lagging (leaning while stepping through).

General Foot Maneuver Errors

a) improper execution:
   i) not obeying Economy of Motion principle / Create a stable base rule:
      1) not stepping correctly:
         A) not stepping with correct foot
         B) not stepping directly to new location
         C) splitting the stance (moving both feet, instead of one)
   ii) creating too many adjustments with feet
   iii) bouncing up and down while executing foot maneuver or stationary
   iv) improper pivoting:
      1) rotating on the heel instead of the ball of the foot
      2) rotating the incorrect foot - i.e. the wrong foot (or both feet)
      3) under / over rotating - not rotating to the proper new angle
      4) not properly rotating the upper body with the lower body
   v) jet legging (splitting timing of lower/upper body – i.e. creating distance with feet first and then the upper body)

Note: Certain general errors that are more commonly seen for a specific type of foot maneuver (such as bobbing) with be repeated in that foot maneuver's section. This is to call attention to the error and how common it is for that specific type of foot maneuver.

Step Out to Meditating Horse

a) improper transition from Attention to Meditating Horse:
- i) stepping out with the right foot instead of the left
- ii) stepping to improper width alignment (see stance errors section)
- iii) stepping to improper depth alignment (see stance errors section)
- iii) adding foot improper rotation (see stance errors section)

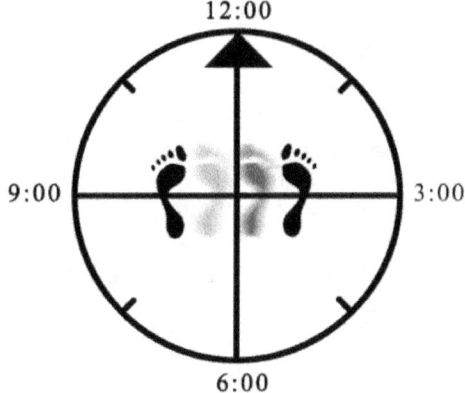

Example of stepping out with wrong foot into meditating Horse

Step Through

a) improper execution:
   i)   not obeying Economy of Motion principle / Create a stable base rule:
        1)   creating too many adjustments with feet:
            A)   breaking the heel (lifting/moving rear of foot before moving front of foot)
            B)   adjusting/rotating feet prior to/during foot maneuvers
            C)   adjusting the foot not used in a foot maneuver
            D)   re-adjusting foot used in foot maneuver, after maneuver
   ii)   improper pivoting:
        1)   executing a twist through instead of a step through (splitting timing of distance/rotation during foot maneuver)
        2)   pivoting prior to or after execution of block / strike (see timing errors section)
   iii)   executing a cat stance as a separate motion – i.e. holding cat stance too long

Comments

a) Common execution errors:
   i)   bobbing up and then down while executing foot maneuver

Example of bobbing during a Step Through (forward or reverse)

Twist Through

a) improper execution:
  i) not obeying Economy of Motion principle / Create a stable base rule:
     1) creating too many adjustments with feet:
        A) re-adjusting foot used in foot maneuver during / after maneuver
        B) re-adjusting foot not used in foot maneuver during / after maneuver
  ii) improper pivoting:
     1) executing a step through instead of a twist through (combining timing of distance/rotation during foot maneuver)
     2) (distance / rotation) pivoting prior to completing the initial step (pivoting while stepping with foot in air)
  iii) executing a twist stance as a separate motion – i.e. holding twist stance too long

b) improper alignments:
  i) stepping to improper width (too narrow / too wide) (see stance errors section)
  ii) stepping to improper depth (too shallow / too deep) (see stance errors section)
  iii) over / under rotating foot / feet / body (improper foot rotation) (see stance errors section)

Comments

a) Common execution errors:
  i) bobbing down and then up while executing foot maneuver

Crossover

a) improper execution:
   i) not obeying Economy of Motion principle / Create a stable base rule:
      1) creating too many adjustments with feet:
         A) re-adjusting feet during, after maneuver
   ii) improper pivoting:
      1) adding foot / body rotation to maneuver
   iii) executing a twist stance as a separate motion – i.e. holding twist stance too long

b) improper alignments:
   i) stepping to improper width (too narrow / too wide) (see stance errors section)
   ii) stepping to improper depth (too shallow / too deep) (see stance errors section)

Comments

a) Common execution errors:
   i) bobbing down and then up while executing foot maneuver

Cover

a) improper execution:
   i) stepping incorrectly:
      1) stepping with wrong foot
   ii) improper pivoting:
      1) pivoting prior to completing the cover step (pivoting while stepping with foot in air)
      2) pivoting prior to or after execution of block / strike (see timing errors section)

b) improper alignments:
   i) stepping to improper width (too narrow / too wide) (see stance errors section)
   ii) stepping to improper depth (too shallow / too deep) (see stance errors section)

Form Specific

Long Form Two cover execution is purposely done stepping forward. This is due to one of the major themes of the form being advancing as a reverse of retreating. This motion breaks the rule of: 'always cover away from the unknown'.

© 2015 EPAKS Publications

Defensive Errors

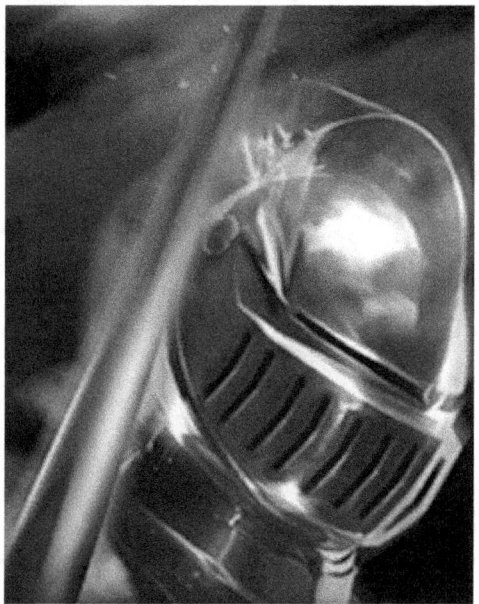

Defense (blocking) is one of the major themes of Long Form Two. Executing these maneuvers properly can make the difference between a successful defense and failure. Just like the stances, the practitioner should become intimately familiar with the proper dimensions utilized in each of the defensive maneuvers.

The primary concepts in dealing with blocking dimensions are the Outer Rim theory and/or the Invisible Box theory. These theories along with the proper dimensions for each block are highlighted in detail in SGM Parker's book, "Infinite Insights into Kenpo, book #3 (Physical Analyzation II)."

Some of the most common defensive mistakes displayed while executing Long Form Two are: not executing blocks to the proper dimensions; not executing blocks to the proper angles; not executing double factor block properly; not executing blocks efficiently (without Economy of Motion); and/or executing blocks with improper timing.

General Defense Errors

a) improper alignments / dimensions :
   i) improper block width (not at edge of body / too wide) (Outer Rim)
   ii) improper block depth (too close / far) (Invisible Box)
   iii) improper block height (too low / too high) (Outer Rim)

b) improper positioning:
   i) hand is not completely closed when executing blocks (minor and/or major)
   ii) improper arm / hand positioning / rotation
   iii) not creating proper Angle of Deflection
   iv) not keeping back straight (leaning)
   v) head not facing correct direction
   vi) muscles not relaxed:
      1) shoulders not relaxed (hunched)
      2) overall muscles not relaxed (too tense)
   vii) improper foot positioning / rotation

c) improper execution:
   i) executed with wrong Method of Execution
   ii) not executing the block smoothly - i.e. mechanical / staccato motion
   iii) not obeying Economy of Motion principle:
      1) not executing the block from Point of Origin (making a cock a separate motion)
      2) executing block outside the Outer Rim / Invisible Box (also see improper alignments)
      3) not executing the block on a direct Path of Travel

Note: The above analysis also applies to double factor blocks.

Note: Typically stance, body, and head positioning is not considered part of most defensive analysis. But, because one of the key goals of American Kenpo forms is the proper coordination between the upper and lower body, these are mentioned here and in the other relevant sections of this chapter.

© 2015 EPAKS Publications

Note: Certain general errors that are more commonly seen for specific types of defensive maneuvers (such as leaning) will be repeated in that maneuver's section. This is to call attention to the error and how common it is for that specific type of maneuver.

Inward Block - Front Arm

a) proper alignments:
    i) height = fist at eye-brow level
    ii) width = blocking arm extended to opposite shoulder
    iii) depth = blocking arm extended to depth of Invisible Box
    iv) execution angle - forward at 45 degrees

b) improper execution:
    i) not obeying Economy of Motion principle:
        1) not executing the block from Point of Origin (making a cock a separate motion)
    ii) not obeying the rule of Margin for Error (also improper alignments):
        1) not anchoring the elbow
        2) not keeping the block vertical – i.e. over reaching
    iii) improper angles of execution
        1) not executed diagonally away from body

Form Specific

a) improper execution:
    i) executing two hammering inward blocks (instead of a hammering and thrusting)

Comments

a) Common execution errors:
    i) execute block to the wrong forward angle. This is due to anticipation of the Outward Hand-sword.

Example of proper Inward Block (right)
(without check)

Improving Your Execution of Long Form Two

Examples of improper Inward Block execution
wrong angle, width - narrow / wide,
height - low / high, depth - narrow / deep

Vertical Outward Block

a) proper alignments:
    i)   height = fist at eye-brow level
    ii)   width = blocking arm extended to same shoulder
    iii)   depth = elbow bent to vertical plane
    iv)   palm facing direct toward you

b) improper execution:
    i)   improper angles of execution
        1)   not executed parallel to body

Improving Your Execution of Long Form Two | 449

c) improper positioning:
- i) not obeying the rule of Margin for Error (also improper alignments):
  1) not anchoring the elbow
  2) not keeping the bock vertical – i.e. over reaching

Comments

a) Common alignment errors:
- i) not keeping blocking arm vertical (improper Margin for Error)

**Example of proper Vertical Outward Block (left)
(with straight punch)**

Examples of improper
Vertical Outward Block execution
improper width - narrow wide, height - high / low,
shrugged shoulders, depth - shallow deep

Improving Your Execution of Long Form Two 451

Universal Block

a) proper alignments:
 i) height =
 Inward blocking arm - fist at eye-brow level
 Downward blocking arm - elbow slightly bent during and after execution of block (not "locked out")
 ii) width =
 Inward Blocking arm - blocking arms extended to opposite shoulder
 Downward Blocking arm - blocking arm extended to same shoulder
 iii) depth =
 Inward Blocking arm - top blocking arm extended to depth of Invisible Box
 Downward Blocking arm - blocking arm extended parallel to front knee after execution
 iv) execution angle =
 Inward Blocking arm - forward at 45 degrees
 Downward Blocking arm - palm facing downward (toward leg)

b) improper execution:
 i) improper angles of execution
 1) not executed to match standard blocking angles (see inward and downward block sections)

c) improper positioning:
 i) not obeying the rule of Margin for Error (also improper alignments):
 Inward Blocking arm:
 1) not anchoring the elbow
 2) not keeping the vertical outward block vertical – i.e. over reaching

© 2015 EPAKS Publications

Form Specific

a) proper positioning:
   i) body positioned / rotated to proper neutral bow dimensions (see Stance Errors section)
   ii) feet positioned / rotated to proper neutral bow dimensions (see Stance Errors section)

b) improper execution:
   i) not rotating body into stance with delivery of block

Comments

a) Common execution errors:
   i) transition into a forward bow during the execution of the block

Example of proper Universal Block (right / left)

Improving Your Execution of Long Form Two

Examples of improper Universal Block execution
(improper angle, improper height, over rotation of body,
improper width, improper depth)

Upward Block

a) proper alignments:
 i) height = blocking arm extended to top of head
 ii) width = blocking arm extended to opposite shoulder
 iii) depth = arm angled forward at 45 degrees away from you
 iv) fist positioned (palm facing directly forward)
 v) ending with angle of deflection (from overhead attack)

b) improper execution:
 i) not obeying the rule of Margin for Error:
  1) executed like 'chicken wing' (strike), no torque, just arm lifting
 ii) improper angles of execution
  1) not executed parallel to body (vertically)

c) improper execution (double factor):
 i) not transitioned along center line - vertically
  1) executed with arm remaining horizontal
  2) executed with arm crossed center line

Form Specific

a) improper positioning:
 i) hand not fully closed (positioned like middle-knuckle)

Improving Your Execution of Long Form Two

Example of proper Upward Block (left)
(with hammer-fist)

The Official EPAKS Guide to Long Form Two

Examples of improper Upward Block execution
improper height, improper angle of rotation,
improper depth, improper width, improper angle

Improving Your Execution of Long Form Two — 457

Downward Block

a) proper alignments:
    i) height = elbow slightly bent during and after execution of block (not "locked out")
    ii) width = blocking arm extended to same shoulder
    iii) depth = blocking arm extended parallel to front knee after execution
    iv) palm facing downward (toward leg)

b) improper execution:
    i) not obeying Economy of Motion principle:
        1) chamber motion done too high (face height instead of parallel to ground)
    ii) improper angles of execution
        1) not executed parallel to body

c) improper positioning:
    i) not keeping back straight (leaning)

Form Specific

a) improper execution:
    i) not rotating body into stance with delivery of block

© 2015 EPAKS Publications

Example of proper Downward Block (left)

Improving Your Execution of Long Form Two

Examples of improper Downward Block execution
improper height - high / low, leaning,
improper width - narrow / wide, improper cocking -
too high

Inside Downward - Palm up Block

a) proper alignments:
   i) height = elbow slightly bent during execution of block (not "locked out")
   ii) depth = blocking arm extended parallel to front knee after execution
   iii) width = blocking arm extended to opposite shoulder
   iv) palm facing diagonally upward

b) improper execution:
   i) not obeying Economy of Motion principle:
      1) cocking weapon prior to delivery

c) improper positioning:
   i) not keeping back straight (leaning)

Form Specific

a) improper execution:
   i) not executed to proper angles of execution
      1) path of travel like standard block (not parrying block)
      2) rotation of hand like standard block (not parrying block)

Comments

a) This block is executed as a parrying block, not as a standard block. This means that the path of travel is diagonally toward the body, not parallel to the body and the hand is rotated to point diagonally upward, not directly upward. Due to these changes, the final positioning of the blocking arm / hand varies slightly from executions of this block in previous forms.

Improving Your Execution of Long Form Two — 461

Example of proper Inside Downward - Palm-Up Block (right)
(from twist stance)

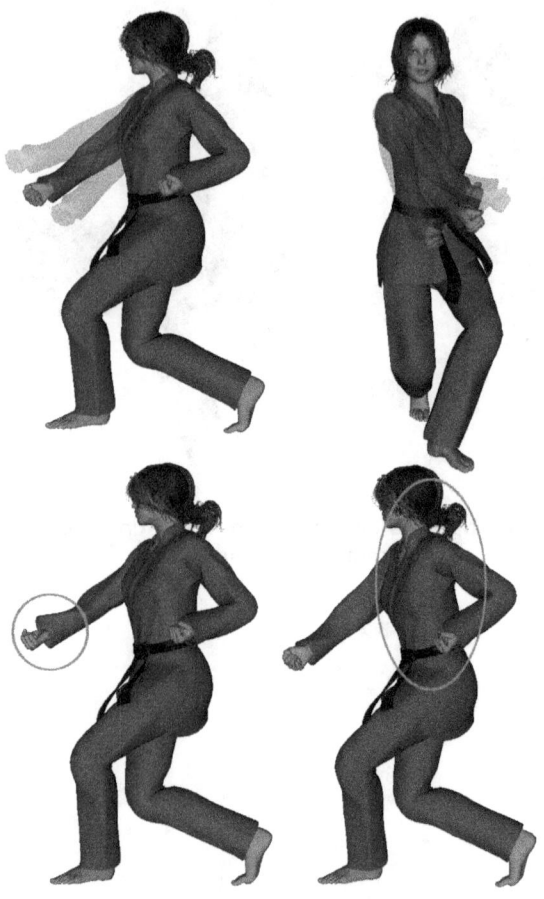

Examples of improper Inside Downward - Palm Up Block execution
improper depth - far / close, improper width - narrow / wide,
improper hand rotation, leaning

Inside Downward - Palm down Block

a) proper alignments:
  i) height = elbow slightly bent during and after execution of block (not "locked out")
  ii) width = blocking arm extended to opposite shoulder
  iii) depth = blocking arm extended parallel to front knee after execution
  iv) palm facing downward (toward leg)

b) improper execution:
  i) not obeying Economy of Motion principle:
    1) cocking weapon prior to delivery
  ii) not keeping back straight (leaning)
  iii) improper angles of execution
    1) not executed parallel to body

c) improper positioning:
  i) not keeping back straight (leaning)

Example of proper Inside Downward - Palm-Down Block (right)

Examples of improper Inside Downward - Palm Down
Block execution
improper depth - far / close, width - narrow / wide,
improper angle of execution, leaning

Improving Your Execution of Long Form Two 465

Push-Down

a) proper alignments:
   i) height = elbow slightly after execution of block (not "locked out")
   ii) width = blocking arm extended to center-line
   iii) depth = blocking arm extended to depth to front knee after execution
   iv) palm facing downward (toward ground)

b) improper execution:
   i) not obeying the rule of Margin for Error:
      1) hand not rotated properly
   iii) improper angles of execution
      1) not executed parallel to body (vertically)

c) improper body positioning:
   i) not keeping back straight (leaning)
   iii) improper hand rotation:
      1) hand not bent properly (fingers pointing downward)
      2) hand not rotated properly (fingers pointing forward / backward)

Form Specific

a) improper body positioning:
   ii) not rotated to forward bow (over / under rotation)

Comments

a) Common execution errors:
   i) over rotation into a twist stance during the execution of this block, combining the block with the next maneuver of the form (rotating into the twist stance)

© 2015 EPAKS Publications

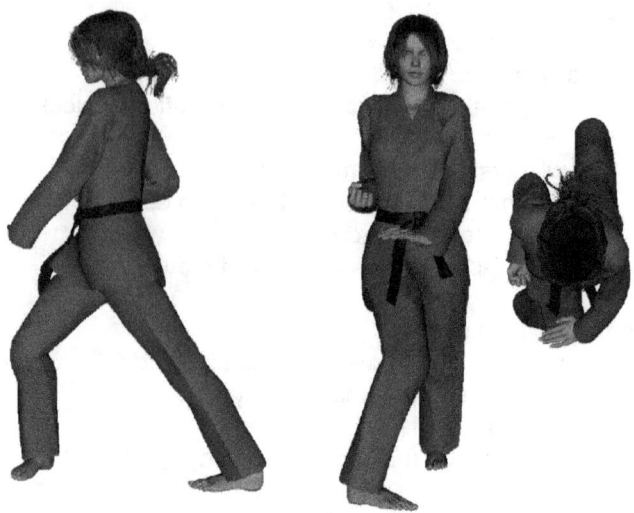

Example of proper Push-Down Block (left)
(from forward bow)

Improving Your Execution of Long Form Two | 467

Examples of improper Inside Downward - Palm Down
Block execution
(improper depth - far / close, width - narrow / wide,
improper hand rotation, improper wrist bend, leaning)

Offensive Errors

Offense (striking) is one of the major themes of Long Form Two. Executing the offensive maneuvers properly can make the difference between a successful offense and failure. Just like stances and blocks, the practitioner should become intimately familiar with the proper dimensions utilized in each of the offensive maneuvers.

Some of the primary concepts in dealing with striking are Angle of Incidence, Directional Harmony, Focus, Alignment, and Method of Execution. These theories along with others are highlighted in detail in SGM Parker's book, "Infinite Insights into Kenpo, book #3 (Physical Analyzation II)."

Improving Your Execution of Long Form Two

Some of the most common offensive mistakes displayed while executing Long Form Two are: not executing strikes to the proper dimensions; not executing strikes to the proper angles; not extending strikes to the proper depth; not executing strikes with the proper point of contact of the weapon; executing strikes with improper timing; improper weapon formation, and/or executing strikes with the improper Method of Execution.

General Offense Errors

a) improper alignments:
    i) executed to improper dimensions
    ii) executed with improper body alignments
    iii) incorrect Point of Contact of weapon with target (hitting with wrong part of weapon)
    iv) improper stance (see Stance Errors section):
        1) not maintaining proper weight distribution
        2) not maintaining alignments
        3) not maintaining proper foot rotation (either or both feet - under / over rotated)
        4) not maintaining proper body rotation (under / over rotation)

b) improper positioning:
    i) improper formation of weapon
    ii) not creating proper Angle of Incidence
    ii) head not facing correct direction
    iv) muscles not relaxed:
        1) shoulders not relaxed (hunched)
        2) overall muscles not relaxed (too tense)
    v) improper arm / hand positioning / rotation
    vi) improper foot positioning / rotation

c) improper execution:
    i) executed with wrong Method of Execution
    ii) not executing the strikes smoothly - i.e. mechanical / staccato motion
    iii) not obeying Economy of Motion principle:
        1) not executing the strike from Point of Origin

Note: Typically stance and head positioning is not considered part of most offensive analysis. But, because one of the key goals of American Kenpo forms is the proper coordination between the upper and lower body, these are mentioned here and in the other relevant sections of this chapter.

Improving Your Execution of Long Form Two

Note: Certain general errors that are more commonly seen for a specific type of offensive maneuver (such as improper weapon formation) with be repeated in that maneuver's section. This is to call attention to the error and how common it is for that specific type of maneuver.

Hand-sword

a) proper alignments:
    i) dimensions:
        1) height - neck level
        2) depth - elbow bent (not hyper-extended)
        3) width - center of body
    ii) body alignments:
        1) hand:
            A) rotated to be diagonal outward
            B) rotated to be diagonal downward
            C) finger pointed diagonally forward
        2) wrist kept straight (not bent up / down and / or side-to-side)
        3) elbow anchored (well below hand height)
        4) shoulders - relaxed
        5) upper body / hips - Neutral Bow rotation
        6) legs / feet - Neutral Bow rotation
    iii) Point of Contact - side of hand
    iv) stance - Neutral Bow

b) proper formation - weapon (hand):
    i) hand - kept flat (not cupped)
    ii) thumb:
        1) pressed tightly against rest of hand (Compact Unit)
        2) bent at top knuckle
        3) not tucked forward onto palm
    iii) fingers:
        1) extended and relatively flat (muscle tension bend allowable on impact)
        2) kept together (Compact Unit)

Improving Your Execution of Long Form Two

c) execution:
 i) Method of Execution - Hammering
 ii) execute directly to target (prevent cocking)
 iii) improper execution:
  1) incorrect speeds / methods:
   A) executed too slow (transforms into push with side of hand)
   B) executed too fast (stance settle unable to keep up with strike)
   C) executed too tense (unable to achieve proper 'snap' of strike) (strike looks 'pushed' out)
   D) strike not tensed at Point of Contact (improper timing / never tensed)
  2) incorrect alignments / angles:
   A) elbow not properly anchored (always kept well below hand)

Form Specific

a) Common execution errors:
 i) cocking the hand back toward the shoulder area just prior to executing the strike in an attempt to gain extra Path of Travel and/or rotation for the strike

Comments

a) Common formation errors:
 i) allowing the thumb to be separated from the fingers

© 2015 EPAKS Publications

Example of a proper hand-sword (left)

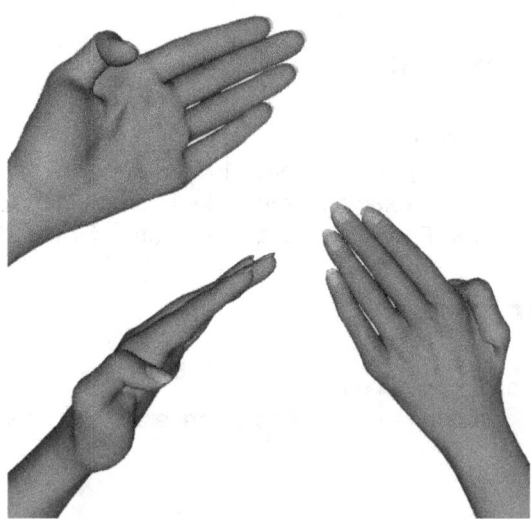

Example of proper hand-sword formation

Improving Your Execution of Long Form Two | 475

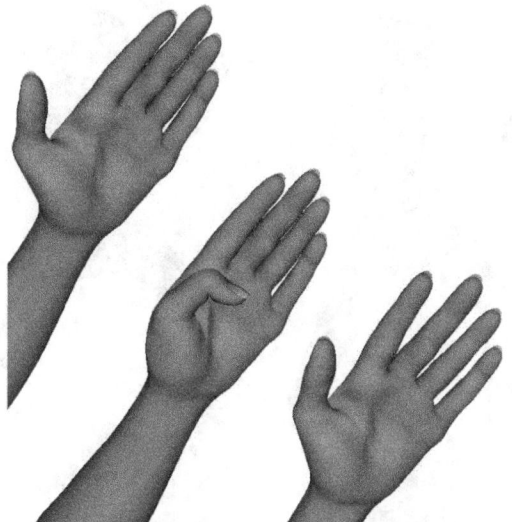

Example of improper hand-sword formation
thumb not tucked, thumb over tucked, fingers
spread

Examples of improper hand-sword execution
improper height - high / low, depth - close / far,
elbow out, rotation - over / under

Horizontal Four-Finger Poke

a) proper alignments:
    i) dimensions:
        1) height - eye level
        2) depth - body facing directly forward with elbow extended forward and slightly bent (not hyper-extended)
        3) width - center of body
    ii) body alignments:
        1) hand:
            A) rotated to be horizontal
            B) fingers pointed directly forward
        2) wrist kept straight (not bent up / down and / or side-to-side)
        3) shoulders - relaxed
        4) upper body / hips - Forward Bow rotation
        5) legs / feet - Forward Bow rotation
    iii) Point of Contact - tip of fingers of hand
    iv) stance - Forward Bow

b) proper formation - weapon (hand):
    i) hand - kept flat (not cupped)
    ii) thumb:
        1) pressed tightly against rest of hand (Compact Unit)
        2) bent at top knuckle
        3) not tucked forward onto palm
    iii) fingers:
        1) extended and relatively flat (muscle tension bend allowable on impact)
        2) slightly spread

c) execution:
  i) Method of Execution - Thrusting
  ii) execute directly to target (prevent arching line of travel)
  iii) improper execution:
    1) incorrect speeds / methods:
      A) executed too slow (transforms into push with fingers)
      B) executed too fast (stance rotation unable to keep up with strike)
      C) executed too tense (unable to achieve proper 'snap' of strike) (strike looks 'pushed' out)
      D) strike not tensed at Point of Contact (improper timing / never tensed)
    2) incorrect alignments / angles:
      A) elbow over bent or hyper-extended

Comments

a) Common formation errors:
  i) allowing the thumb to be separated from the fingers

b) Common execution errors:
  i) over rotate beyond a Forward Bow
  ii) aim strike high and bend wrist downward to compensate

Improving Your Execution of Long Form Two

Example of a proper horizontal four-finger poke (left)

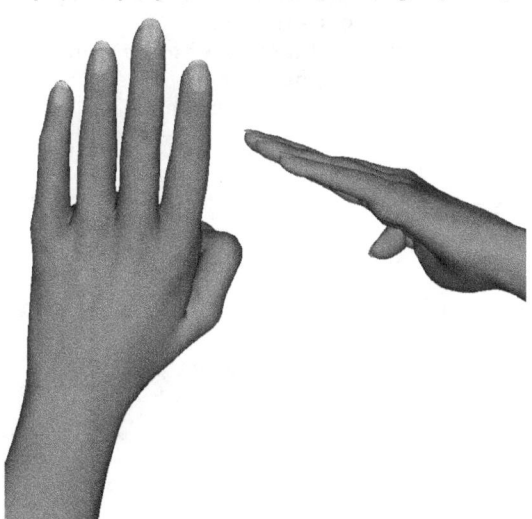

Example of proper horizontal four-finger poke formation

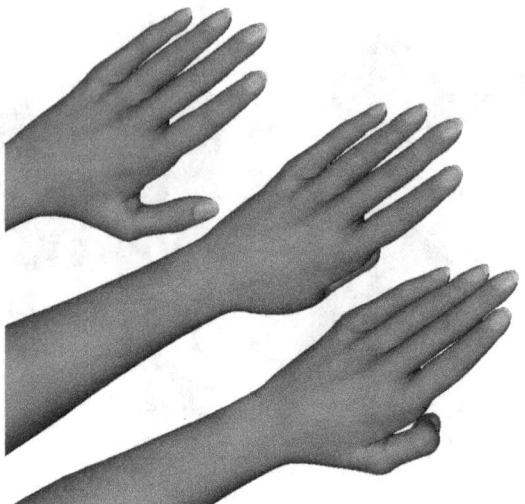

Example of improper horizontal four-finger poke formation
thumb not tucked, thumb over tucked, fingers together

Improving Your Execution of Long Form Two

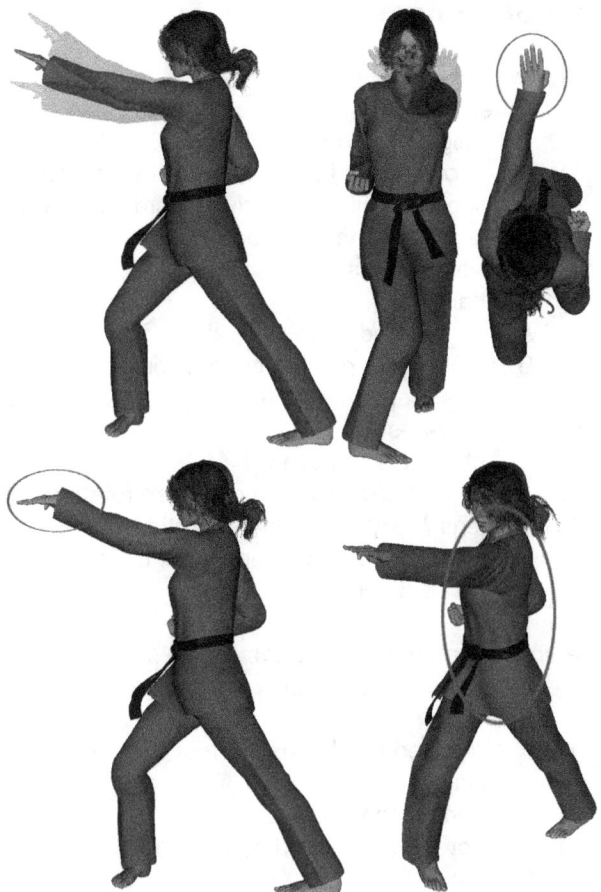

Examples of improper horizontal four-finger poke execution
improper height - high / low, width - narrow / wide,
wrist bent to side,
wrist bent donward, over rotated

Vertical Four-Finger Poke

a) proper alignments:
    i)   dimensions:
        1)   height - rib level
        2)   depth - body in side horse with elbow at ribs and fingers pointing directly forward, vertically
        3)   width - in-line with body
    ii)   body alignments:
        1)   hand:
            A)   rotated to be vertical
            B)   fingers pointed directly forward
        2)   wrist kept straight (not bent up / down and / or side-to-side)
        3)   shoulders - relaxed
        4)   upper body / hips - side Horse rotation
        5)   legs / feet - side Horse rotation
    iii)   Point of Contact - tip of fingers of hand
    iv)   stance - side Horse

b) proper formation - weapon (hand):
    i)   hand - kept flat (not cupped)
    ii)   thumb:
        1)   pressed tightly against rest of hand (Compact Unit)
        2)   bent at top knuckle
        3)   not tucked forward onto palm
    iii)   fingers:
        1)   extended and relatively flat (muscle tension bend allowable on impact)
        2)   slightly spread

Improving Your Execution of Long Form Two

- c) execution:
  - i) Method of Execution - Thrusting
  - ii) execute directly to target (prevent arching line of travel)
  - iii) improper execution
    1) incorrect speeds / methods:
       - A) executed too slow (transforms into push with fingers)
       - B) executed too fast (stance rotation unable to keep up with strike)
       - C) executed too tense (unable to achieve proper 'snap' of strike) (strike looks 'pushed' out)
       - D) strike not tensed at Point of Contact (improper timing / never tensed)
    2) incorrect alignments / angles:
       - A) incorrect elbow bend:
         - I) over bent (strike not horizontal)
         - II) too-extended (strike not backed by ribs)

Form Specific

- a) Common execution errors:
  - i) over extend the elbow, not allowing ribs to back strike
  - ii) over bend the elbow, so strike is not executed horizontally

Comments

- a) Common formation errors:
  - i) allowing the thumb to be separated from the fingers

© 2015 EPAKS Publications

Example of a proper vertical four-finger poke (right)

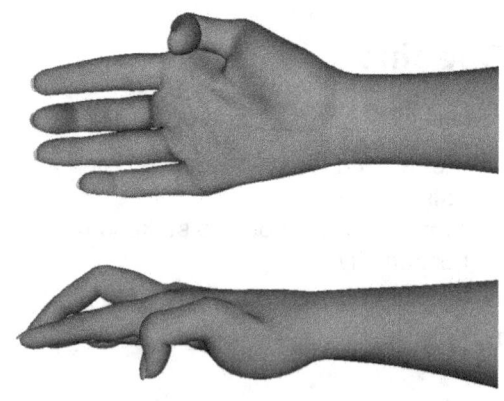

Example of proper vertical four-finger poke formation

Improving Your Execution of Long Form Two | 485

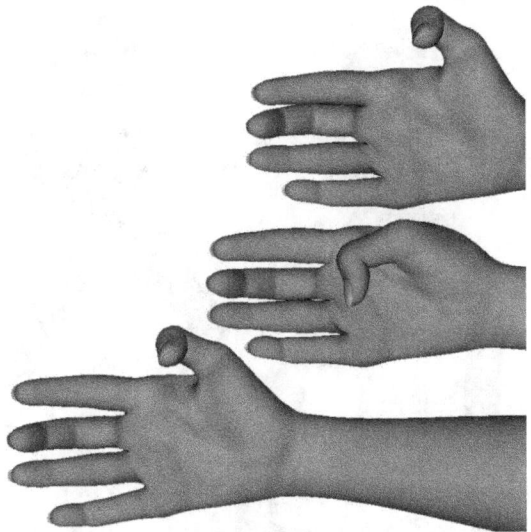

Example of improper vertical four-finger poke formation
thumb not tucked, thumb over tucked, fingers spread

Examples of improper vertical four-finger poke execution
improper height - high / low, depth - too deep,
improper width - narrow / wide, wrist bent to side,
over rotated

Straight Punch

a) proper alignments:
    i) dimensions:
        1) height - upper abdomen to lower shoulder level
        2) depth - elbow bent (forearm parallel to ground)
        3) width - directly ahead
    ii) body alignments:
        1) hand - horizontal (palm parallel to ground)
        2) wrist kept straight (not bent up / down and / or side-to-side)
        3) elbow directly in-line with fist (horizontally)
        4) shoulders - relaxed
        5) upper body / hips - offset Horse to Forward Bow rotation
        6) legs / feet - offset Horse to Forward Bow rotation
    iii) Point of Contact - index / middle finger knuckles
    iv) stance - offset Horse to Forward Bow positioning / do not allow:
        1) over rotation of body / feet
        2) improper weight distribution
        3) feet not remaining flat to floor

b) proper formation - weapon (hand):
    i) fingers - standard fist (tightly bent and kept together to form Compact Unit)
    ii) thumb:
        1) wrapped under bent fingers (Compact Unit)
        2) do not allow to separate from contact with fingers

c) execution:
  i) Method of Execution - Thrusting
  ii) execute directly to target (prevent arching line of travel)
  iii) improper execution:
    1) incorrect speeds / methods:
      A) executed too slow (transforms into push with knuckles)
      B) executed too fast (stance adjustment unable to keep up with strike)
      C) executed too tense (unable to achieve proper 'snap' of strike) (strike looks 'pushed' out)
      D) strike not tensed at Point of Contact (improper timing / never tensed)

Form Specific

a) improper alignments:
  i) side Horse:
    1) attempt to align shoulder behind weapon - causing over rotation of stance
    2) not punching to proper height (shoulder)
  ii) Forward Bow:
    1) over reach with strike, causing over rotation
    2) under rotation into Forward Bow
    3) punching too high (parallel to floor)
  ii) Step Through:
    1) over reach with strike, causing over rotation
    2) under rotation into Forward Bow positioning
    3) not keeping base stance flat on floor
    4) not keeping height constant (bobbing)
    5) punching too high (parallel to floor)

Comments

a) Common errors:
  i) side Horse:

1) not maintaining a proper offset horse, but to rotate into a neutral bow or a forward bow and/or allow the rear heel to come off of the floor during this process. The straight punches in Long Form Two in this section are purposely delivered on an angle with only the elbow in-line with the punch, but not the rest of the body. This is done purposely for the minimization of torque and the maximization of back-up mass during the execution of these maneuvers i.e. to isolate the power principle back-up mass.

Note: See Stance Errors - Offset Horse section for information on this subject.

ii) Step Through:
   1) not maintaining a flat base foot while kicking and punching simultaneously, but lifting to just the ball of foot
   2) not punching parallel to floor, but rather punching too high (usually at shoulder to face level)

Example of a proper straight punch (right) (from side horse)

Example of a proper straight punch with front hand
(left)
(from side horse)

Example of a proper straight punch (right)
(from forward bow)

Improving Your Execution of Long Form Two

Example of a proper straight punch (left)
(with kick - from forward bow positioning)

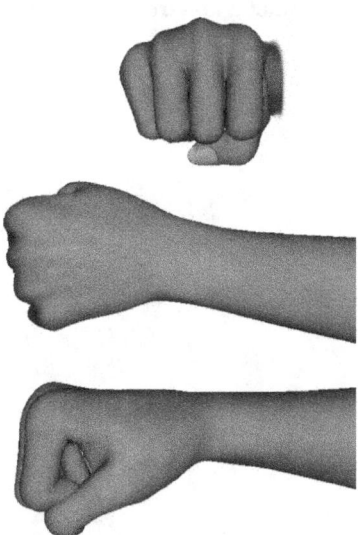

Example of proper punch formation

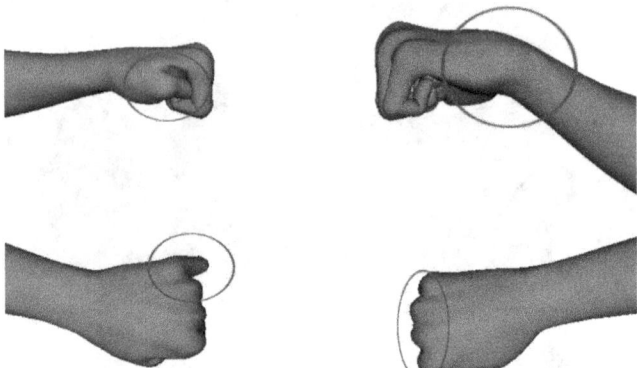

Examples of improper Straight Punch - weapon formation / alignment
formation - tucked thumb / hanging pinky finger
wrist: vertical angle - over bent, wrist: horizontal angle - contact with wrong knuckles

Improving Your Execution of Long Form Two

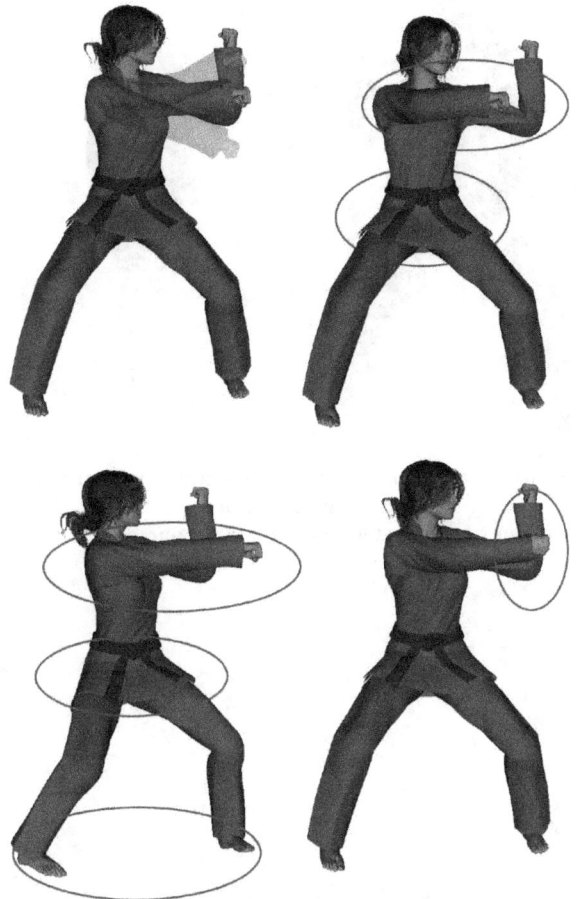

Examples of improper punch execution (from side horse)
improper height - high / low, depth - under rotated,
depth - over rotated, fist rotation - not horizontal

Examples of improper punch execution with front
hand (from side horse)
improper height - high / low, width - narrow / wide

Improving Your Execution of Long Form Two   495

Examples of improper punch execution (from forward bow)
improper height - high / low, width - narrow / wide, foot not flat, over reaching

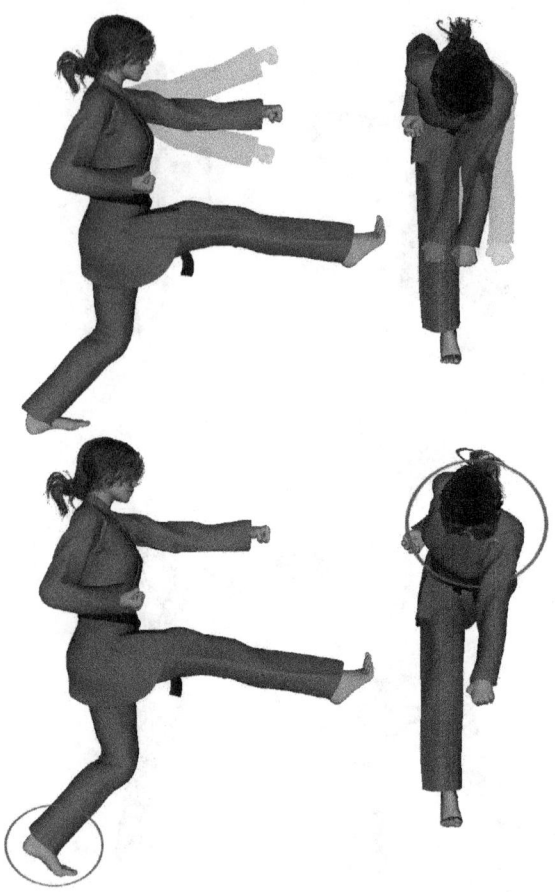

Examples of improper punch execution (with kick) improper height - high / low, width - narrow / wide, foot not flat, over rotation

Vertical Punch (high)

a) proper alignments:
    i)   dimensions:
        1)   height - shoulder to face level
        2)   depth - arm extended forward and slight bend in elbow (not hyper-extended)
        3)   width - in-line with body
    ii)   body alignments:
        1)   hand:
            A)   rotated to be vertical
            B)   knuckles pointed directly forward
        2)   wrist bent downward to have knuckles pointing forward
        3)   elbow pointing directly downward
        4)   shoulders - relaxed
        5)   upper body / hips - side Horse rotation
        6)   legs / feet - side Horse rotation
    iii)   Point of Contact - first two knuckles of fist
    iv)   stance - side Horse positioning

b) proper formation - weapon (hand):
    i)   fingers - standard fist (tightly bent and kept together to form Compact Unit)
    ii)   thumb:
        1)   wrapped under bent fingers (Compact Unit)
        2)   do not allow to separate from contact with fingers

c) execution:
   i) Method of Execution - Snapping
   ii) execute directly to target (prevent arching line of travel / cocking)
   iii) improper execution:
   1) incorrect speeds / methods:
      A) executed too slow (transforms into push with fist)
      B) executed too fast (stance change unable to keep up with strike)
      C) executed too tense (unable to achieve proper 'snap' of strike) (strike looks 'pushed' out)
      D) strike not tensed at Point of Contact (improper timing / never tensed)
   2) incorrect alignments / angles:
      A) incorrect elbow bend:
         I) over bent (full reach of strike not achieved)
         II) too-extended (elbow hyper-extended)

Form Specific

a) Common execution errors:
   i) not executed with proper Method of Execution (snapping)

Improving Your Execution of Long Form Two | 499

Example of a proper high vertical punch (left)
(with side kick - from side horse)

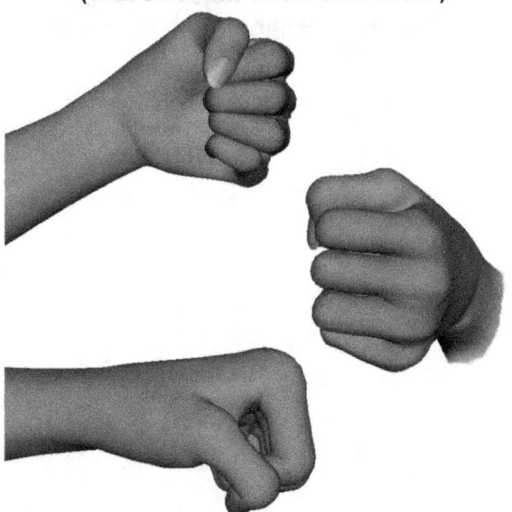

Example of proper vertical punch formation
(high height zone)

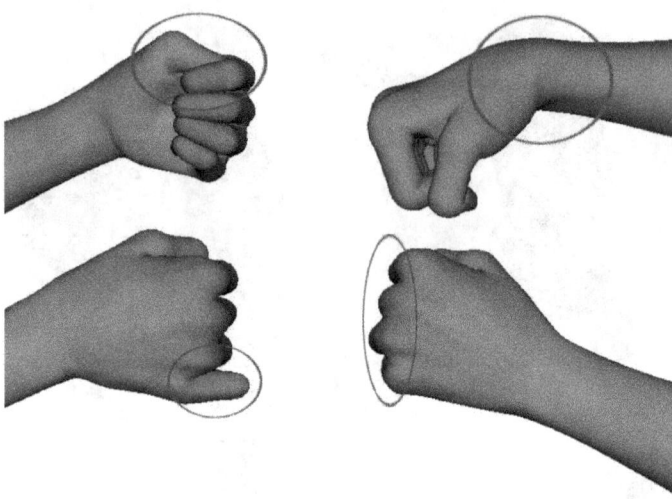

Examples of improper Vertical Punch - weapon formation / angle
formation - tucked thumb, wrist: horizontal angle - over bent
formation - hanging pinky finger, wrist: vertical angle - contact with wrong knuckles

Improving Your Execution of Long Form Two 501

Examples of improper vertical punch execution (from side horse)
improper height - high / low, width - narrow / width,
wrist not bent enough, punch not fully extended

Side Kick

a) proper alignments:
    i) dimensions:
        1) height - shin level
        2) depth - knee slightly bent (not hyper-extended)
        3) width - center of body
    ii) body alignments:
        1) foot:
            A) rotated to be parallel to ground
            B) toes pointed directly to side (to toe slightly downward)
        2) ankle bent to expose edge of foot
        3) upper body / hips - side Horse rotation
    iii) Point of Contact - side of foot (knife edge)
    iv) stance - side Horse positioning

b) proper formation - weapon (foot):
    i) foot - kept flat
    ii) toes:
        1) extended and relatively flat (not bent forward)
        2) kept together (Compact Unit)

Improving Your Execution of Long Form Two 503

- c) execution:
  - i) Method of Execution - Snapping
  - ii) execute directly to target (prevent cocking / arching line of travel)
  - iii) improper execution:
    1) improper speeds / methods:
       - A) executed too slow (transforms into push with side of foot)
       - B) executed too long (weight shifted to stable foot)
       - C) executed too tense (unable to achieve proper 'snap' of strike) (strike looks 'pushed' out)
       - D) strike not tensed at Point of Contact (improper timing / never tensed)
       - E) strike kick 'pumped' - i.e. overly chambered
    2) improper alignments / angles:
       - A) weapon not fully extended
       - B) leaning

Form Specific

- a) Common execution errors:
  - i) weight transferred to supporting foot to point of almost balancing on it. Should be minimal (to no) weight transfer to supporting foot
  - ii) foot re-chambered after kick (pumped)

Comments

- a) Common alignment errors:
  - i) allowing the toes to be over rotated and pointing to far downward to point of diagonally striking with foot
  - ii) over rotating hip to reverse bow positioning (and Thrusting Method of Execution)

© 2015 EPAKS Publications

Example of a proper side kick (right)
(with punch - from side horse)

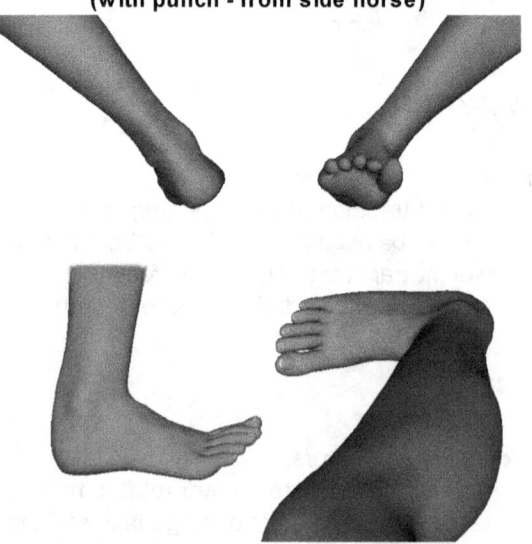

Example of proper side kick formation

Improving Your Execution of Long Form Two

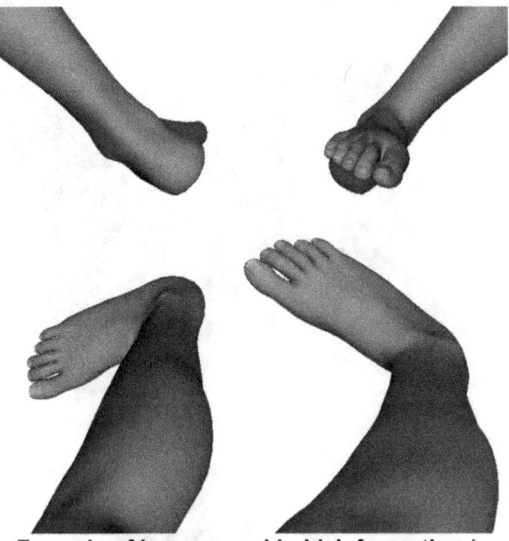

Example of improper side kick formation / alignment
ankle improperly bent, toes rolled over,
improper rotation - over / under

506   The Official EPAKS Guide to Long Form Two

Examples of improper side kick execution
improper height - high, width - narrow / wide,
depth - not fully extended

Hammer-fist

a) proper alignments:
    i)   dimensions:
           1)   height - groin level
           2)   depth - striking arm extended to depth of Invisible Box
           3)   width - center of body
    ii)   body alignments:
           1)   hand:
                A)   rotated to be vertical
                B)   knuckles pointed directly downward
           2)   wrist bent front / backward to point knuckles downward (not bent side-to-side)
           3)   shoulders - relaxed
           4)   upper body / hips - Forward Bow rotation
           5)   legs / feet - Forward Bow rotation
    iii)   Point of Contact - side of hand
    iv)   stance - Forward Bow

b) proper formation - weapon (hand):
    i)   fingers - standard fist (tightly bent and kept together to form Compact Unit)
    ii)   thumb:
           1)   wrapped under bent fingers (Compact Unit)
           2)   do not allow to separate from contact with fingers

c) execution:
   i) Method of Execution - Hammering
   ii) execute directly to target (prevent cocking)
   iii) improper execution:
   1) improper speeds / methods:
      A) executed too slow (transforms into push with fist)
      B) executed too fast (stance rotation unable to keep up with strike)
      C) executed too tense (unable to achieve proper 'snap' of strike) (strike looks 'pushed' out)
      D) strike not tensed at Point of Contact (improper timing / never tensed)
   2) improper alignments / angles:
      A) elbow over bent or hyper-extended

Form Specific

a) Common execution errors:
   i) wrist not bent properly to strike with side of hand

Comments

a) Common execution errors:
   i) over rotate beyond a Forward Bow

Improving Your Execution of Long Form Two   509

Example of a proper forward, underhand, reverse hammer-fist
(right)
(with block - from forward bow)

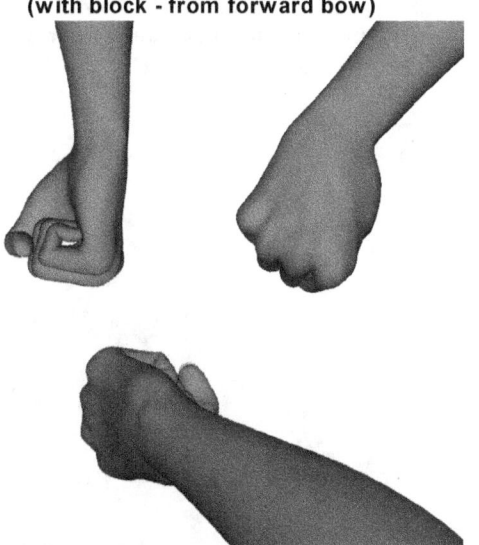

Example of proper forward, underhand,
reverse, hammer-fist formation

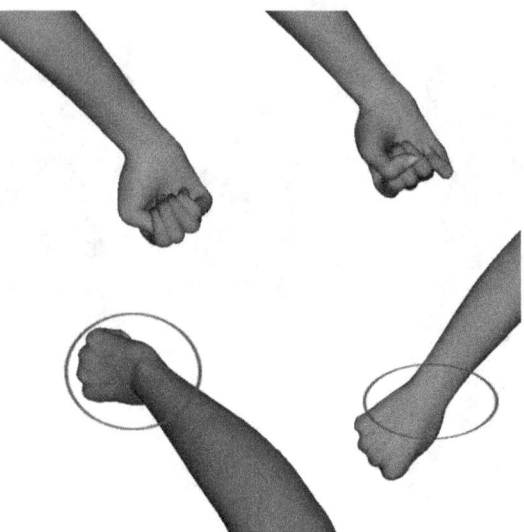

Example of improper hammer-fist
formation / alignment
thumb tucked, pinky out,
wrist bent to side, wrist no bent propery

Improving Your Execution of Long Form Two | 511

Examples of improper forward hammer-fist execution
improper depth - close / far width - narrow / wide,
over rotation, foot not flat

Claw

a) proper alignments:
   i) dimensions:
      1) height - lower face
      2) depth - elbow bent (not hyper-extended)
      3) width - directly ahead
   ii) body alignments:
      1) hand vertical (palm pointing forward to ground)
      2) wrist bent to expose heel-of-palm
      3) elbow below hand (anchored)
      4) shoulders - relaxed
      5) upper body / hips - Neutral Bow rotation
      6) legs / feet - Neutral Bow rotation
   iii) Point of Contact - tips of fingers (and possibly thumb)
   iv) stance - Neutral Bow

b) proper formation - weapon (hand):
   i) fingers
      1) slightly bent to expose tips of fingers (not nails of fingers)
      2) slightly spread (Margin for Error)
   ii) thumb:
      1) slightly bent to expose tip (not nail)
      2) slightly spread (Margin for Error)

Improving Your Execution of Long Form Two

c) execution:
   i) Method of Execution - Clawing
   ii) execute directly to target (prevent cocking)
   iii) improper execution:
      1) improper speeds / methods:
         A) executed too slow (transforms into downward pull with fingers)
         B) executed too tense (unable to achieve proper 'snap' of strike) (strike looks 'pulled' downward)
         C) strike not tensed at Point of Contact (improper timing / never tensed)

Comments

a) Common errors:
   i) formation:
      1) over bending of fingers / thumb causes a nails to rake skin - not finger tips

   ii) alignment:
      1) not anchoring elbow

© 2015 EPAKS Publications

514 | The Official EPAKS Guide to Long Form Two

Example of a proper overhead claw (left)
(prior to execution / stance rotation)

Example of a proper overhead claw (right)

Improving Your Execution of Long Form Two

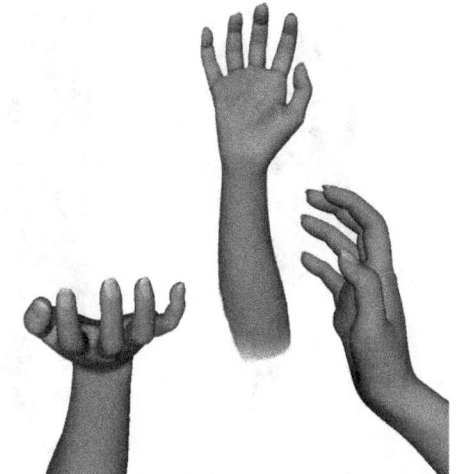

Example of proper overhead claw formation

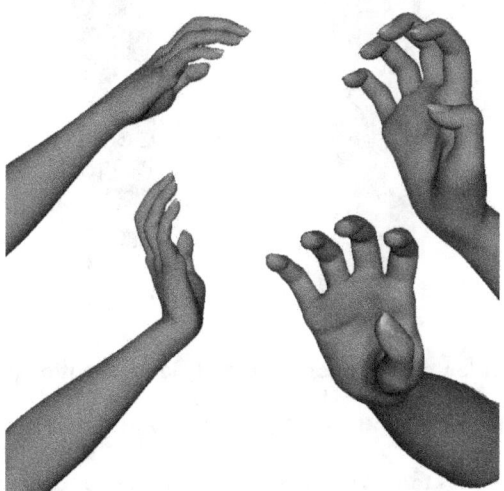

Examples of improper claw formation / alignment
wrist - not bent, formation - fingers too bent,
wrist - over bent, formation - thumb tucked

Examples of improper overhead claw execution (with hammer-fist)
improper depth - shallow / deep, width - narrow / wide,
height - too low, elbow alignment - not anchored

Improving Your Execution of Long Form Two | 517

Examples of improper overhead claw execution
improper depth - shallow / deep, width - narrow / wide,
height - too low, elbow alignment - not anchored

Outward Back-knuckle

a) proper alignments:
    i)   dimensions:
        1)   height - jaw to temple
        2)   depth - elbow bent (not hyper-extended)
        3)   width - same side of body as striking hand
    ii)   body alignments:
        1)   hand - vertical (palm perpendicular to ground)
        2)   wrist kept straight (not bent up / down and / or side-to-side)
        3)   elbow below strike (anchored)
        4)   shoulders - relaxed
        5)   upper body / hips - Neutral Bow rotation
        6)   legs / feet - Neutral Bow rotation
    iii)   Point of Contact - index / middle finger back of knuckles
    iv)   stance - Neutral Bow

b) proper formation - weapon (hand):
    i)   fingers - standard fist (tightly bent and kept together to form Compact Unit)
    ii)   thumb:
        1)   wrapped under bent fingers (Compact Unit)
        2)   do not allow to separate from contact with fingers

Improving Your Execution of Long Form Two

c) execution:
  i) Method of Execution - Snapping
  ii) execute directly to target (prevent cocking)
  iii) improper execution:
    1) improper speeds / methods:
      A) executed too slow (transforms into push - not snap)
      B) executed too fast (stance settle unable to keep up with strike)
      C) executed too tense (unable to achieve proper 'snap' of strike) (strike looks 'pushed' out)
      D) strike not tensed at Point of Contact (improper timing / never tensed)
    2) improper alignments / angles:
      A) incorrect elbow bend:
        I) over bent (full reach of strike not achieved)
        II) too-extended (elbow hyper-extended)

Comments

a) Common execution errors:
  i) over rotate beyond a Neutral Bow (or into Forward Bow)
  ii) over reach - elbow not kept bent (hyper extended)

Example of a proper outward back-knuckle (left / right)
(front / rear hand)

Improving Your Execution of Long Form Two

Example of proper back-knuckle formation

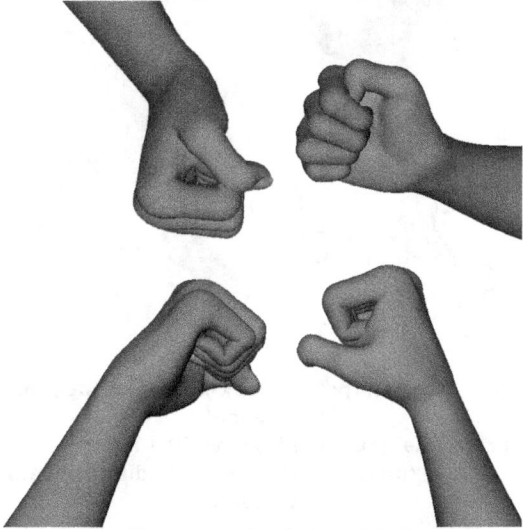

Examples of improper back-knuckle formation / alignment
wrist back backward, thumb not tucked,
wrist bent forward, hanging thumb

Examples of improper back-knuckle execution
(rear hand)
improper height - high / low, width - narrow / wide
stance over rotated, over reach - bending with elbow
extended

Improving Your Execution of Long Form Two 523

Examples of improper back-knuckle execution
(front hand)
improper height - high / low, width - narrow / wide
stance over rotated, over reach - bending with elbow
extended

Inverted Vertical Back-knuckle

a) proper alignments:
    i) dimensions:
        1) height - face level
        2) depth - arm extended forward and slight bend in elbow (not hyper-extended)
        3) width - in-line with body
    ii) body alignments:
        1) hand:
            A) rotated to be vertical (thumb downward)
            B) knuckles pointed directly to the side
        2) wrist kept straight (not bent up / down and / or side-to-side)
        3) elbow almost in-line with fist (horizontally) (slightly anchored)
        4) shoulders - relaxed
        5) upper body / hips - Neutral Bow rotation
        6) legs / feet - Neutral Bow rotation
    iii) Point of Contact - back of first two knuckles of fist
    iv) stance - Neutral Bow

b) proper formation - weapon (hand):
    i) fingers - standard fist (tightly bent and kept together to form Compact Unit)
    ii) thumb:
        1) wrapped under bent fingers (Compact Unit)
        2) do not allow to separate from contact with fingers

Improving Your Execution of Long Form Two   525

c) execution:
   i) Method of Execution - Round-housing
   ii) execute directly to target (prevent cocking)
   iii) improper execution:
   1) improper speeds / methods:
      A) executed too slow (transforms into push with fist)
      B) executed too tense (unable to achieve proper 'snap' of strike) (strike looks 'pushed' out)
      C) strike not tensed at Point of Contact (improper timing / never tensed)
   2) improper alignments / angles:
      A) elbow bend
         I) over bent (full reach of strike not achieved)
         II) too-extended (elbow hyper-extended)

Form Specific

a) Common execution errors:
   i) not executed to proper depth
      1) executed to almost parallel in front of body
      2) executed almost like straight, inverted, vertical punch

Comments

a) Common execution errors:
   i) executed with shrugged shoulders

© 2015 EPAKS Publications

Example of a proper inverted vertical back-knuckle strike (left)

Example of proper inverted, vertical, back-knuckle formation

Improving Your Execution of Long Form Two 527

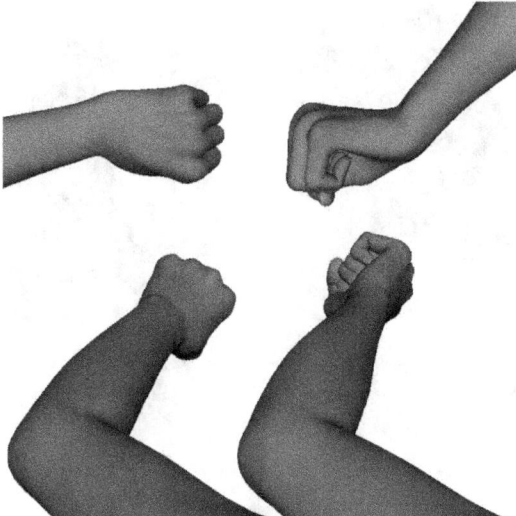

Examples of improper Inverted Vertical
Back-knuckle
wrist bent to side, wrist bent forward,
strike under rotated, strike over rotated

Examples of improper inverted, vertical, Back-knuckle strike execution
improper height - high / low, shrugged shoulders, elbow over extended / over bent, leaning

Improving Your Execution of Long Form Two   529

Straight Kick

a) proper alignments:
    i) dimensions:
        1) height - groin level
        2) depth - knee slightly bent (not hyper-extended)
        3) width - center of body
    ii) body alignments:
        1) foot:
            A) heel pointing directly downward
        2) toes bent back to expose ball of foot (toes pointing upward)
        3) ankle bent to point toes forward
        4) knee directly inline with foot and hip
        5) upper body / hips - Forward Bow rotation
    iii) Point of Contact - ball of foot
    iv) stance - Forward Bow positioning

b) proper formation - weapon (foot):
    i) foot - kept flat
    ii) toes:
        1) bent upward to expose ball of foot
    iii) ankle bent forward to point at target (ankle = wrist of foot - for punch)

© 2015 EPAKS Publications

- c) execution:
    - i) Method of Execution - Snapping
    - ii) execute directly to target (prevent cocking / arching line of travel)
    - iii) improper execution:
        1) improper speeds / methods:
            - A) executed too slow (transforms into push with ball of foot)
            - B) executed too tense (unable to achieve proper 'snap' of strike) (strike looks 'pushed' out)
            - C) strike not tensed at Point of Contact (improper timing / never tensed)
        2) improper alignments / angles:
            - A) incorrect extension:
                - I) knee over bent (full reach of strike not achieved)
                - II) over extended (knee hyper-extended)
            - B) incorrect positioning:
                - I) ankle not bent forward
                - II) toes not bent backward (exposing toe tips to contact)

Form Specific

- a) execution errors:
    - i) foot re-chambered after kick (pumped). Doing this causes kicking foot to have to be re-extended (extra motion) to position for next maneuver (buckle)
    - ii) lifting heel of supporting foot during kick execution (caused by over extending reach of kick)

Comments

- a) Common alignment errors:
    - i) never bending toes upward to expose ball of foot
    - iii) over / under rotating hip / body at perceived point of contact of kick

Improving Your Execution of Long Form Two | 531

iii) leaning, either backwards or forwards, during execution of kick

Example of a proper front kick (left) (with punch)

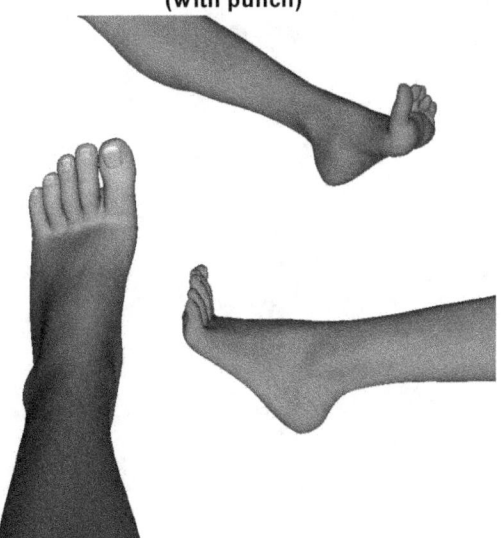

Example of proper front kick formation

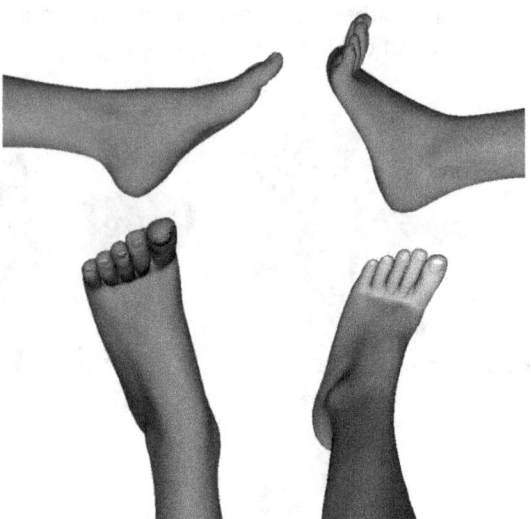

Example of improper front kick
formation / alignment
toes not bent, ankle bent up,
ankle bent to side, over rotated

Improving Your Execution of Long Form Two 533

Examples of improper front kick execution
knee hyper-extended & too high,
knee under extended,
foot not flat, leaning backwards

Vertical Punch (middle)

a) proper alignments:
    i) dimensions:
        1) height - rib level
        2) depth - body in side horse with elbow at ribs and fingers pointing directly forward, vertically
        3) width - in-line with body
    ii) body alignments:
        1) hand:
            A) rotated to be vertical
            B) knuckles pointed directly forward
        2) wrist kept straight (not bent up / down and / or side-to-side)
        3) shoulders - relaxed
        4) upper body / hips - side Horse rotation
        5) legs / feet - side Horse rotation
    iii) Point of Contact - first two knuckles of fist
    iv) stance - side Horse

b) proper formation - weapon (hand):
    i) fingers - standard fist (tightly bent and kept together to form Compact Unit)
    ii) thumb:
        1) wrapped under bent fingers (Compact Unit)
        2) do not allow to separate from contact with fingers

Improving Your Execution of Long Form Two — 535

- c) execution:
    - i) Method of Execution - Thrusting
    - ii) execute directly to target (prevent arching line of travel)
    - iii) improper execution:
        1) improper speeds / methods:
            - A) executed too slow (transforms into push with fist)
            - B) executed too fast (stance change unable to keep up with strike)
            - C) executed too tense (unable to achieve proper 'snap' of strike) (strike looks 'pushed' out)
            - D) strike not tensed at Point of Contact (improper timing / never tensed)
        2) improper alignments / angles:
            - A) elbow bend:
                - I) over bent (strike not horizontal)
                - II) too-extended (strike not backed by ribs)

Form Specific

- a) Common execution errors:
    - i) over extend the elbow, not allowing ribs to back strike
    - ii) over bend the elbow, so strike is not executed horizontally

© 2015 EPAKS Publications

Example of a proper middle height vertical punch (right)

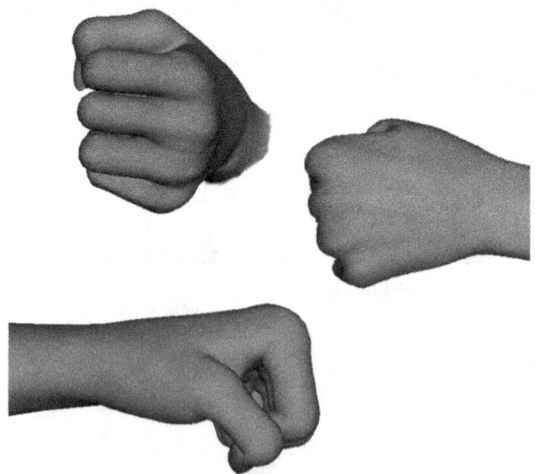

Example of proper vertical punch formation
(middle height zone)

Improving Your Execution of Long Form Two | 537

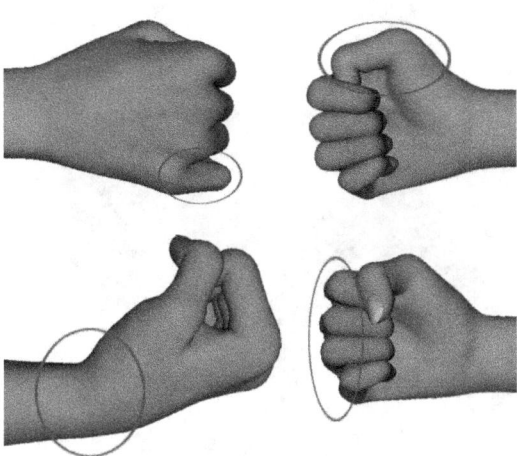

Examples of improper Vertical Punch - weapon formation / angle
formation - hanging pinky finger / tucked thumb,
wrist: horizontal angle - over bent, wrist: vertical angle - contact with wrong knuckles

Examples of improper vertical punch execution (from side horse)
improper height - high / low, width - narrow / width, depth - too extended

Buckle

a) proper alignments:
   - i) dimensions:
     1) height - shin / calf level
     2) depth - side Horse depth
     3) width - inline with hip / body
   - ii) body alignments:
     1) shin rotated directly to side (perpendicular to Point of Reference)
     1) legs / feet - side Horse rotation
     2) hips / upper body = side Horse rotation
   - iii) Point of Contact - shin of leg
   - iv) stance - side Horse

b) execution:
  i) Method of Execution - Buckling
  ii) improper execution:
    1) no dropping of weight (settling) during execution of maneuver
    2) improper alignment / angles:
      A) shin over / under rotated to apply pressure properly
      B) ankle over / under bent to side
      C) knee not bent properly to apply pressure

Form Specific

a) execution errors:
  i) shin under rotated (not in side Horse positioning)

Comments

a) Common alignment errors:
  i) ankle over bent to side

b) Common execution errors:
  i) no dropping of weight (settling) during execution of maneuver
  ii) shifting weight too much on buckling leg

Improving Your Execution of Long Form Two | 541

Example of a proper buckle (right)
(with vertical punch)

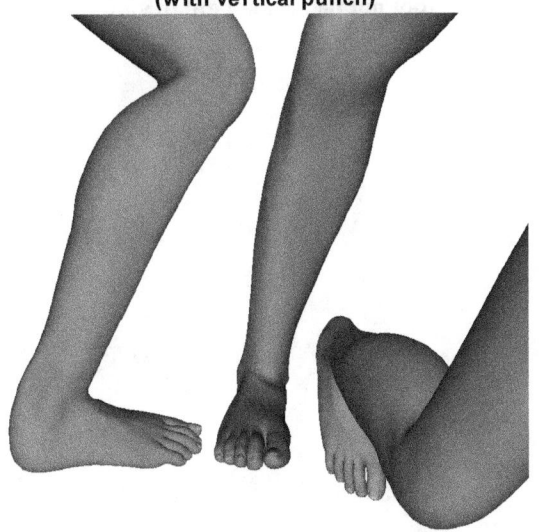

Example of proper buckle alignment

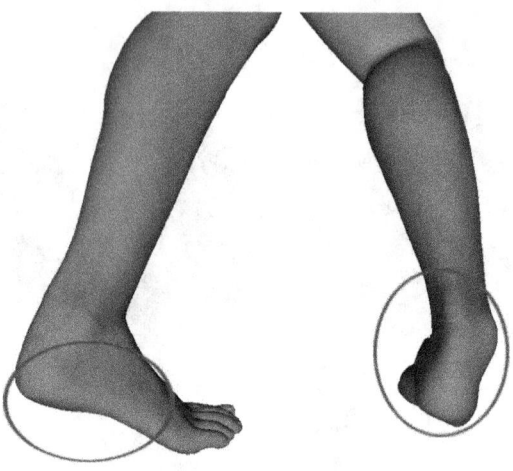

**Example of improper buckle alignment
foot not flat, ankle bent to side**

Improving Your Execution of Long Form Two 543

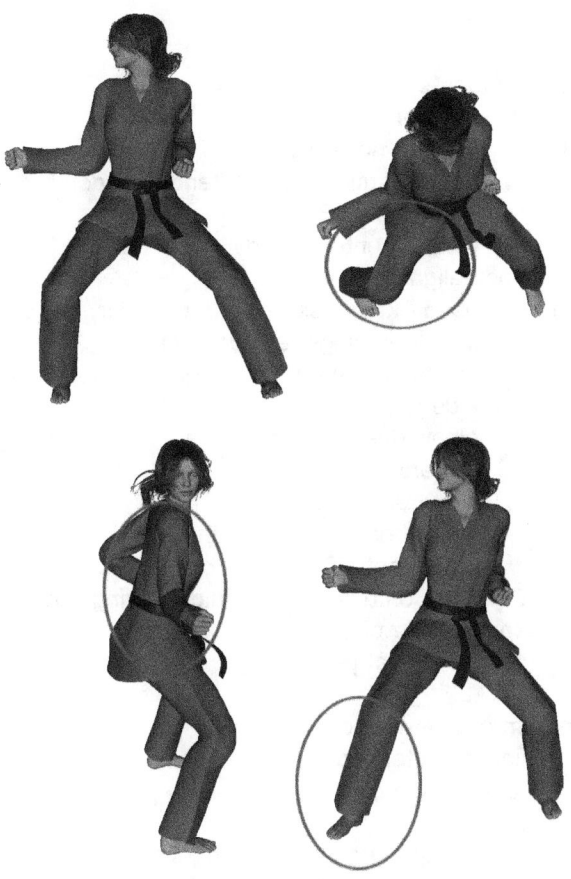

Examples of improper buckle execution
improper weight distribution, over rotated,
leaning, under rotated

Half-knuckle

a) proper alignments:
    i) dimensions:
        1) height - nose level
        2) depth - striking arm extended to depth of about half Invisible Box
        3) width - center of body
    ii) body alignments:
        1) hand - knuckles upward, palm forward, middle knuckles diagonally downward
        2) wrist kept straight (not bent up / down and / or side-to-side)
        3) elbow directly inline below fist (angled diagonally forward)
        4) shoulders - relaxed
        5) upper body / hips - Twist rotation
        6) legs / feet - Twist rotation
    iii) Point of Contact - index / middle / ring finger middle-knuckles (avoid pinky knuckle)
    iv) stance - Twist positioning

b) proper formation - weapon (hand):
    i) fingers - standard fist (tightly bent and kept together to form Compact Unit)
    ii) thumb:
        1) wrapped under bent fingers (Compact Unit)
        2) do not allow to separate from contact with fingers

Improving Your Execution of Long Form Two

c) execution:
    i) Method of Execution - Hammering
    ii) improper execution:
        1) improper speeds / methods:
            A) executed too slow (transforms into push with knuckles)
            B) executed too fast (stance change unable to keep up with strike)
            C) executed too tense (unable to achieve proper 'snap' of strike) (strike looks 'pushed' out)
            D) strike not tensed at Point of Contact (improper timing / never tensed)
        2) improper alignments / angles:
            A) elbow not anchored (aka no "chicken winging")

Form Specific

a) execution errors:
    i) not executed with proper strike (middle knuckles)

Comments

a) Common alignment errors:
    i) arm extended too far forward (over reaching)
    ii) elbow not anchored properly (not inline with knuckles)

b) Common execution errors:
    i) strike executed on arch not line

546　　The Official EPAKS Guide to Long Form Two

Example of a proper half-knuckle (left)
(with instep kick)

Example of proper helf-knuckle formation

Improving Your Execution of Long Form Two

Examples of improper half-knuckle -
weapon formation / alignment
wrist bent, fist not closed propery,
thumb tucked

Examples of improper half-knuckle execution
depth - shallow / deep, improper height - high / low,
width - wide, elbow not anchored

Instep Kick

a) proper alignments:
    i) dimensions:
        1) height - shin level
        2) depth - knee slightly bent (not hyper-extended)
        3) width - center of body
    ii) body alignments:
        1) foot:
            A) rotated to be parallel to ground
            B) toes pointed directly to side (to toe slightly upward)
        2) ankle slightly bent to expose inside of foot
        3) upper body / hips - Twist rotation
    iii) Point of Contact - inside of foot
    iv) stance - Twist positioning

b) proper formation - weapon (foot):
    i) foot - kept flat
    ii) toes:
        1) extended and relatively flat (not bent forward)
        2) kept together (Compact Unit)

c) execution:
   i) Method of Execution - Thrusting
   ii) execute directly to target (prevent arching line of travel)
   iii) improper execution:
      1) improper speeds / methods:
         A) executed too slow (transforms into push with foot)
         B) executed too tense (unable to achieve proper 'snap' of strike) (strike looks 'pushed' out)
         C) strike not tensed at Point of Contact (improper timing / never tensed)
      2) improper alignments / angles:
         A) incorrect extension:
            I) not executed at all
         B) incorrect positioning:
            I) ankle over / under bent (side to side)

Form Specific

a) Common execution errors:
   i) not executed at all (only crossover is executed)

Comments

a) Common alignment errors:
   i) leaning away during execution

Improving Your Execution of Long Form Two   551

Example of a proper instep kick (left)
(with half-knuckle)

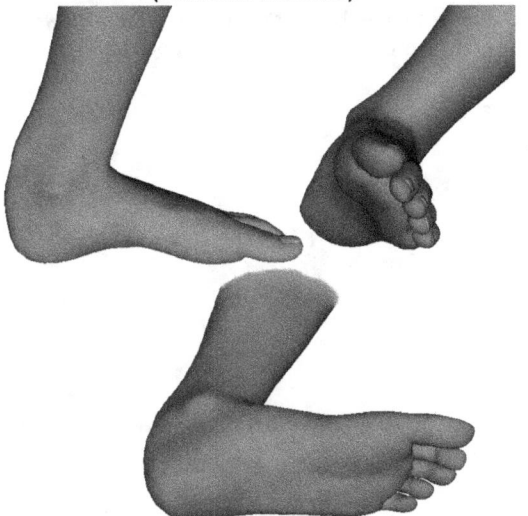

Example of proper instep kick formation

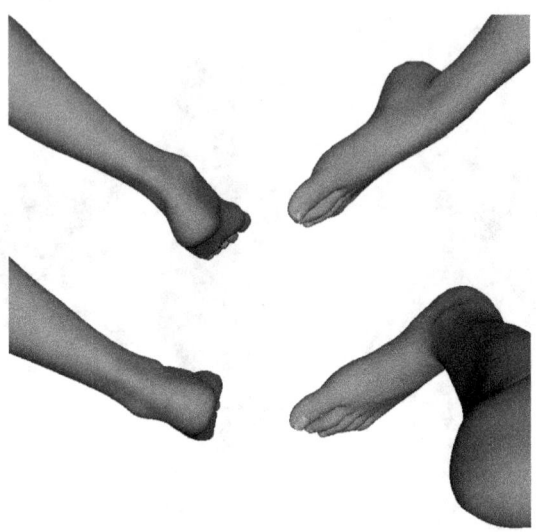

Example of improper instep kick
formation / alignment
ankle improperly bent - too much / too forward /
too little, improper rotation - over

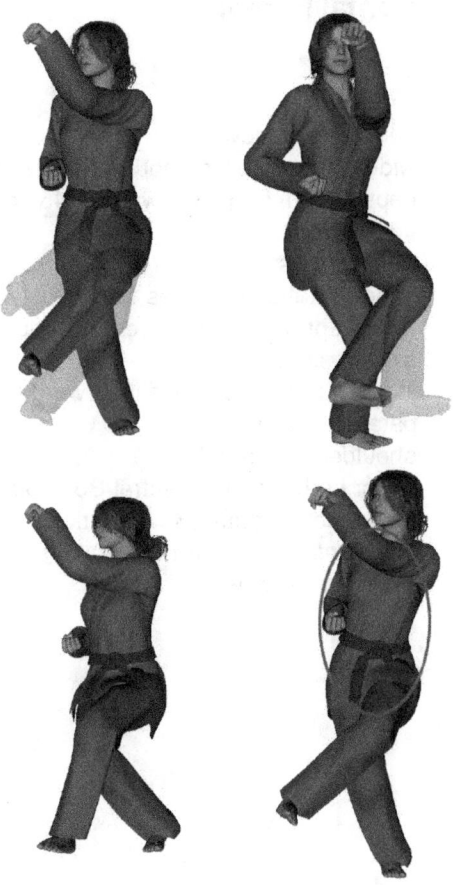

Examples of improper instep kick execution
improper height - high / low, width - wide,
not executed, leaning away

Upward Horizontal Forearm

a) proper alignments:
    i)   Dimensions:
        1)   height = chin level
        2)   width = shoulder to shoulder, horizontally
        3)   depth = arm angled forward at 45 degrees away from you
    ii)   body alignments:
        1)   hand - rotation matches forearm
        2)   wrist kept straight (not bent up / down and / or side-to-side)
        3)   forearm rotated diagonally upward / relatively parallel to ground
        4)   shoulders - relaxed
        5)   upper body / hips - Neutral Bow rotation
        6)   legs / feet - Neutral Bow rotation
    iii)   Point of Contact - forearm (bone)
    iv)   stance - Neutral Bow

Improving Your Execution of Long Form Two

b) execution:
   i) Method of Execution - Thrusting
   ii) execute directly to target (prevent arcing path of travel)
   iii) improper execution:
      1) improper speeds / methods:
         A) executed too slow (transforms into push with forearm)
         B) executed too tense (unable to achieve proper 'snap' of strike) (strike looks 'pushed' out)
         C) strike not tensed at Point of Contact (improper timing / never tensed)
      2) improper alignments / angles:
         A) incorrect extension:
            I) elbow over / under extended
            II) final height too high / low
         B) incorrect rotation:
            I) forearm rotated to make contact with muscle (not bone)

Comments

a) Common alignment errors:
   i) forearm not kept parallel to Point of Focus (over extended)

b) Common execution errors:
   i) forearm kept parallel to ground during entire execution
   ii) forearm executed too high (not at chin level)

Example of a proper upward forearm (right)

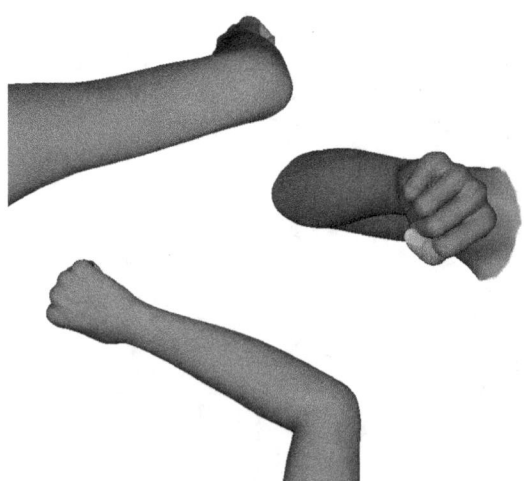

Example of proper upward forearm formation

Improving Your Execution of Long Form Two | 557

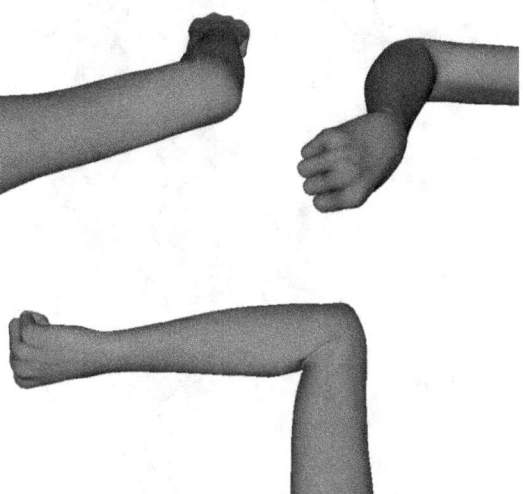

Example of improper upward forearm
forearm not rotated to expose bone,
wrist bent, elbow over bent

Examples of improper upward forearm
execution
improper height - high / low, width - wide /
narrow,
leaning, improper rotation - over / under

Vertical Two-Finger Poke

a) proper alignments:
- i) dimensions:
  - 1) height - eye level
  - 2) depth - elbow fully extended forward
  - 3) width - in-line with body
- ii) body alignments:
  - 1) hand:
    - A) rotated to be vertical
    - B) fingers pointed directly forward
  - 2) wrist kept straight (not bent up / down and / or side-to-side)
  - 3) shoulders - relaxed
  - 4) upper body / hips - Neutral / Forward Bow rotation
  - 5) legs / feet - Neutral / Forward Bow rotation
- iii) Point of Contact - tip of fingers of hand
- iv) stance - Neutral Bow

b) proper formation - weapon (hand):
- i) hand - kept flat (not cupped)
- ii) thumb:
  - 1) pressed tightly against rest of hand (Compact Unit)
  - 2) bent at top knuckle
  - 3) not tucked forward onto palm
- iii) fingers:
  - 1) first two fingers extended and relatively flat (muscle tension bend allowable on impact)
  - 2) second two fingers bent at first and second joints (from tip)

© 2015 EPAKS Publications

c) execution:
   i) Method of Execution - Thrusting
   ii) execute directly to target (prevent arching line of travel)
   iii) improper execution
      1) incorrect speeds / methods:
         A) executed too slow (transforms into push with fingers)
         B) executed too fast (stance rotation unable to keep up with strike)
         C) executed too tense (unable to achieve proper 'snap' of strike) (strike looks 'pushed' out)
         D) strike not tensed at Point of Contact (improper timing / never tensed)
      2) incorrect alignments / angles:
         A) incorrect elbow bend:
            I) over bent (not fully extended)
            II) too-extended (elbow hyper-extended)

Form Specific

a) Common execution errors:
   i) strike executed on arcing angle (not directly)
   ii) wrist over-bent to side to compensate for wrong height angle

Comments

a) Common formation errors:
   i) first two fingers not kept together (back-up mass)

Improving Your Execution of Long Form Two

Example of a proper vertical two-finger poke (left)
(with rear hand)

Example of a proper vertical two-finger poke (right)
(with front hand)

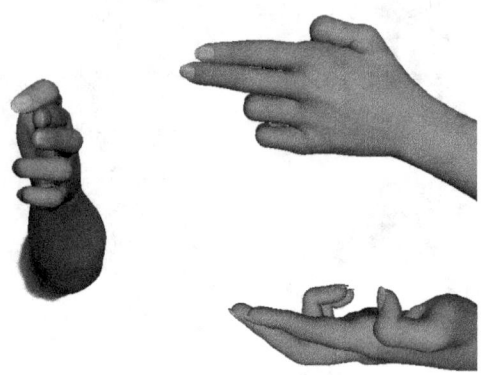

Example of proper vertical two-finger poke formation

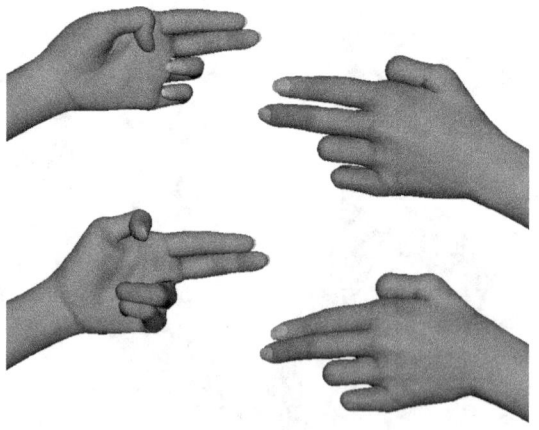

Example of improper vertical two-finger poke
formation / alignment
thumb tucked, fingers spread,
fingers bent improperly, wrist over bent
vertically

Improving Your Execution of Long Form Two

Examples of improper vertical two-finger poke
execution
(rear hand)
improper height - high, wide - too narrow / wide,
leaning, improper rotation - over rotated, foot not flat

Examples of improper vertical two-finger poke
execution
(front hand)
improper height - high / low, wide - too narrow / wide,
leaning, shrugged shoulders

Vertical Back-knuckle

a) proper alignments:
    i) dimensions:
        1) height - lower to mid face
        2) depth - elbow slightly bent at full extension
        3) width - directly ahead
    ii) body alignments:
        1) hand inverted (palm pointing diagonally upward)
        2) wrist kept straight (not bent up / down and / or side-to-side)
        3) elbow inline with hand (vertically)
        4) shoulders - relaxed
        5) upper body / hips - Neutral Bow rotation
        6) legs / feet - Neutral Bow rotation
    iii) Point of Contact - index / middle finger knuckles
    iv) stance - Neutral Bow

b) proper formation - weapon (hand):
    i) fingers - standard fist (tightly bent and kept together to form Compact Unit)
    ii) thumb:
        1) wrapped under bent fingers (Compact Unit)
        2) do not allow to separate from contact with fingers

c) execution:
    i) Method of Execution - Snapping
    ii) execute directly to target (prevent cocking / pumping)
    iii) improper execution:
        1) improper speeds / methods:
            A) executed too slow (transforms into upward push with knuckles)
            B) executed too tense (unable to achieve proper 'snap' of strike) (strike looks 'pushed' upward)
            C) strike not tensed at Point of Contact (improper timing / never tensed)

Form Specific

a) Common execution errors:
    i) weapon cocked (pumped) before execution (not from Point of Origin)
    ii) weapon not fully extended or hyper-extended
    ii) leaning (typically forward) with execution (typically for extra reach)

Comments

a) Common errors:
    i) formation:
        1) over bending of wrist (forward)

    ii) alignment:
        1) not properly anchoring elbow

    iii) execution:
        1) executed with an arch at the end of travel (instead of linear - diagonally)

Improving Your Execution of Long Form Two

Example of a proper vertical back-knuckle (right)

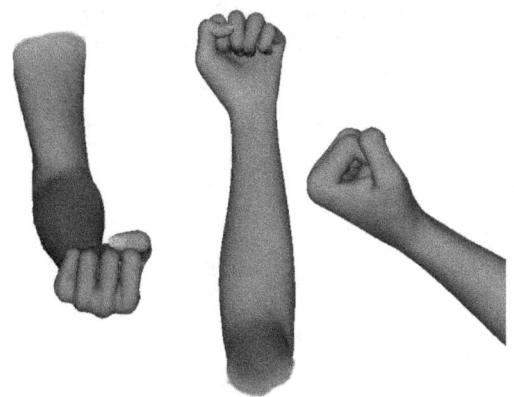

Example of proper vertical back-knuckle formation

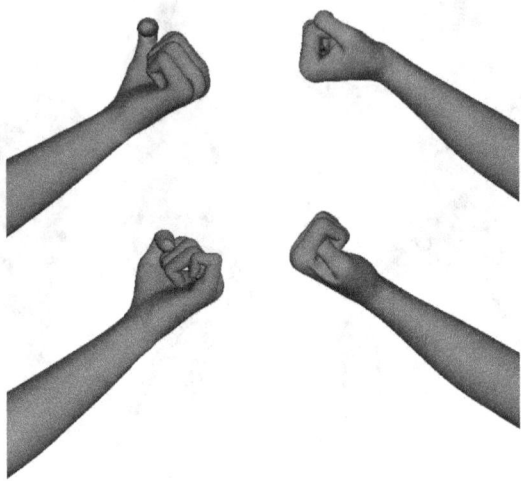

Examples of improper vertical back-knuckle
weapon formation / alignment
thumb hanging, wrist over bent,
pinky handing, thumb tucked

Improving Your Execution of Long Form Two 569

**Examples of improper vertical back-knuckle execution
improper height - low / high, width - narrow / wide,
leaning (weight distribution), not fully extended**

Outward Overhead Elbow

a) proper alignments:
    i) dimensions:
        1) height - face level
        2) depth - striking elbow extended to approximately 1/2 depth of Invisible Box
        3) width - directly ahead
    ii) body alignments:
        1) hand:
            A) directly above (diagonally) elbow
            B) standard fist formation
        2) elbow - bent (to form Compact Unit)
        3) shoulders - relaxed
        4) upper body / hips - Neutral Bow rotation
        5) legs / feet - Neutral Bow rotation
    iii) Point of Contact - tip of elbow
    iv) stance - Neutral Bow

b) proper formation - weapon (elbow):
    i) elbow - bent (tightly bent to form Compact Unit)

- c) execution:
    - i) Method of Execution - Hammering
    - ii) execute in overhead, downward arc to target
    - iii) improper execution:
        1) improper speeds / methods:
            - A) executed too slow (transforms into push with elbow)
            - B) executed too fast (stance rotation unable to keep up with strike)
            - C) executed too tense (unable to achieve proper 'snap' of strike) (strike looks 'pushed')
            - D) strike not tensed at Point of Contact (improper timing / never tensed)
        2) improper alignments / angles:
            - A) elbow under bent (no Compact Unit)
            - B) elbow too bent (improper alignments)
            - C) hand not directly in-line with elbow (diagonally above)

Form Specific

- a) Common execution errors:
    - i) arc of strike not directly vertical
        - A) should pass over top of head
        - B) should not pass in front of face / chest

Comments

- a) Common alignment errors:
    - i) leaning (to create more power)
    - ii) hand not vertically aligned with elbow (bad vertical alignment)

© 2015 EPAKS Publications

Example of a proper outward, overhead elbow (left)

Example of proper outward, overhead elbow formation

Improving Your Execution of Long Form Two

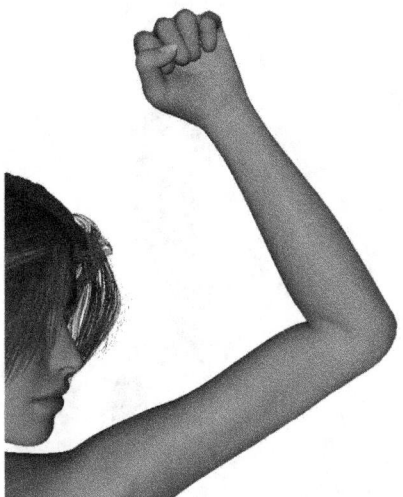

Example of improper outward, overhead elbow
formation / alignment
elbow not properly bent
(no Compact Unit)

Examples of improper outward, overhead
elbow execution
improper width - narrow / wide,
improper arc (not over head)
improper execution (outward), leaning

Inward Vertical Forearm

a) proper alignments:
    i) dimensions:
        1) height - fist at eye-brow level
        2) depth - striking arm extended to depth of Invisible Box
        3) width - striking arm extended to opposite shoulder
        4) execution angle - forward at 45 degrees
    ii) body alignments:
        1) hand:
            A) rotated to be diagonal forward
            B) directly vertical (in-line with elbow)
        2) wrist kept straight (not bent up / down and / or side-to-side)
        3) elbow directly below hand (vertically in-line)
        4) shoulders - relaxed
        5) upper body / hips - Neutral Bow rotation
        6) legs / feet - Neutral Bow rotation
    iii) Point of Contact - side of forearm
    iv) stance - Neutral Bow

b) proper formation:
    i) hand
        1) closed to standard fist
    ii) forearm
        1) kept vertical
        2) pointing forward at 45 degree angle
    iii) elbow:
        1) directly below hand and forearm vertically

c) execution:
    i) Method of Execution - Hammering
    ii) execute directly to target
    iii) improper execution:
        1) incorrect speeds / methods:
            A) executed too slow (transforms into push with forearm)
            B) executed too fast (stance rotation unable to keep up with strike)
            C) executed too tense (unable to achieve proper 'snap' of strike) (strike looks 'pushed' out)
            D) strike not tensed at Point of Contact (improper timing / never tensed)
        2) incorrect alignments / angles:
            A) elbow not properly anchored
            B) forearm not kept vertical
            C) not executed forward at 45 degree angle

Form Specific

a) Common execution errors:
    i) strike executed as thrust (not hammer) - due to cocking weapon too low

Improving Your Execution of Long Form Two

Example of a proper inward, vertical forearm strike (left)

Example of proper inward, vertical forearm formation

578 The Official EPAKS Guide to Long Form Two

Example of improper inward, vertical forearm
formation / alignment
not vertical, under / over rotated

Improving Your Execution of Long Form Two

Examples of improper inward, vertical forearm
execution
improper width - wide / narrow, height - high / low,
depth - close / far,
shrugged shoulders

© 2015 EPAKS Publications

Inward Overhead Elbow

a) proper alignments:
    i)   dimensions:
        1)   height - lower chest level
        2)   depth - striking elbow extended to approximately 1/2 depth of Invisible Box
        3)   width - directly ahead
    ii)   body alignments:
        1)   hand:
            A)   directly above (vertically) elbow
            B)   standard fist formation
        2)   elbow - bent (to form Compact Unit)
        3)   shoulders - relaxed
        4)   upper body / hips - Neutral Bow rotation
        5)   legs / feet - Neutral Bow rotation
    iii)   Point of Contact - tip of elbow
    iv)   stance - Neutral Bow

b) proper formation - weapon (elbow):
    i)   elbow - bent (tightly bent to form Compact Unit)

Improving Your Execution of Long Form Two 581

c) execution:
    i) Method of Execution - Hammering
    ii) execute directly downward (linear) to target
    iii) improper execution:
        1) improper speeds / methods:
            A) executed too slow (transforms into push with elbow)
            B) executed too fast (stance rotation unable to keep up with strike)
            C) executed too tense (unable to achieve proper 'snap' of strike) (strike looks 'pushed')
            D) strike not tensed at Point of Contact (improper timing / never tensed)
        2) improper alignments / angles:
            A) elbow under bent (no Compact Unit)
            B) elbow too bent (improper alignments)
            C) hand not directly in-line with elbow (directly above)

Comments

a) Common alignment errors:
    i) leaning (to create more power)
    ii) hand not vertically aligned with elbow (bad vertical alignment)

582   The Official EPAKS Guide to Long Form Two

Example of a proper inward, overhead elbow (left)

Example of proper inward, overhead elbow formation

Improving Your Execution of Long Form Two

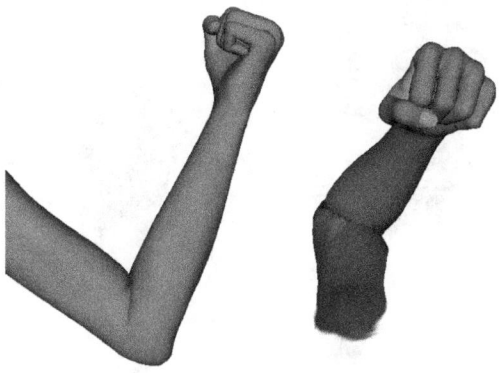

Example of improper inward, overhead elbow
formation / alignment
elbow not properly bent (no Compact Unit),
improper hand / elbow alignment (vertically)

Examples of improper inward, overhead
elbow execution
improper height - high / low,
width - wide / narrow,
shrugged shoulders, leaning

Inward Horizontal Elbow

a) proper alignments:
    i) dimensions:
        1) height - jaw level
        2) depth - striking elbow extended to approximately 1/4 depth of Invisible Box
        3) width - directly ahead
    ii) body alignments:
        1) hand:
            A) slightly lower (vertically) than elbow
            B) standard fist formation (horizontal rotation)
        2) elbow - bent (to form Compact Unit)
        3) shoulders - relaxed
        4) upper body / hips - Horse rotation
        5) legs / feet - Horse rotation
    iii) Point of Contact - tip of elbow
    iv) stance - Horse

b) proper formation - weapon (elbow):
    i) elbow - bent (tightly bent to form Compact Unit)

c) execution:
  i) Method of Execution - Thrusting
  ii) execute directly forward to target
  iii) improper execution:
    1) improper speeds / methods:
      A) executed too slow (transforms into push with elbow)
      B) executed too fast (stance rotation unable to keep up with strike)
      C) executed too tense (unable to achieve proper 'snap' of strike) (strike looks 'pushed')
      D) strike not tensed at Point of Contact (improper timing / never tensed)
    2) improper alignments / angles:
      A) elbow under bent (no Compact Unit)
      B) elbow too bent (improper alignments)

Form Specific

a) Common execution errors:
  i) strike not completed with stance settle (improperly timed)

Comments

a) Common alignment errors:
  i) elbow over bent
  ii) elbow not bent enough (no Compact Unit)
b) Common execution errors:
  i) strike not executed to front (instead toward side)

Improving Your Execution of Long Form Two

Example of a proper inward, horizontal elbow (right)

Example of proper inward, horizontal elbow formation

Example of improper inward, horizontal elbow
formation / alignment
elbow not properly bent (no Compact Unit),
eblow over bent (bad alignment)

Improving Your Execution of Long Form Two

Examples of improper inward, horizontal
elbow execution
improper height - high / low, leaning
improper hand alignment,
improper direction

Outward Horizontal Elbow

a) proper alignments:
    i) dimensions:
        1) height - jaw level
        2) depth - striking elbow extended directly to side
        3) width - directly to side
    ii) body alignments:
        1) hand:
            A) in-line (vertically) with elbow
            B) standard fist formation (horizontal rotation)
        2) elbow - bent (to form Compact Unit)
        3) shoulders - relaxed
        4) upper body / hips - Horse rotation
        5) legs / feet - Horse rotation
    iii) Point of Contact - tip of elbow
    iv) stance - Horse

b) proper formation - weapon (elbow):
    i) elbow - bent (to form Compact Unit)

c) execution:
   i) Method of Execution - Thrusting
   ii) execute directly to side
   iii) improper execution:
      1) improper speeds / methods:
         A) executed too slow (transforms into push with elbow)
         B) executed too fast (stance rotation unable to keep up with strike)
         C) executed too tense (unable to achieve proper 'snap' of strike) (strike looks 'pushed')
         D) strike not tensed at Point of Contact (improper timing / never tensed)
      2) improper alignments / angles:
         A) elbow under bent (no Compact Unit)
         B) hand too far below elbow (improper alignments)

Comments

a) Common alignment errors:
   i) elbow not bent enough (no Compact Unit)
b) Common execution errors:
   i) strike not executed to side (instead diagonally forward)

Example of a proper outward, elbow (double)

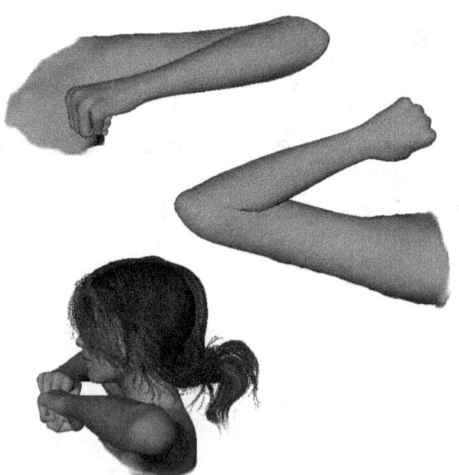

Example of proper outward elbow formation

Improving Your Execution of Long Form Two

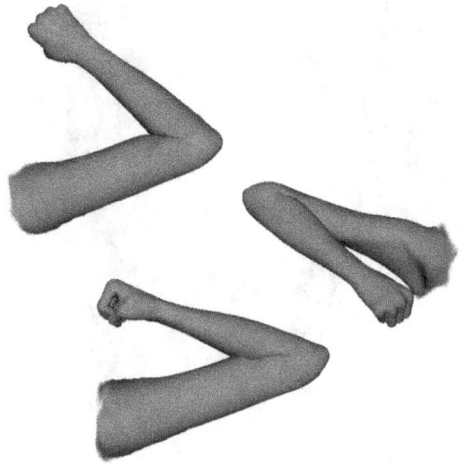

Example of improper upward elbow formation / alignment
elbow not properly bent (no Compact Unit),
hand not in-line with elbow (too low),
hand not rotated properly

594 The Official EPAKS Guide to Long Form Two

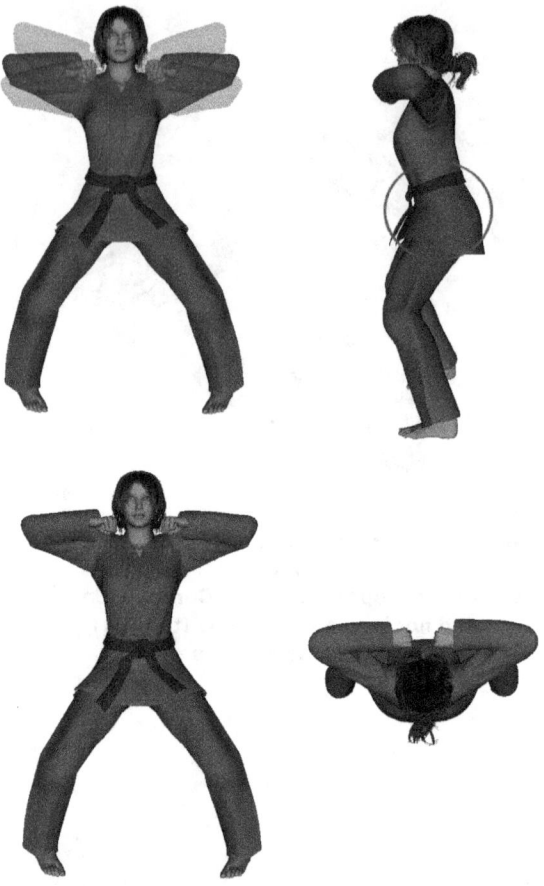

Examples of improper outward elbow execution
improper height - high / low, leaning
shoulders shrugged,
improper direction (not extended to sides)

Improving Your Execution of Long Form Two

Upward Elbow

a) proper alignments:
    i)   dimensions:
        1)   height - face level
        2)   depth - elbow extended directly forward
        3)   width - directly ahead
    ii)   body alignments:
        1)   hand:
            A)   directly in-line (vertically) with elbow
            B)   standard fist formation (vertical rotation)
        2)   elbow - bent (to form Compact Unit)
        3)   shoulders - relaxed
        4)   upper body / hips - Horse rotation
        5)   legs / feet - Horse rotation
    iii)   Point of Contact - tip of elbow
    iv)   stance - Horse

b) proper formation - weapon (elbow):
    i)   elbow - bent (to form Compact Unit)

- c) execution:
    - i) Method of Execution - Thrusting
    - ii) execute directly upward to target
    - iii) improper execution:
        1) improper speeds / methods:
            - A) executed too slow (transforms into push with elbow)
            - B) executed too fast (stance rotation unable to keep up with strike)
            - C) executed too tense (unable to achieve proper 'snap' of strike) (strike looks 'pushed')
            - D) strike not tensed at Point of Contact (improper timing / never tensed)
        2) improper alignments / angles:
            - A) elbow under bent (no Compact Unit)
            - B) hand not directly in-line with elbow (too high / low)

Comments

- a) Common alignment errors:
    - i) leaning (to create more power)
    - ii) hand not vertically aligned with elbow (bad vertical alignment)
    - iii) hand not rotated vertically (like vertical punch)
    - iv) elbow not aligned to center of body (bad width)

Improving Your Execution of Long Form Two | 597

Example of a proper upward elbow (left)

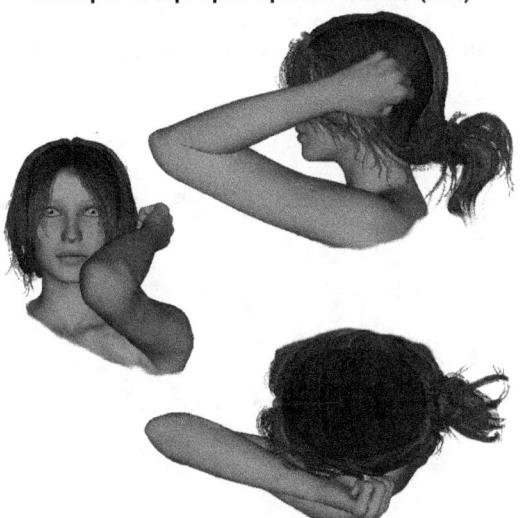

Example of proper upward elbow formation

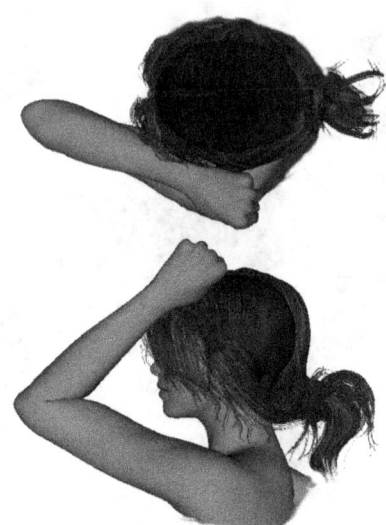

Example of improper upward elbow formation
improper fist rotation,
elbow not properly bent (no Compact Unit)

Improving Your Execution of Long Form Two   599

Examples of improper upward elbow execution
improper width - wide / narrow,
height - high / low,
shrugged shoulders, leaning

Back Elbow

a) proper alignments:
    i)   dimensions:
        1)   height - kidney level
        2)   depth - elbow extended directly backward
        3)   width - directly behind
    ii)   body alignments:
        1)   hand:
            A)   directly in-line (horizontally) with elbow
            B)   standard fist formation (chamber rotation)
        2)   elbow - bent (to form Compact Unit)
        3)   shoulders - relaxed
        4)   upper body / hips - Horse rotation
        5)   legs / feet - Horse rotation
    iii)   Point of Contact - tip of elbow
    iv)   stance - Horse

b) proper formation - weapon (elbow):
    i)   elbow - bent (to form Compact Unit)

Improving Your Execution of Long Form Two

c) execution:
    i) Method of Execution - Hammering
    ii) execute directly backward to target
    iii) improper execution:
        1) improper speeds / methods:
            A) executed too slow (transforms into push with elbow)
            B) executed too fast (stance rotation unable to keep up with strike)
            C) executed too tense (unable to achieve proper 'snap' of strike) (strike looks 'pushed')
            D) strike not tensed at Point of Contact (improper timing / never tensed)
        2) improper alignments / angles:
            A) elbow under bent (no Compact Unit)
            B) hand not directly in-line with elbow (too high / low)
            C) shoulder shrugged

Comments

a) Common alignment errors:
    i) leaning (to create more power)
    ii) hand not vertically aligned with elbow (bad vertical alignment)
    iii) hand not rotated vertically (like chambered position)

b) Common execution errors:
    i) not fully extended

Example of a proper backward elbow (right)

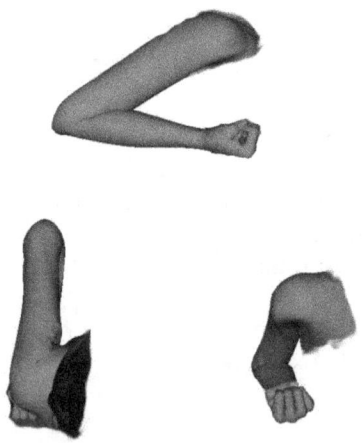

Example of proper backward elbow formation

Improving Your Execution of Long Form Two

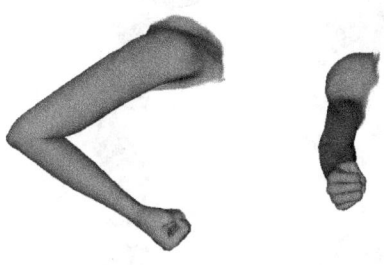

Example of improper backward elbow formation
elbow not properly bent (no Compact Unit), improper hand rotation

Examples of improper backward elbow
execution
improper width - wide / narrow,
height - high / low,
shrugged shoulders,
not fully extended

Improving Your Execution of Long Form Two | 605

Improvement Priorities

The following chart is designed to help the practitioner correct some of the errors illustrated in this section. It provides the practitioner with a chart that maps the commonality of errors against the severity of errors.

To start fixing errors in Long Form Two, start with the errors in the upper right hand corner and work downward and to the left of the graph. This will ensure the most sever errors and common errors are fixed first.

```
                                    Improper Block - Dimensions
                                    Improper Stance - Dimensions
  ^                  Improper Weapon Formation
  ^
  |                               Improper Strike - Dimensions
More Severe                       Improper Kick - Dimensions
  |     Improper Cover Step       Improper Execution Paths
  |     Improper Step into Horse
  |                  Improper Strike / Body Alignment

  |                       Over / Under Rotation Executing Blocks / Strikes
  -                           Improper Stance - Weight Distribution
  |                                          Leaning in Stance

  |                                  Improper Stance - Foot Directionality
Less Severe    Improper Cocking of Weapon
  |            Improper Step Thru - Height
  |                              Improper Stance Direction
  v            Improper Method of Execution
  v
                       Improper Double Factor Blocking

               Improper Breathing
                                              Improper Gaze Direction
```

<< Less Common   -   More Common >>

© 2015 EPAKS Publications

Chapter 11 - Frequently Asked Questions

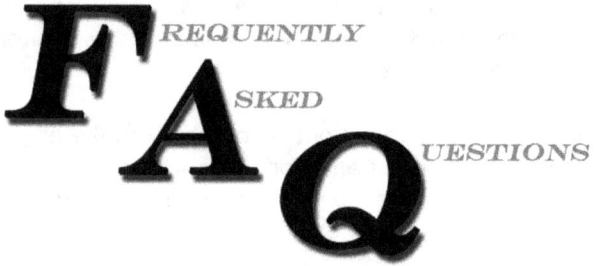

This section highlights information presented in other sections of this guide, but presents it in a question and answer format. One of the things the Q&A format allows for is presenting information from a different perspective. This perspective change can sometimes allow the reader to more quickly and firmly grasp the presented information. It also can combine information across multiple areas of the guide together. Thus, allowing the reader to understand connections that are not as obvious as in other formats.

Why is this form call Long Form Two?

First, because it is the second long form of the American Kenpo system. Short Form One is the first form of the system, but is also the first SHORT form of the system. Long Form Two is basically the extension to Short Form Two, and thus shares it's numerical designation.

Second, because of it's timing. The "one's" demonstrate one-in-one timing, whereas the "two's" demonstrate two-in-one timing - meaning there are two upper body actions for every single lower body action.

Third, because it is a long form. In simple terms Long Form Two builds upon Short Form Two. By this one can deduce that Long Form Two includes the basic information presented in Short Form Two and more. For a more comprehensive explanation of this see the "Understanding Long Form Two" section of this book.

What is the timing of Long Form Two?

The timing of Long Form Two is called two-in-one timing or sometimes referred to as double beat timing. What that means is that for every foot / body maneuver there are two defense / offensive maneuvers. Both Long Form Two and Short Form Two share this timing. Other forms do not necessarily share this timing sequence. For instance, the One's have a one-in-one timing sequence.

Why are the "two's" called the reverses of the "one's"?

One primary reason is due to the fact that the "two's" advance, while the "one's" retreat. And, as such, the "two's" move in the reverse direction of the "one's".

There is only one exception to the "rule" that the "one's" retreat, and it is the first downward block of Long Form One. There are a few reasons why Long Form One advances at this point in the form. For further information as is relates to this subject, refer to The Official EPAKS Guide to Long Form One: the Analysis of Long Form One section and the Frequently Asked Questions section.

© 2015 EPAKS Publications

What's the difference between isolating power principles and an isolation?

Isolation moves are another form of call-out or highlighted maneuvers. They are designed to visually and physically isolate specific maneuvers such that they stand out in a form. The purpose of this is to draw attention to the maneuvers, so that the initiated practitioner is subtly directed to analyze these maneuvers further for the purpose of exposing their true meaning in the form.

An isolation maneuver shows one or more of the following:
    i) previews of things to come
    ii) new information
    iii) missing information

On the other hand, Isolating Power Principles is a specialized way of maneuvering such that a specific Power Principle is highlighted. The purpose of this is to draw attention to the isolated Power Principle for further analysis. These type of maneuvers are not tied to the three (3) purposes with which an isolation is limited.

Although both terms are similar in definition, they are very different in purpose and practice. This can be quickly shown by comparing the isolation of Long Form One with maneuvers isolating the Power Principles in Short / Long Form Two.

© 2015 EPAKS Publications

What is the purpose of the "cup and saucer" position in Long Form Two?

The "cup and saucer" position can be thought of as a "chambered" position, but for both arms. It is a formalized way of cocking both arms to one side of the body in preparation for a future maneuver - to the opposite side of the body. Just like the "chambered" position, the "cup and saucer" position is not practical for defensive purposes, but is used more for placing the arms into a common, cocked position. And, is just a two handed variation of the "chambered" position.

What is the difference between an opposite and a reverse?

For a quick explanation; all reverses are opposites, but not all opposites are reverses. Opposites tend to be conceptual, reverses tend to be physical. For a more in-depth analysis of these terms, see The Official EPAKS Guide to Long Form One - Appendix 3.

Why should I do an instep kick instead of a crossover in this form?

The instep kick is needed because it is an integral part of a number of major categories demonstrated in the form. Replacing the kick with a crossover will detract from information presented in these categories.

For more information on this subject, see the "Variations to Long Form Two" and "Analysis of Long Form Two" sections of this book.

Should I check with my alternate hand throughout the execution of the form?

Even though Short Form Two introduced checking with the alternate hand, Long Form Two still falls into the 'dictionary' forms (i.e. the lower forms), therefore the unused hand is often drawn back into a chambered position. This does not mean that the alternate hand can't be positioned as a check, just that it is not part of the standard execution of the form.

To get a more in-depth answer to this question see the "Variations to Long Form Two / Form Execution - Variations."

© 2015 EPAKS Publications

Why are there universal blocks in this form?

One answer has to do with the logical progression of maneuvers and where they are demonstrated in the forms. In Short Form One, only blocking with the front arm was introduced. In Long Form One, blocking with the rear hand was introduced along with striking with the rear hand. In Short Form two, striking with the front hand was introduced along with blocking and striking at the same time. In Long Form Two, striking and striking at the same time and blocking and blocking (i.e. Universal blocks) at the same time is introduced.

Note: One should learn of this progression to determine if it is expanded upon in future forms.

Why are there no kicks in the forms until Long Form Two?

The answer has to do with the logical progression of maneuvers and where they are demonstrated in the forms. In Short Form One, only defense with the upper body was introduced. In Long Form One, striking with the upper body was introduced. In Short Form two, blocking and striking simultaneously with the upper body was introduced. In Long Form Two, striking with the lower body is introduced.

Note: One should learn of this progression to determine if it is expanded upon in future forms.

Why are some vertical punches in Long Form Two to the middle height zone when it is a high height zone punch?

All basics have at least one height / depth / width zone in which they can be used effectively, but some basics can be used in many different zones and situations. For instance, the straight punch is most often used to the middle height zone and is not effective at the high height zone without modification. The vertical punch, on the other hand, can be used just as effectively at both the high and middle height zones. Long Form Two demonstrates this fact.

We do Long Form Two differently - is that OK?

The quick answer is that one should always execute a form as their instructor wishes it to be done.

The long answer is that this book attempts to set a standard of execution that was laid out by SGM Parker in the system he founded (i.e. created), known as American Kenpo. One of the goals of the system is to build a comprehensive logical knowledge base of human movement as it relates to the martial arts. In order to do this, SGM Parker created the forms of the system with one of the fundamental goals being the fulfillment of the saying: everything has an opposite and a reverse. One purpose of this book series is an attempt to give an understanding to how that goal was accomplished. Also, it is one primary reason why every move in the standard execution of the form is detailed as to how it helps accomplish this goal and what variations do to detract from that goal. This does not mean that one cannot do the form however they wish - they can and do. It means only that there was a purpose and a design to the forms and that the forms are not just a random collection of basics put together in a haphazard manner.

It should be noted that every effort has been made to detail not only the what and why of the form design, but also the original intent of the design. This was done not only through SGM Parker himself, but also through input from a large number of his first generation students.

Given the above rationale, there are still a number of reasons why there are varying ways to execute this form - see the "Execution of Long Form Two" and "Variations to Long Form Two" sections for more information.

Why are there a lot of downward type blocks in Long Form Two?

This has to do with the quantity of block types that can be demonstrated with the upper body. If the in / out / up / down sequence is examined, there are:
    1 - inward block types (with 1 purposefully omitted)
    2 - outward block types
    1 - upward block types (with 1 purposefully omitted)
    3 - downward block types (with 1 purposefully omitted)

Also, to include the push-down blocks (with 1 purposefully omitted) adds another type of downward block, to arrive at 4 in total.

From this analysis one can quickly see that there are more effective downward block types than any other block - double the next closest type. Because of this and because one of the purposes of the forms is to complete as many categories as possible through demonstration, it is only logical that there are more downward blocks than any other type.

Note: The above analysis is limited to only the major blocks. In other words, parries and smothering blocks of all types are purposefully omitted.

Why are there three outward, overhead elbows but only two inward, overhead elbows in Long Form Two?

This has to do with the fact that most American Kenpo forms make an attempt to start and complete in the same general position. Because of this when the inside, downward, palm-down blocks are completed, the practitioner is placed one complete stance depth behind the position were the form started. In order to get both sides of both the outward, overhead elbows and the inward, overhead elbows (left and right) while also returning to the original starting position of the form, three repetitions of the first and two of the second are needed.

Why do we step away on the first downward block of Long Form Two?

There is a distinctive thread that is created by the first downward block of the first four forms (Short / Long One through Short / Long Two). In order to complete this thread the first downward block must be executed in this manner.

For more information on this subject, see the "Analysis of Long Form Two" section of this book.

© 2015 EPAKS Publications

How does leaning effect me?

Leaning can be done in a number of ways. First, one can just lean while settled in a stance (leaning); or, one can lean while maneuvering between stances (jet lagging). Either way, the back is not kept perpendicular to the ground.

In the case of a settled stance, leaning can decrease both the stability of a stance and decrease maneuverability of the stance. A straight back places the weight and position of the body in the center of the stance, i.e. the Intersection Position. From the Intersection Position it is more efficient to go in any possible direction. Also, when leaning it is easier for the attacker to make the defender go in one direction over another, because the defender's body is already positioned favoring a direction, which can be exploited.

In the case of maneuvering between stances, leaning creates precession. Precession is the wobble of a rotation that is not perfectly aligned vertically with its axis. For example the earth has a precession in its rotation. A precession, in this case, creates inefficiencies in rotation, breaking the principle of Economy of Motion. Also, leaning can create Jet Lagging. Jet Lagging is created by allowing the head and upper body to follow the lower body (instead of with the lower body) while stepping through in reverse. Since the purpose of stepping away is to create distance, letting the upper body lag behind the lower body exposes the face to the opponent for a longer period of time than necessary – creating a defensive problem, which can be exploited by the opponent.

Did SGM Parker create Long Form Two?

Yes. For further information about the history of Long Form Two read the "History of Long Form Two" section of this book.

What is meant by a 'dictionary' form?

Dictionary forms (i.e. Short Form One, Long Form One, Short Form Two, Long Form Two) concentrate more on 'defining' motion over theories and concepts. The 'encyclopedia' forms (i.e. the higher forms), rely more heavily on theories and concepts. While the 'appendix' forms (i.e. the sets) rely on concentrated information about a subject (i.e. kicking, blocking, finger strikes, etc.).

Why shouldn't we visualize an opponent while executing this form?

Visualizing an opponent is a good mental exercise for learning how to focus a maneuver to a specific point in space. By visualizing, one can pretend to be blocking an incoming attack, giving the blocks more urgency and focus. But, as in all American Kenpo forms, there is no intention for there to be an imaginary opponent. Rather, that the form demonstrates: the rules and principles of motion, that everything has a reverse and an opposite, and gives and example. Visualizing an opponent can detract from this goal and lead the practitioner into treating the form as a preordained imaginary fight, rather than a demonstration of motion study and analysis.

© 2015 EPAKS Publications

If I'm not visualizing an imaginary opponent, where and what should I look at when doing the form?

When executing Long Form Two, the practitioner should keep their gaze at eye level and parallel to the floor at all times.

| Quizzes | 627 |

Chapter 12 - Quizzes

This section contains quizzes that can be used to test one's understanding of Long Form Two. They are designed to be used by the reader themselves, or by an instructor to query a student's understanding of the information presented in the form. There are two groups of tests presented: 1) beginner to intermediate and 2) advanced. And, each group is broken down into two types of tests: 1) multiple choice and 2) fill in the blank.

The answers to each of the quizzes can be found in Appendix A at the back of this guide.

© 2015 EPAKS Publications

Multiple Choice - Beginner / Intermediate

1) The inward block and downward block sequences in Long Form Two are related because:
   a) both utilize open hand strikes
   b) both utilize gravitational marriage as their primary power principle
   c) both block and strike with the same hand
   d) both utilize kicks
   e) both use one in one timing

2) The outward and upward block sequences of Long Form Two are related because
   a) both are executed only on the horizontal plane
   b) both are executed only on the vertical plane
   c) both use the forward bow to extend the reach of the rear hand
   d) both use the horse stance to extend the reach of the front hand
   e) both deliver defensive and offensive moves simultaneously

3) A major purpose of the inward block sequence stance shifting in Long Form Two is
   a) for enhancing gravitational marriage
   b) for introducing the forward bow
   c) for extending rear hand reach
   d) all of the above
   e) none of these

4) Long Form Two starts exactly the same as
   a) Short Form One
   b) Long Form One
   c) Short Form Two
   d) all of the above
   e) none of these

5) The in/out/up/down sequences in Long Form Two extends
   a) Short Form One
   b) Long Form One
   c) Short Form Two
   d) all of the above
   e) none of these

6) The outward block sequence in Long Form Two introduces
   a) offensive moves
   b) two-in-one timing
   c) multiple simultaneous offensive moves
   d) the rear hand
   e) defensive moves

7) The upward block sequence in Long Form Two introduces
   a) two-in-one timing
   b) multiple defensive moves
   c) horizontal blocks
   d) the rear hand
   e) front hand offense

8) Long Form One and Long Form Two triple maneuvers differ, in that
   a) Long Form One are all front/rear/front - Long Form Two are all rear/front/rear
   b) Long Form One are all defensive - Long Form Two are all offensive
   c) Long Form One are all path of travel - Long Form Two are not
   d) all of the above
   e) none of these

9) The theme stance of Long Form Two is the
   a) neutral bow
   b) forward bow
   c) horse stance
   d) twist stance
   e) wide kneel

10) The isolation in Long Form Two
    a) previews Short Form Three
    b) is all doubles
    c) is all strikes
    d) all of the above
    e) none of these

11) Why would you spread your fingers on the first eye poke of Long Form Two
    a) more back up mass
    b) more margin for error
    c) better economy of motion
    d) all of the above
    e) none of these

12) The step-throughs and twist-throughs of Long Form Two differ by
    a) rotation
    b) timing
    c) distance
    d) all of the above
    e) none of these

13) A major theme introduced in Long Form Two is
    a) two-in-one timing
    b) open handed strikes
    c) punching
    d) checking
    e) kicking

14) Which strike is NOT introduced in Long Form Two
    a) outward back knuckle
    b) vertical back knuckle
    c) inverted vertical roundhouse
    d) uppercut
    e) vertical two-finger poke

15) Which foot maneuver is introduced in Long Form Two
   a) step through forward
   b) 90 degree cover
   c) 180 degree cover
   d) all of the above
   e) none of these

16) Which maneuver(s) of Long Form Two is/are cocked using body rotation
   a) both the step through forward and the rear cross over
   b) only the double outward elbows
   c) the vertical forearm strike and outward overhead elbow strike
   d) all of the above
   e) none of these

17) The rear hand strikes in Long Form Two shift to forward bows
   a) always
   b) never
   c) only from the horse stance
   d) only during step-through
   e) depends upon the sequence

18) The heel of the foot is the primary striking surface of which strike
   a) ball kick
   b) knife-edge kick
   c) instep (arch) kick
   d) all of the above
   e) none of these

19) The two-in-one timing on the last move of the downward block sequence in Long Form Two is formed by
   a) a punch and a kick
   b) a punch and a buckle
   c) a punch and a claw
   d) a punch and an elbow
   e) there is no two-in-one timing

© 2015 EPAKS Publications

20) The front kick in Long Form Two should be executed
    a) without stepping through
    b) without changing the height of the stance
    c) without changing the depth of the stance
    d) without changing the width of the stance
    e) without line of sight of the weapon

21) The instep (arch) kick in Long Form Two should be executed
    a) without changing the height of the stance
    b) without changing the width of the stance
    c) without cocking the weapon
    d) all of the above
    e) none of these

22) The "theme" timing in Long Form Two is:
    a) one-in-two
    b) one-in-one
    c) two-in-one
    d) two-in-two
    e) varies throughout the form

23) Which of these foot maneuvers is NOT in Long Form Two:
    a) step-through
    b) twist-through
    c) cover
    d) all of the above
    e) none of these

24) The strikes in Long Form Two most closely related to the heel-palm strike in Short Form Two are:
    a) straight punch, front kick, inward-overhead elbow
    b) side kick, outward hand-sword, outward back-knuckle
    c) straight punch, front kick, overhead claw
    d) straight four-finger thrust, vertical punch, overhead claw
    e) outward hand-sword, vertical punch, side kick

25) How do the straight punches of Long Form One and Long Form Two differ from all the back-knuckle strikes of Long Form Two:
   a) back hand strikes vs front hand strikes
   b) different Method of Execution
   c) circular motion vs linear motion
   d) all of the above
   e) none of these

Fill in the Blank - Beginner / Intermediate

1) The ___ block sequence on the plus(+) pattern of Long Form Two demonstrates offensive moves on all three height zones.

2) The ___ block sequence delivers offensive maneuvers only to the middle height zone.

3) Like Short Form Two, the upward block sequence in Long Form Two completes the ___ pattern.

4) The front kick strike of Long Form Two is the ___ zone version of the heel palm strike of Short Form Two.

5) The ___ block is demonstrated in Short Form Two but not Long Form Two.

6) The primary purpose of the forward bow with the forward underhand reverse hammer fist is to extend the ___ of the rear hand.

7) The outward block sequence of Long Form Two purposely eliminates ___ rotation.

8) The shifting of stances and strikes into an ever more complete circle is called degrees of ___.

9) The vertical equivalent to the heel palm of Short Form Two in Long Form Two is the ___.

10) The ___ block sequence demonstrates all the new close handed striking surfaces of Long Form Two.

11) The blocks and forearm strikes in Long Form Two are executed on a ___ of travel.

12) The open handed striking surface category of Short Form Two is extended by the ____ and ____ strikes of Long Form Two.

13) The concept of ____ is the primary reason for the difference between the blocks and forearm strikes of Long Form Two.

14) The ____ line of the 'x' pattern in Long Form Two is emphasized.
(Hint: use the clock principle)

15) The ____ strikes of Long Form Two are all near the end of the form.

16) The last maneuver in the inward block sequence of Long Form Two demonstrates power generation in the ____ direction of the same sequence in Long Form One.

17) Long Form Two is the last of the _____ forms.

18) In Long Form Two, the first major deviation of the in/out/up/down pattern occurs prior to the execution of the first ____ block.

19) The isolation of Long Form Two shows the doubles of the ____ strike in Long Form One.

20) The step into the isolation in Long Form One demonstrates the ____ direction of the step into the isolation of Long Form Two.

21) The ____ strike in Long Form Two uses the same point of contact as the strike of the same name in Short Form Two, but with a different degree of opening.

22) The ____ strike in Long Form Two uses the top of the knuckles of the fist as it's point of contact.

23) The offensive moves of Long Form One are expanded upon by being executed on the ___ pattern in Long Form Two.

24) The primary purpose of the training horse stances of Long Form One and Long Form Two is to execute the ___ sequences.

25) The finger poke and punch strikes of Long Form Two are executed on a ___ of travel.

Multiple Choice - Advanced

1) Why are there so many front hand strikes in Long Form Two?
   a) to show the opposite front hand maneuvers in Short Form One
   b) to show the opposite rear hand maneuvers of Long Form One
   c) to expand upon the front hand maneuvers of Short Form Two
   d) all of the above
   e) none of these

2) A major foot/hand strike category is completed in Long Form Two by
   a) the outward/downward/half-knuckle sequences
   b) the inward/upward/push-down sequences
   c) the inside-downward palm up/down/push-down sequences
   d) the outward/downward/isolation sequences
   e) none of these

3) Which striking sequence demonstrates sophisticated motion
   a) inward block/hand-sword
   b) claw/back-knuckle
   c) upper-cut/forearm
   d) all of the above
   e) none of these

4) The first and last eye poke sequences of Long Form Two are related by
   a) both have the primary power principle of back up mass
   b) they are matched as a vertical/horizontal pair
   c) they introduce a new striking surface
   d) all of the above
   e) none of these

© 2015 EPAKS Publications

5) Why is there no checking hand in the first maneuver of Long Form Two?
   a) to match Short Form Two
   b) to create line of sight for rear hand
   c) to facilitate economy of motion
   d) to create realistic positioning in the maneuver
   e) to create full path for travel for the rear hand strike

6) The first downward block in Long Form Two completes a major category with the first downward block of
   a) Short Form One
   b) Long Form One
   c) Short Form Two
   d) all of the above
   e) none of these

7) The hidden stomp after the front kick in Long Form Two shows
   a) the opposite to the hidden stomp in Long Form One
   b) settling
   c) weight transfer
   d) body harmony
   e) there is no stomp

8) The reverse path of the first downward block/punch maneuver in Long Form Two is
   a) the inward block/hand-sword
   b) the outward block/punch
   c) the inside downward palm down/punch
   d) the inside downward palm up/punch
   e) the push down/elbow

9) The reverse of the push down/outward overhead elbow maneuver in Long Form Two is
   a) the double outward elbows in the Long Form Two isolation
   b) the outward elbow in Long Form One
   c) the up/back elbow in the Long Form Two isolation
   d) all of the above
   e) none of these

10) The punch/inside vertical forearm sequence of Long Form Two is reversed by
    a) the inward block/punch sequence in Long Form One
    b) the outward block/punch sequence in Short Form Two
    c) the uppercut/forearm strike in Long Form Two
    d) the downward block/inverted vertical roundhouse in Long Form Two
    e) the outward block/punch in Long Form One

11) What is one of the purposes of the universal block in Long Form Two?
    a) simultaneous defense and offense
    b) double defensive moves
    c) one-in-one timing
    d) enhancing back-up mass
    e) to reverse the cup and saucer position

12) The defense/offense category continued in Long Form Two is
    a) the block/strike/step/kick category
    b) the front hand/rear hand/opposite hand/double hands category
    c) the block/strike/double block/double strike category
    d) all of the above
    e) none of these

13) The side kick of Long Form Two should be executed
    a) with minimal weight transfer
    b) with full weight transfer
    c) with rotation of the hip
    d) to the middle height zone
    e) as high as possible

14) One of the main reasons to change coordination between moves is
    a) to show the opposite of the moves
    b) to show the reverse of the moves
    c) to change the emphasis of the moves
    d) to alter the moves
    e) to change the sequence of the moves

15) Long Form Two introduces:
    a) striking with the elbow
    b) the minor angles of the clock
    c) realistic positioning
    d) all of the above
    e) none of these

16) The elbows of Long Form Two expand upon the elbow of Long Form One by
    a) being executed to new planes
    b) being executed simultaneously
    c) using circular motion
    d) all of the above
    e) none of these

17) The elbows in the isolation of Long Form Two are related to the punches in the isolation in Long Form One in that
    a) they show the reverse line
    b) they show the opposite line
    c) they show the same line
    d) all of the above
    e) none of these

18) Why is the twist stance the 'theme' stance of Long Form Two
    a) because it is obtained so many ways and times in the form
    b) because it is a sophisticated basic
    c) because it is only used as transitory stance
    d) because it is the only stance that utilizes all of the power principles
    e) because it is not used in any other forms up to Long Form Two

19) The straight punches to the 4:30 / 7:30 lines of Long Form Two
    a) provide no new information
    b) introduce striking to the 'x' pattern
    c) introduce a new method of execution
    d) fill in the bottom half of the 'x' pattern started in Long Form One
    e) fill in the rear hand punch category

20) The first two hand-swords of Long Form Two
    a) provide no new information
    b) introduce the reverse line to the same strikes in Short Form Two
    c) introduce striking to the diagonal plane
    d) fill in the open handed strike category
    e) fill in the missing method of execution

21) Contouring is demonstrated in Long Form Two with the
    a) straight punches
    b) side kicks
    c) inward and outward overhead elbows
    d) isolation
    e) buckles

22) The weapon introduced in Short Form Two, but demonstrated with a different weapon formation in Long Form Two is:
    a) round-house punch
    b) half-knuckle
    c) heel-palm
    d) back-knuckle
    e) four-finger poke

23) The triple vertical outward blocks of Long Form One are related to the triple vertical two-finger pokes of Long Form Two by being
    a) opposites - linear / circular
    b) opposites - front / rear - rear / front
    c) opposites - defense / offense
    d) all of the above
    e) none of these

24) The isolation of Long Form Two adds the following information to the isolation of Long Form One:
    a) new angles and new directions
    b) new contact points and new weapons
    c) new timing and new ranges
    d) all of the above
    e) none of these

25) The inside, downward palm down, palm up, and push-down sequence of Long Form One is changed in Long Form Two:
    a) to demonstrate Opposing Forces
    b) to demonstrate Point of Reference
    c) to demonstrate the blocks while moving
    d) to demonstrate Offensive Defense
    e) to demonstrate Point of Origin

Fill in the Blank - Advanced

1) All the mid height, vertical, front hand ___ in Long Form Two can be related by their variation in foot maneuvers.

2) The reverse line of the first offensive maneuver in the outward block sequence is demonstrated in the ___.

3) The strikes of Long Form Two demonstrate ___ degrees of rotation.

4) The reverse rotation of the step to the first downward block in Long Form Two is demonstrated by the first downward block in ___.

5) The ___ directions (i.e. paths) of the Short Form Two middle-knuckle and Long Form Two hammer-fist form an almost complete circle, vertically.

6) The triple maneuvers of both Long Form One and Long Form Two add usage of the ___ end of the body in relation to previous maneuvers of the forms.

7) One characteristic of Long Form Two is its increased complexity of ___ maneuvers.

8) The major power principle of the push down in Long Form Two is ___.

9) The rotating twist stances of Long Form Two ___ the outward overhead elbow strikes.

10) The ___ of Long Form Two should be delivered as compact units.

11) The block/___ pattern started in Long Form One and expanded in Short Form Two, is further extended in Long Form Two.

12) The downward block sequence of Long Form Two _____ the sequence of the downward block sequence in Short / Long Form One.

13) The upward blocks in all the forms up to and including Long Form Two use _____ torque.

14) In order to change the perceived emphasis of a maneuver, one must change it's ___ with other maneuvers.

15) One major difference between the foot maneuvers in all the forms prior to Long Form Two and Long Form Two is ___.

16) The ___ strikes of Long Form Two do NOT rely upon depth penetration to be effective

17) A ___ basic is one that has a single movement but multiple effects.

18) ___ing the vertical back-knuckle punch in Long Form Two causes the Economy of Motion principle to be broken.

19) Threading is demonstrated with the ___ strikes of Long Form Two.

20) The term ___ is defined by a specific geometric figure missing a side.
Hint: multiple words

21) The foot maneuvers of Long Form Two emphasis the ___ angles of the Eight Major Angles of Attack, Defense, and Balance.

22) ___ vs ___ motion is an important theme of Long Form Two

23) The ___ strike of Long Form Two uses the same striking surface as the hand-sword strike in Short Form Two, but with a different weapon formation .

24) The ___ sequence of Long Form Two switches directions without stepping.

25) The ___ sequence of Long Form Two demonstrates multiple opposing offensive maneuvers simultaneously.

Appendix A - Quiz Answers

These are the answers to the quizzes presented earlier in the guide. The answer section order matches the quiz section order presented earlier.

Multiple Choice Answers - Beginner / Intermediate

1) c
2) e
3) c
4) e
5) d
6) c
7) b
8) d
9) d
10) d
11) b
12) b
13) e
14) d
15) e
16) c
17) e
18) e
19) b
20) b
21) d
22) c
23) e
24) c
25) c

Fill in the Blank Answers - Beginner / Intermediate

1) outward
2) inside downward palm up
3) plus or major angle
4) low
5) extended outward
6) reach
7) body
8) rotation
9) push-down
10) upward
11) path
12) poke, claw
13) intent
14) 1:30-7:30
15) elbow
16) reverse
17) dictionary
18) upward
19) elbow
20) opposite (reverse acceptable)
21) half-fist
22) back-knuckle
23) x (minor angle acceptable)
24) isolation
25) line

Multiple Choice Answers - Advanced

1) d
2) a
3) c
4) d
5) e
6) d
7) e
8) c
9) e
10) a
11) b
12) b
13) a
14) c
15) e
16) d
17) d
18) a
19) d
20) a
21) e
22) b
23) d
24) d
25) e

Fill in the Blank Answers - Advanced

1) strikes
2) isolation
3) 270
4) Long Form One
5) reverse
6) opposite
7) foot (basic is also acceptable)
8) gravitational marriage
9) cock (align, position also acceptable)
10) elbows
11) strike
12) reverses
13) isolated
14) coordination
15) timing
16) claw
17) sophisticated
18) pump (cock is also acceptable)
19) vertical two-finger poke
20) open ended triangle
21) minor
22) circular / linear
23) hammer-fist
24) half-knuckle / instep (arch) kick
25) isolation

Appendix B - The Kenpo Kards

The Kenpo Kards is a project by EPAKS that presents all of the American Kenpo self-defense techniques, forms, and sets to a quick reference card which can be used for research, study and entertainment. The Kenpo Kards were released in three (3) decks - beginner, intermediate, and advanced. Along with the Kards, EPAKS produced a guidebook to help in the usage of both the Kards and understanding of some of the foundational layout of American Kenpo.

Along with the physical version of the Kards and guidebook, EPAKS has released a digital version of each. The Kenpo Kards app is available on both the Google Play store and the Amazon App store. The digital guidebook is available on the Google Play store, the Amazon digital book store, and the Barnes and Noble digital book store.

© 2015 EPAKS Publications

| 652 | The Official EPAKS Guide to Long Form Two |

The Kenpo Kard app allows the user to quickly sort and/or choose Kards to study, and allows for the user to play back the list for practicing alone or with up to five (5) partners. The app has options to select the speed to play the list, choose which yellow belt techniques to use in the sorting (old / new / both), and select the highest technique one has learned. This app is invaluable in helping to understand relations between techniques as well as to quickly group techniques by similarities - such as same attack, same side forward, same web of knowledge grouping, just to name a few.

One of the most important things the reader should understand is it is not the intent of the Kenpo Kards project to teach the practitioner how to do American Kenpo. Rather, it is to help the practitioner to explore and understand the information contained in the parts of the system they have learned from their instructor.

The Front of the Kard

The Official EPAKS Guide to Long Form Two

The first thing one will notice about the front of the Kard is the signification of Long Form Two. It is the most prominent image on the Kard. This layout is part of a theme that is shared among all of the Kards in the form Dek. As the forms increase in complexity, the signification becomes less prominent while at the same time the figures on the Kard become more prominent.

The next thing one should notice is that the figure on the Kard is executing a prominent move of Long Form Two. This is part of another theme that is shared among all the Kards in the forms Dek. The figure and any other images (aside from the signification) will highlight the some of the most important pieces of information and/or physical attributes of the form being illustrated. It is the intent that a person familiar with the form should be able to quickly ascertain which form is being illustrated without having to read the text.

The Back of the Kard

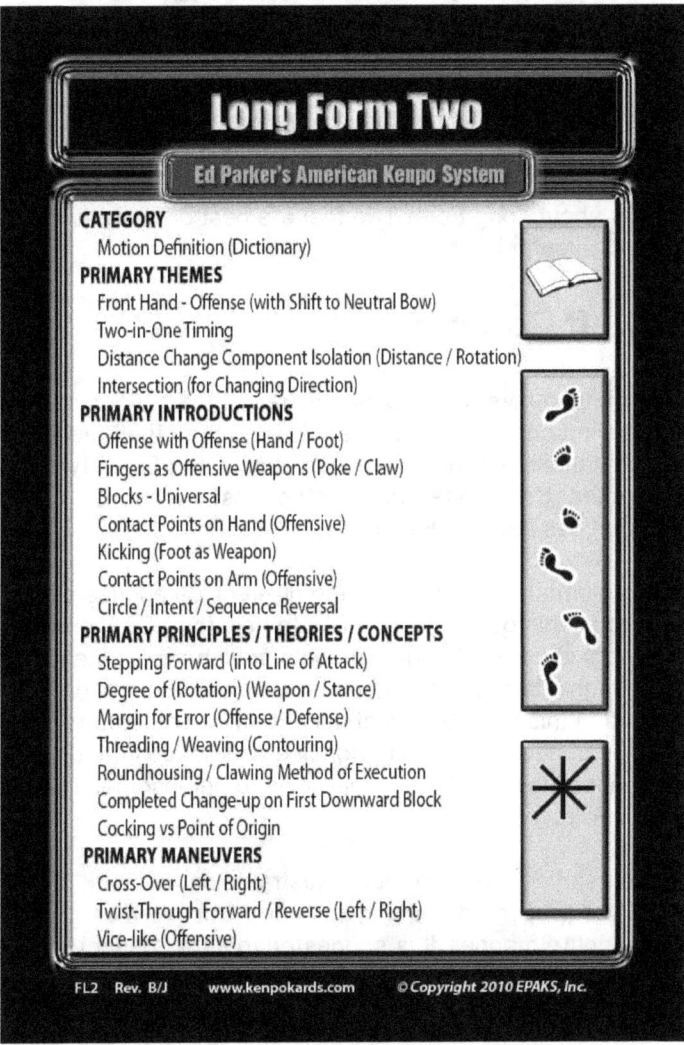

The back of the Kard can quickly be described as a microcosm of this guidebook. If you have read the book up to this point, the information presented on the Kard should be very easy to understand without much further explanation. What follows is a breakdown of the design and intent of the Kard.

The back of the Kard is divided into two columns. The left column is a textual summary of the major information presented in Long Form Two. The right column is a quick overview of other attributes about Long Form Two that are best or more quickly illustrated through images.

The Left Column

The left column lays out a quick overview of the major information presented in Long Form Two. It should be noted that due to space limitations, not all information about Long Form Two can be presented. So, a wide variety of the most important information has been included.

The left column is broken down into different 'categories of information.' This design is intended to help the practitioner in absorbing and comprehending the information more categorically and in a highly targeted manner. Because the information is presented in this way, the practitioner can be presented with related information that is very concise and concentrated, thereby enabling the a lot of information to be absorbed in a short period of time.

As stated earlier, the information illustrated on the back of the Kard is also presented in this guidebook - but in a more detailed and descriptive manner. It is suggested that the reader use this guidebook to help research, clarify, and expand upon the information presented on the Kard.

The Right Column

The right column has three (3) rows.

1) The top row illustrates what category of form Long Form Two falls into - in this case Dictionary (see Dictionary / Encyclopedia / Appendix analogy earlier in this book).

2) The middle row illustrates the theme stance of the form - in this case the Twist. It also show some of the other prominent stances of this form - in this case the cat and forward bow.

3) The bottom row lays out the important patterns of Long Form Two - in this case the directional and foot patterns.

Appendix C - Body English

Definition:

An idiom referring to the subtle extra body maneuvers used to enhance Body Momentum during the execution of a maneuver.

Usage / Purpose:

Body English is a term used to describe 'enhanced' body momentum, most typically during the execution of self-defense maneuvers. This 'enhanced' body momentum is achieved by coordinating upper body rotation with lower body rotation to maximize offensive moves. Although Body English is used for all types of moves, the term Body English is most often referenced when referring to offensive, upper body, moves.

The term Body English is derived from the billiards (pool) slang "putting English on the ball", which refers to placing spin on the cue ball to position it, for the next move, at a predetermined location.

Discussion:

So one might ask - "isn't Body English always executed with proper Body Momentum?" The short answer is, no. The long answer is, one can execute an offensive move properly and effectively, yet still not have Body English. This typically arises from non-optimized coordination (timing) between the upper body and the lower body. The result being a maneuver that is still effective, but not optimal.

© 2015 EPAKS Publications

Appendix C - Body English

For example: consider a right inward elbow (towards 10:30H) strike, to an opponent's solar plexus (assume the opponent is in the proper positioning and the same size), while shifting from a right forward bow into a right neutral bow. The strike should be coordinated such that the lower body shift is in-sync with the upper body shift and the elbow movement. The tricky part of the previous statement is: what does in-sync mean? Does it mean that the lower body starts moving at the same time as the upper body movement and the elbow movement? Only some movement at the same time? Or, all movements at different times? And, there is still one more thing to consider: what about the 'shift' from the forward bow to the neutral bow? Does the lower body move at all - i.e. is only the upper body and elbow moving? To answer these questions, is to explain the overall concept of Body English.

To start with, assume that no matter what happens with the coordination of the different body parts, each variation completes having all required body momentum focused at the point of contact with the opponent. In other words, each variation is executed to try and maximize the effectiveness of the strike. Or, in the shortest possible words - executed properly. Also, because there are essentially three moving parts (elbow, upper body, lower body), there is a total of six possible combinations (1 x 2 x 3). This analysis will not consider each possible combination, just the two most relevant.

© 2015 EPAKS Publications

Option #1 - Everything moves at the same time

This is the option the majority of beginning practitioners would choose. On the face of it, this option seems to be the best and most practical option. Everything starts and finishes at the same time. At first glance, this choice seems logically to be the optimal way to execute the maneuver, right? In short, no. Under further scrutiny, this type of motion proves to be not so optimal. This is because one of the most important things to consider about this maneuver is that not every element of the maneuver is the same distance from the focal point (the solar plexus). Which immediately implies that not everything will be executed at its most optimal speed. This can be deduced due to the fact that different distances automatically dictates that each element's speed must be regulated to remain coordinated from the beginning all the way to the end. Because of this, maximum speed, and thus maximum power, can never be truly achieved for the maneuver as a whole.

Movement of this type:
- can be very effective, but never completely optimal
- looks very clean and polished, but not dynamic
- looks very mechanical to the trained eye

Also, if the above maneuver starts from a neutral bow (not a forward bow), the lower body is essentially eliminated from the execution of the maneuver. Which leaves only the upper body (and weapon) to generate all of the power for the strike. The only contribution the lower body can potentially add is settling. Which will help to enhance power, but not to its fullest potential.

© 2015 EPAKS Publications

Option #2 - The lower body and upper body elements move independently

This option, or movement of a similar type, epitomizes Body English. It allows the practitioner to maximize each element in relation to the final position in coordination with the other moving elements of the same maneuver. It is more complex and harder to coordinate than option #1, but with practice, can achieve more effective results. A major characteristic of this type of movement is that both acceleration and deceleration of the individual elements are coordinated independently of one another to achieve an in-sync and maximized effect at the point of contact.

One way in which this type of movement optimizes overall effectiveness is by allowing the upper body acceleration to be sped up by borrowing from the lower body's momentum, thus achieving a faster speed at the moment of impact - and therefore more power. The lower body, once it has helped the upper body achieve maximum speed, can then be varied to enhance other elements of the execution (such as settling, shifting, regulating gap, etc.). The net effect of this type of movement is true optimization of each individual element and therefore the overall move.

Movement of this type:
- can be tailored to achieve truly optimal results
- looks very dynamic, but not as clean and polished
- looks more practiced to the trained eye

Also, if starting from a neutral bow, the lower body can be engaged, using shifting, slight rotations, and settling to enhance the effectiveness of the strike. The reason this can be achieved is because of the same reason option #1 is not optimal - distance. The lower body, which in this example is potentially the closest element to the focal point, can be engaged to fill in the 'timing gap' between the upper body starting and making contact. As stated in the definition, the lower body maneuvers are subtle, but the effects are demonstrable.

© 2015 EPAKS Publications

In summary, Body English is essentially the optimal regulation of each element of a move independently in such a way as to help maximize the overall effectiveness of the move. This can be visually apparent by seeing each of the elements of a move coordinated at different times and speeds to achieve an effective, in-sync, and optimized move.

Appendix D - Intent

Definition:

The objective, rationale, purpose, design, aim, motivation, function, or meaning for a specific action, motion, or thought.

Usage / Purpose:

Intent is the determining factor as to whether the nature of a particular move or action is offensive or defensive.

In legal terms, intent can be the difference between being incarcerated for a few years or a lifetime. For example, causing the death of another by accident is not nearly as serious an offense as planning and executing the murder of another human being. In order to be convicted for the more serious offense, the prosecution must prove that the defender thought about and then committed the crime. This is proving intent. In other words, proving what the mindset of the offender was, up to and during the execution of the crime. Without that proof, one can only be convicted of a lesser offense and thus a lesser sentence. And sometimes that means that the only way for the prosecution to get to the intent is through a confession. That is, getting the defendant to tell them what they were thinking before and during the execution of the crime.

© 2015 EPAKS Publications

Discussion:

At first thought, one might think that looking at a specific maneuver can determine whether it is a defensive or offensive maneuver. For example, seeing someone punch another person is obviously offensive. In contrast, seeing someone parry an oncoming punch is obviously defensive. But, under further scrutiny, just seeing a maneuver can't always determine the intent of the maneuver. For example, seeing an oncoming punch being blocked - is that maneuver defensive or offensive? It depends. Whether it is defensive or offensive is determined by one factor - the intent of the practitioner deflecting the punch. Did the practitioner intend to only deflect the punch? If so, then the maneuver was defensive. Or, did the practitioner intent to hurt the arm of the attacker? If so, then the maneuver was offensive. Both cases depend upon one element; the state of the defender's mind when executing the maneuver.

Keep in mind the definition of a block:
    Force against force, against a weapon in flight, without intent to cause injury.

And the definition of a strike:
    Any move or action that has the intent to cause injury or harm.

One of the key elements of the above definitions is the intent part. If at any time the intent is to cause injury, any move ceases being defensive and is considered offensive - i.e. a strike.

In summary, without knowing intent, one cannot always determine whether a move is defensive or offensive in nature.

Further research:

Any maneuver can be broken down into one of the following categories:
Defensive defense
Offensive defense
Defensive offense
Offensive offense

It is beyond the scope this section to get into the specific definitions and examples of the above categories, but is left to the reader research further.

Appendix E - Addendums and Further Insights

Note 1

Even though the striking surface of both the hand-sword and hammer-fist are technically the same surface, a difference can be noted because each are executed with completely different hand positioning. The hand-sword can be related to the pokes, claws, and heel-palm striking surface category - where the hammer-fist can be related to the punch, back-knuckle, and half-knuckle striking surface category.

As a further note: the hand-sword striking surface can be directly related to the side kick and in-step arch kick striking surface category - as they are opposites (high weapon vs low weapon); and are also both open weapons. In contrast, the front kick striking surface is more closely related to the punch striking surface category, rather than the more obvious strike, the heel-palm striking surface category. This is true even though the first weapon comparison are opposites, while the second weapon comparison are both open, which seems at first to be the more obvious choice.

Note 2

The major striking surface of the poke vs claw can be directly related to the striking surface of the punch vs back-knuckle. Each of which uses the front (tip) of the weapon vs the side (front / back) of the tip of the weapon. Even though these surfaces are close in proximity, they are distinct in execution and analysis.

© 2015 EPAKS Publications

Note 3

Even though the claw and heel-palm hand positioning is very similar and can often be used as a single, sophisticated maneuver; they are distinct. The heel-palm hand positioning is slightly more open (bend of fingers) with the fingers and thumb more tightly grouped. Where as the claw is typically executed with fingers slightly more bent, slightly more spread and thumb not grouped with fingers. Also, keep in mind that the heel-palm can also lend itself to being converted immediately into a four-finger poke just as easily as a claw.

Note 4

Due to the positioning prior to (cup and saucer) and the Path of Travel of the execution of the Outward block and Middle-knuckle strikes during the execution of the form Short Form Two, it can be considered that these two maneuvers are reverses of one another. If the form is executed without the cup and saucer positioning (i.e. without the 'V' step) the positioning of the Middle-knuckle strike changes (Point of Origin) and this effects the path the Middle-knuckle strike travels and thus alters whether the strike remains a reverse or not. In this second case (without the 'V' step) the left Middle-knuckle strike would only be an opposite, not a reverse.

Index

- A -

Addendums	666
Addendums and Futher Insights	666
Advanced	
Analysis	252
Analysis - Downward Block Sequence	269
Analysis - Elbow, Isolation Sequence	285
Analysis - Form Close	288
Analysis - Form Overview	255
Analysis - Half-knuckle Sequence	272
Analysis - Inside, Vertical Forearm Strike Sequence	281
Analysis - Inside-Downward, Palm down Block Sequence	277
Analysis - Inside-Downward, Palm up Block Sequence	275
Analysis - Inward Block Sequence	256
Analysis - Inward, Overhead Elbow Strike Sequence	283
Analysis - Outward Block Sequence	261
Analysis - Push-Down Block Sequence	279
Analysis - Summary	289
Analysis - Transition Inward / Outward	260
Analysis - Transition Upward / Downward	268
Analysis - Upward Block Sequence	264
Analysis - Walk Through	254
Downward Block Sequence - Analysis	269
Elbow, Isolation Sequence - Analysis	285
Form Close - Analysis	288
Form Overview - Analysis	255

© 2015 EPAKS Publications

- Advanced
  - Half-knuckle Sequence - Analysis … 272
  - Inside, Vertical Forearm Strike Sequence - Analysis … 281
  - Inside-Downward, Palm down Block Sequence - Analysis … 277
  - Inside-Downward, Palm up Block Sequence - Analysis … 275
  - Inward Block Sequence - Analysis … 256
  - Inward, Overhead Elbow Strike Sequence - Analysis … 283
  - Outward Block Sequence - Analysis … 261
  - Push-Down Block Sequence - Analysis … 279
  - Quiz - Fill in the Blank … 643
  - Quiz - Multiple Choice … 637
  - Quiz Answers - Fill in the Blank … 650
  - Quiz Answers - Multiple Choice … 649
  - Summary - Analysis … 289
  - Transition Inward / Outward - Analysis … 260
  - Transition Upward / Downward - Analysis … 268
  - Upward Block Sequence - Analysis … 264
  - Walk Through - Analysis … 254
- Analysis … 192
  - Advanced … 252
  - Advanced - Downward Block Sequence … 269
  - Advanced - Elbow, Isolation Sequence … 285
  - Advanced - Form Close … 288
  - Advanced - Form Overview … 255
  - Advanced - Half-knuckle Sequence … 272
  - Advanced - Inside, Vertical Forearm Strike Sequence … 281
  - Advanced - Inside-Downward, Palm down Block Sequence … 277
  - Advanced - Inside-Downward, Palm up Block Sequence … 275
  - Advanced - Inward Block Sequence … 256

Index 671

Analysis	192
Advanced - Inward, Overhead Elbow Strike Sequence	283
Advanced - Outward Block Sequence	261
Advanced - Push-Down Block Sequence	279
Advanced - Summary	289
Advanced - Transition Inward / Outward	260
Advanced - Transition Upward / Downward	268
Advanced - Upward Block Sequence	264
Advanced - Walk Through	254
Beginning / Intermediate	196
Beginning / Intermediate - Downward Block Sequence	219
Beginning / Intermediate - Elbow, Isolation Sequence	241
Beginning / Intermediate - Form Close	245
Beginning / Intermediate - Form Overview	199
Beginning / Intermediate - Half-knuckle Sequence	224
Beginning / Intermediate - Inside, Vertical Forearm Strike Sequence	237
Beginning / Intermediate - Inside-Downward, Palm down Block Sequence	232
Beginning / Intermediate - Inside-Downward, Palm up Block Sequence	229
Beginning / Intermediate - Inward Block Sequence	200
Beginning / Intermediate - Inward, Overhead Elbow Strike Sequence	239
Beginning / Intermediate - Outward Block Sequence	206
Beginning / Intermediate - Push-Down Block Sequence	234
Beginning / Intermediate - Summary	246
Beginning / Intermediate - Transition Inward / Outward	205

© 2015 EPAKS Publications

Analysis	192
Beginning / Intermediate - Transition Outward / Upward	211
Beginning / Intermediate - Transition Upward / Downward	218
Beginning / Intermediate - Upward Block Sequence	212
Beginning / Intermediate - Walk Through	198
Concepts	375
Definitions	375
Downward Block Sequence - Advanced	269
Downward Block Sequence - Beginning / Intermediate	219
Elbow, Isolation Sequence - Advanced	285
Elbow, Isolation Sequence - Beginning / Intermediate	241
Form Close - Advanced	288
Form Close - Beginning / Intermediate	245
Form Overview - Advanced	255
Form Overview - Beginning / Intermediate	199
Half-knuckle Sequence - Advanced	272
Half-knuckle Sequence - Beginning / Intermediate	224
Inside, Vertical Forearm Strike Sequence - Advanced	281
Inside, Vertical Forearm Strike Sequence - Beginning / Intermediate	237
Inside-Downward, Palm down Block Sequence - Advanced	277
Inside-Downward, Palm down Block Sequence - Beginning / Intermediate	232
Inside-Downward, Palm up Block Sequence - Advanced	275
Inside-Downward, Palm up Block Sequence - Beginning / Intermediate	229
Inter vs Intra Form	195

Index

Analysis	192
Inward Block Sequence - Advanced	256
Inward Block Sequence - Beginning / Intermediate	200
Inward, Overhead Elbow Strike Sequence - Advanced	283
Inward, Overhead Elbow Strike Sequence - Beginning / Intermediate	239
Opposite / Reverse	301
Outward Block Sequence - Advanced	261
Outward Block Sequence - Beginning / Intermediate	206
Principles	375
Push-Down Block Sequence - Advanced	279
Push-Down Block Sequence - Beginning / Intermediate	234
Reverse / Opposite	296, 301
Rules	375
Summary - Advanced	289
Summary - Beginning / Intermediate	246
Theories	375
Transition Inward / Outward - Advanced	260
Transition Inward / Outward - Beginning / Intermediate	205
Transition Outward / Upward - Beginning / Intermediate	211
Transition Upward / Downward - Advanced	268
Transition Upward / Downward - Beginning / Intermediate	218
Upward Block Sequence - Advanced	264
Upward Block Sequence - Beginning / Intermediate	212
Walk Through - Advanced	254
Walk Through - Beginning / Intermediate	198
Answers	
Quiz - Fill in the Blank - Advanced	650

Answers
- Quiz - Fill in the Blank - Beginner / Intermediate — 648
- Quiz - Multiple Choice - Advanced — 649
- Quiz - Multiple Choice - Beginner / Intermediate — 647

Appendix
- Addendums and Futher Insights — 666
- Body English — 658
- Intent — 663

- B -

Base Set Coordination
- Form Execution — 146

Basics
- Detailed Usage — 177
- Form — 170
- Quick Reference — 172

Beginner / Intermediate
- Quiz - Fill in the Blank — 634
- Quiz - Multiple Choice — 628
- Quiz Answers - Fill in the Blank — 648
- Quiz Answers - Multiple Choice — 647

Beginning / Intermediate
- Analysis — 196
- Analysis - Downward Block Sequence — 219
- Analysis - Elbow, Isolation Sequence — 241
- Analysis - Form Close — 245
- Analysis - Form Overview — 199
- Analysis - Half-knuckle Sequence — 224
- Analysis - Inside, Vertical Forearm Strike Sequence — 237
- Analysis - Inside-Downward, Palm down Block Sequence — 232

Index

Beginning / Intermediate

Analysis - Inside-Downward, Palm up Block Sequence	229
Analysis - Inward Block Sequence	200
Analysis - Inward, Overhead Elbow Strike Sequence	239
Analysis - Outward Block Sequence	206
Analysis - Push-Down Block Sequence	234
Analysis - Summary	246
Analysis - Transition Inward / Outward	205
Analysis - Transition Outward / Upward	211
Analysis - Transition Upward / Downward	218
Analysis - Upward Block Sequence	212
Analysis - Walk Through	198
Downward Block Sequence - Analysis	219
Elbow, Isolation Sequence - Analysis	241
Form Close - Analysis	245
Form Overview - Analysis	199
Half-knuckle Sequence - Analysis	224
Inside, Vertical Forearm Strike Sequence - Analysis	237
Inside-Downward, Palm down Block Sequence - Analysis	232
Inside-Downward, Palm up Block Sequence - Analysis	229
Inward Block Sequence - Analysis	200
Inward, Overhead Elbow Strike Sequence - Analysis	239
Outward Block Sequence - Analysis	206
Push-Down Block Sequence - Analysis	234
Summary - Analysis	246
Transition Inward / Outward - Analysis	205
Transition Outward / Upward - Analysis	211
Transition Upward / Downward - Analysis	218
Upward Block Sequence - Analysis	212

© 2015 EPAKS Publications

Beginning / Intermediate
    Walk Through - Analysis   198
Blocks - Downward
    Errors   457
Blocks - Inside Downward (Palm Up)
    Errors   460, 463
Blocks - Inward
    Errors   445
Blocks - Push-Down
    Errors   465
Blocks - Universal
    Errors   451
Blocks - Upward
    Errors   454
Blocks - Vertical Outward
    Errors   448
Body English   658
Breathing
    Errors   386

- C -

Coordination
    Form Execution   141

- D -

Defense - General
    Errors   443
Defensive
    Errors   441
Downward Block Sequence
    Advanced - Analysis   269
    Analysis - Advanced   269

Downward Block Sequence
    Analysis - Beginning / Intermediate   219
    Beginning / Intermediate - Analysis   219

- E -

Elbow, Isolation Sequence
    Advanced - Analysis   285
    Analysis - Advanced   285
    Analysis - Beginning / Intermediate   241
    Beginning / Intermediate - Analysis   241
Errors
    Blocks - Downward   457
    Blocks - Inside Downward (Palm Up)   460, 463
    Blocks - Inward   445
    Blocks - Push-Down   465
    Blocks - Universal   451
    Blocks - Upward   454
    Blocks - Vertical Outward   448
    Breathing   386
    Defense   441
    Defense - General   443
    Foot Maneuvers   432
    Foot Maneuvers - Cover   440
    Foot Maneuvers - Crossover   439
    Foot Maneuvers - General   434
    Foot Maneuvers - Step Out (Meditating Horse)   435
    Foot Maneuvers - Step Through   436
    Foot Maneuvers - Twist Through   438
    Gaze   385
    General - Overview   382
    Improvement Priorities   605
    Offense - General   470
    Offensive   468

© 2015 EPAKS Publications

Errors
- Stance - 45 Degree Cat — 408
- Stance - Forward Bow — 402
- Stance - General — 390
- Stance - Meditating Horse — 391
- Stance - Neutral Bow — 396
- Stance - Offset Horse — 414
- Stance - Overview — 388
- Stance - Reverse Bow — 420
- Stance - Twist — 427
- Strikes - Back Elbow — 600
- Strikes - Buckle — 539
- Strikes - Claw — 512
- Strikes - Half-knuckle — 544
- Strikes - Hammer-fist — 507
- Strikes - Hand-sword — 472
- Strikes - Horizontal Four-Finger Poke — 477
- Strikes - Instep Kick — 549
- Strikes - Inverted Vertical Back-knuckle — 524
- Strikes - Inward Horizontal Elbow — 585
- Strikes - Inward Overhead Elbow — 580
- Strikes - Inward Vertical Forearm — 575
- Strikes - Outward Back-knuckle — 518
- Strikes - Outward Horizontal Elbow — 590
- Strikes - Outward Overhead Elbow — 570
- Strikes - Side Kick — 502
- Strikes - Straight Kick — 529
- Strikes - Straight Punch — 487
- Strikes - Upward Elbow — 595
- Strikes - Upward Horizontal Forearm — 554
- Strikes - Vertical Back-knuckle — 565
- Strikes - Vertical Four-Finger Poke — 482
- Strikes - Vertical Punch (high) — 497
- Strikes - Vertical Punch (middle) — 534
- Strikes - Vertical Two-Finger Poke — 559

Index   679

Errors
   Timing   383
Executio
   Striking Errors - Buckle   539
   Striking Errors - Instep Kick   549
   Striking Errors - Inward Vertical Forearm   575
   Striking Errors - Straight Kick   529
   Striking Errors - Upward Horizontal Forearm   554
   Striking Errors - Vertical Two-Finger Poke   559
Execution   56
   Blocking Errors - Downward   457
   Blocking Errors - Inside Downward (Palm Up)   460, 463
   Blocking Errors - Inward   445
   Blocking Errors - Push-Down   465
   Blocking Errors - Universal   451
   Blocking Errors - Upward   454
   Blocking Errors - Vertical Outward   448
   Breathing Errors   386
   Defensive Errors   441
   Defensive Errors - General   443
   Errors - Improvement Priorities   605
   Foot Maneuver Errors   432
   Foot Maneuver Errors - Cover   440
   Foot Maneuver Errors - Crossover   439
   Foot Maneuver Errors - General   434
   Foot Maneuver Errors - Step Out (Meditating Horse)   435
   Foot Maneuver Errors - Step Through   436
   Foot Maneuver Errors - Twist Through   438
   Form Standard - Pace   138
   Form Standard - Video   137
   Gaze Errors   385
   General Errors - Overview   382
   Improving   379
   Offensive Errors   468

© 2015 EPAKS Publications

Execution	56
Offensive Errors - General	470
Salutation, Standard	25, 41
Salutation, Standard - Illustration	29
Stance Errors - 45 Degree Cat	408
Stance Errors - Forward Bow	402
Stance Errors - General	390
Stance Errors - Meditating Horse	391
Stance Errors - Neutral Bow	396
Stance Errors - Offset Horse	414
Stance Errors - Overview	388
Stance Errors - Reverse Bow	420
Stance Errors - Twist	427
Standard - Illustration	45
Striking Errors - Back Elbow	600
Striking Errors - Claw	512
Striking Errors - Half-knuckle	544
Striking Errors - Hammer-fist	507
Striking Errors - Hand-sword	472
Striking Errors - Horizontal Four-Finger Poke	477
Striking Errors - Inverted Vertical Back-knuckle	524
Striking Errors - Inward Horizontal Elbow	585
Striking Errors - Inward Overhead Elbow	580
Striking Errors - Outward Back-knuckle	518
Striking Errors - Outward Horizontal Elbow	590
Striking Errors - Outward Overhead Elbow	570
Striking Errors - Side Kick	502
Striking Errors - Straight Punch	487
Striking Errors - Upward Elbow	595
Striking Errors - Vertical Back-knuckle	565
Striking Errors - Vertical Four-Finger Poke	482
Striking Errors - Vertical Punch (high)	497
Striking Errors - Vertical Punch (middle)	534
TimingErrors	383
Various Standards	58

Index 681

Execution - "V" step
    Form Standard — 136
Execution - Base Set Coordination
    Form Standard - Base Set Coordination — 146
Execution - Coordination
    Form Standard - Coordination — 141
Execution - Form Coordination Variations — 158
Execution - Form Variations — 154
Execution - Maneuver Coordination
    Form Standard - Maneuver Coordination — 144
Execution - no "V" step
    Form Standard — 62
    Form Standard - Illustration — 88
Execution - Standard Coordination
    Form Standard - Standard Coordination — 150

- F -

FAQ — 606
    Did SGM Parkger create this form? — 623
    Difference between isolating power and isolation — 610
    How does leaning effect me? — 622
    Should I check throughout the form? — 614
    Timing of Form? — 608
    We do Long Form Two differently - is that OK? — 618
    What is a dictionary form? — 624
    What is purpose of 'cup and saucer'? — 611
    Where to look executing form — 626
    Why are some vertical punches at middle height zone — 617
    Why are there a lot of downward type blocks in Long Form Two? — 619
    Why are there different number of inward and outward overhead elbows? — 620

© 2015 EPAKS Publications

The Official EPAKS Guide to Long Form Two

- FAQ — 606
  - Why are there no kicks in the forms until Long Form Two? — 616
  - Why are there universal blocks in this form? — 615
  - Why do we step away on the first downward block of this form? — 621
  - Why named Long Form Two? — 607
  - Why not visualize opponent? — 625
  - Why should I do an instep kick? — 613
  - Why Two's are reverses of One's? — 609
- Fill in the Blank
  - Advanced - Quiz — 643
  - Beginner / Intermediate - Quiz — 634
  - Quiz Answers - Advanced — 650
  - Quiz Answers - Beginner / Intermediate — 648
- Foot Maneuver
  - Errors — 432
- Foot Maneuver - Cover
  - Errors — 440
- Foot Maneuver - Crossover
  - Errors — 439
- Foot Maneuver - General
  - Errors — 434
- Foot Maneuver - Step Out (Meditating Horse)
  - Errors — 435
- Foot Maneuver - Step Through
  - Errors — 436
- Foot Maneuver - Twist Through
  - Errors — 438
- Form Close
  - Advanced - Analysis — 288
  - Analysis - Advanced — 288
  - Analysis - Beginning / Intermediate — 245
  - Beginning / Intermediate - Analysis — 245
- Form Coordination - Variations — 158

Form Coordination Variations - Execution	158
Form Execution - Variations	154
Form Overview	
Advanced - Analysis	255
Analysis - Advanced	255
Analysis - Beginning / Intermediate	199
Beginning / Intermediate - Analysis	199
Form Variations - Execution	154
Futher Insights	666

- G -

Gaze	
Errors	385
General	
Errors - Overview	382

- H -

Half-knuckle Sequence	
Advanced - Analysis	272
Analysis - Advanced	272
Analysis - Beginning / Intermediate	224
Beginning / Intermediate - Analysis	224
History	16
Accumulative Journal 1.0	18
Accumulative Journal 2.0	20
Basic Booklet	18
During SGM Parker's Life	18
Encyclopedia of Kenpo	20
Inifinite Insight into Kenpo #5	18
Post SGM Parker Death	20

© 2015 EPAKS Publications

- I -

Illustration	
Fom Execution - no "V" step	88
Salutation, Standard Execution	29
Signifying, Standard Execution	45
Improvement Priorities	
Errors	605
Inside, Vertical Forearm Strike Sequence	
Advanced - Analysis	281
Analysis - Advanced	281
Analysis - Beginning / Intermediate	237
Beginning / Intermediate - Analysis	237
Inside-Downward, Palm down Block Sequence	
Advanced - Analysis	277
Analysis - Advanced	277
Analysis - Beginning / Intermediate	232
Beginning / Intermediate - Analysis	232
Inside-Downward, Palm up Block Sequence	
Advanced - Analysis	275
Analysis - Advanced	275
Analysis - Beginning / Intermediate	229
Beginning / Intermediate - Analysis	229
Intent	663
Inter vs Intra Form Analysis	195
Introduction	14
Inward Block Sequence	
Advanced - Analysis	256
Analysis - Advanced	256
Analysis - Beginning / Intermediate	200
Beginning / Intermediate - Analysis	200
Inward, Overhead Elbow Strike Sequence	
Advanced - Analysis	283

Inward, Overhead Elbow Strike Sequence
    Analysis - Advanced   283
    Analysis - Beginning / Intermediate   239
    Beginning / Intermediate - Analysis   239

- K -

Kenpo Kards
    Back of Kard   655
    Front of Kard   653
    Overview   651

- M -

Maneuver Coordination
    Form Execution   144
Multiple Choice
    Advanced - Quiz   637
    Beginner / Intermediate - Quiz   628
    Quiz Answers - Advanced   649
    Quiz Answers - Beginner / Intermediate   647

- O -

Offense
    Errors   468
Offense - General
    Errors   470
Opposite / Reverse
    Analysis   301
Outward Block Sequence
    Advanced - Analysis   261
    Analysis - Advanced   261
    Analysis - Beginning / Intermediate   206

© 2015 EPAKS Publications

Outward Block Sequence
    Beginning / Intermediate - Analysis   206

- P -

Pace
    Form Execution   138
Push-Down Block Sequence
    Advanced - Analysis   279
    Analysis - Advanced   279
    Analysis - Beginning / Intermediate   234
    Beginning / Intermediate - Analysis   234

- Q -

Quiz
    Advanced - Fill in the Blank   643
    Advanced - Multiple Choice   637
    Answers - Fill in the Blank - Advanced   650
    Answers - Fill in the Blank - Beginner / Intermediat   648
    Answers - Multiple Choice - Advanced   649
    Answers - Multiple Choice - Beginner / Intermediate   647
    Answers - Overview   646
    Beginner / Intermediate - Fill in the Blank   634
    Beginner / Intermediate - Multiple Choice   628
    Overview   627

- R -

Reverse / Opposite
    Analysis   296, 301

- S -

Salutation	23
Execution, Standard	25, 41
Execution, Standard - Illustration	29
Standard Execution	25, 41
Variations	38, 54
Salutation and Signifying	22
Signifying	39
Execution, Standard - Illustration	45
Variations	54
Signing	39
Stance	
Errors - Overview	388
Stance - 45 Degree Cat	
Errors	408
Stance - Forward Bow	
Errors	402
Stance - General	
Errors	390
Stance - Meditating Horse	
Errors	391
Stance - Neutral Bow	
Errors	396
Stance - Offset Horse	
Errors	414
Stance - Reverse Bow	
Errors	420
Stance - Twist	
Errors	427
Standard	
Form Execution - "V" step	136
Form Execution - Base Set Coordination	146

© 2015 EPAKS Publications

Standard
    Form Execution - Coordination   141
    Form Execution - Illustration - no "V" step   88
    Form Execution - Maneuver Coordination   144
    Form Execution - no "V" step   62
    Form Execution - Pace   138
    Form Execution - Standard Coordination   150
    Form Execution - Video   137
    Salutation Execution   25, 41
    Salutation Execution - Illustration   29
    Signifying Execution - Illustration   45
Standard Coordination
    Form Execution   150
Strikes - Back Elbow
    Errors   600
Strikes - Buckle
    Errors   539
Strikes - Claw
    Errors   512
Strikes - Half-knuckle
    Errors   544
Strikes - Hammer-fist
    Errors   507
Strikes - Hand-sword
    Errors   472
Strikes - Horizontal Four-Finger Poke
    Errors   477
Strikes - Instep Kick
    Errors   549
Strikes - Inverted Vertical Back-knuckle
    Errors   524
Strikes - Inward Horizontal Elbow
    Errors   585
Strikes - Inward Overhead Elbow
    Errors   580

Index 689

Strikes - Inward Vertical Forearm	
Errors	575
Strikes - Outward Back-knuckle	
Errors	518
Strikes - Outward Horizontal Elbow	
Errors	590
Strikes - Outward Overhead Elbow	
Errors	570
Strikes - Side Kick	
Errors	502
Strikes - Straight Kick	
Errors	529
Strikes - Straight Punch	
Errors	487
Strikes - Upward Elbow	
Errors	595
Strikes - Upward Horizontal Forearm	
Errors	554
Strikes - Vertical Back-knuckle	
Errors	565
Strikes - Vertical Four-Finger Poke	
Errors	482
Strikes - Vertical Punch (high)	
Errors	497
Strikes - Vertical Punch (middle)	
Errors	534
Strikes - Vertical Two-Finger Poke	
Errors	559
Summary	
Advanced - Analysis	289
Analysis - Advanced	289
Analysis - Beginning / Intermediate	246
Beginning / Intermediate - Analysis	246

© 2015 EPAKS Publications

- T -

Timing	
Errors	383
Transition Inward / Outward	
Advanced - Analysis	260
Analysis - Advanced	260
Analysis - Beginning / Intermediate	205
Beginning / Intermediate - Analysis	205
Transition Outward / Upward	
Analysis - Beginning / Intermediate	211
Beginning / Intermediate - Analysis	211
Transition Upward / Downward	
Advanced - Analysis	268
Analysis - Advanced	268
Analysis - Beginning / Intermediate	218
Beginning / Intermediate - Analysis	218

- U -

Understanding	
American Kenpo forms	166
Long Form Two	169
Upward Block Sequence	
Advanced - Analysis	264
Analysis - Advanced	264
Analysis - Beginning / Intermediate	212
Beginning / Intermediate - Analysis	212

- V -

Variations - Form Coordination	158
Variations - Form Execution	154

© 2015 EPAKS Publications

Index

Video
    Form Execution   137

- W -

Walk-Through
    Advanced - Analysis   254
    Analysis - Advanced   254
    Analysis - Beginning / Intermediate   198
    Beginning / Intermediate - Analysis   198

www.ingramcontent.com/pod-product-compliance
Lightning Source LLC
Chambersburg PA
CBHW050313240426
43673CB00042B/1393